Catholic Literary France

Catholic Literary France

from Verlaine to the Present Time

Sister Mary Jerome Keeler

Essay Index Reprint Series

 BOOKS FOR LIBRARIES PRESS
FREEPORT, NEW YORK

First Published 1938
Reprinted 1969

STANDARD BOOK NUMBER:
8369-1219-5

LIBRARY OF CONGRESS CATALOG CARD NUMBER:
76-90649

PRINTED IN THE UNITED STATES OF AMERICA

1503977

Acknowledgment

The author wishes to thank the editors of *Thought, The Catholic World, The Month, Studies, The Torch, Magnificat,* and *The Ampleforth Journal,* for permission to reproduce in whole or in part articles published in these periodicals. She also wishes gratefully to acknowledge the suggestions and assistance received from the late Dr. Romanus Butin, S.M., and Dr. William Roach of the Catholic University of America, Professor Louis Cons of Harvard University, Professor Raymond Brugère of the University of Iowa, and Very Reverend Bonaventure Schwinn, O.S.B., of St. Benedict's College. None of these, however, are in any way responsible for the opinions and sentiments set forth in the book.

Preface by the General Editor

DISTINGUISHED FRENCH SCHOLARS IN SECULAR universities, no less than Catholic authorities in the field of French letters, have expressed their approval of the selection of authors made for this volume. Without exception, they are representative figures of universal interest, quite independently of whatever their relations may be with the Church of their fathers.

Names such as those of Verlaine, Huysmans, Bourget, Bazin — to mention but the first four as they occur here — are familiar to everyone. Distinctively French, these men are at the same time part of the cultured *élite* of the world. Yet if one or other choice may naturally appear less popular in the public eye, it does not follow that the significance of such a writer is therefore negligible in the comprehensive picture presented here of Catholic Literary France. Each has contributed his own distinctive share to the literature of our day. Perhaps the least known may for that very reason prove the most interesting of all.

No other book of this kind exists today. "It will fill a real gap — the lack of an adequate treatment of French Catholic literature by a Catholic and in English," was the observation made by an eminent specialist in a letter written to the author in connection with the manuscript of her book. "One of the things that most appeals to me," he continued, *"is the fact that you have been extremely impartial and have not attempted to make all your authors good authors just because they have Catholic tendencies."* That, indeed, is a distinctive merit of the book, deserving to be stressed, since it gives the imprint of reliability to the volume. So, too, the weight of religion has never been thrown into the balance to estimate the importance of a writer, save where it had actually served him as an inspiration to higher and nobler work.

One fact there is which this book makes obvious. A new breath has blown through the land of ancient song, a new spirit has awakened to shake the pulse and quicken into throbbing action the life of Catholic Literary France, the wine of a new vintage has been poured out in more rich and generous abundance, there is a fresh exhilaration of Catholic thought and sentiment that arouses our wonder and our gratitude. Yet French critics would not have us interpret this as in any sense a renaissance or a revival, words that would imply for them a previous failure and surcease in the Catholic literature of their land. We honor their attitude.

The period covered in this book opens with Verlaine and continues down to our day. For the author to have begun with our own twentieth century might have been more simple, but also less accurate. Great movements do not spring up and fulfill themselves within strict calendar limits. They cannot be contained within century partitions. They have a way of growing quietly and slowly, of perhaps lying dormant in long spells of inclement weather, but at last unfolding and opening wide in their own due time, like the blossoming rose or the night-blooming cereus. So we must go back further than our century if we would trace to its origins the present interesting phase in the development of French Catholic letters. Verlaine has been chosen as merely the first significant manifestation of the new spirit, little as we would wish to propose him as the ideal representative of the Catholic Faith, whether in his life or in his general work, fine and truly Catholic though some of this has certainly been. He is the only one, however, of all the authors considered here who died at an earlier date than the year 1900. That still leaves the twentieth century as the true culminating and flowering period of this literary movement, almost unconscious of itself and entirely unorganized.

Besides the writers included in this book, as the author herself more fully explains, many others might have been chosen who have not less distinguished themselves and may even have accomplished far greater good. And yet, with no discredit to themselves, they do not fit into the special and restricted category of this volume. A single example will suffice.

There is one book which might well be considered the most influential that Catholic France has produced within the recent decades. That certainly is true if our judgment is to be based on the beauty and attractiveness of the personality portrayed in it, its wide diffusion over all the earth, the multiplication of editions in countless languages, its inspiration that penetrates wherever the feet of zealous missionaries travel to the ends of civilization and to the most distant savage tribes. It is the humble volume first published under the title *L'Histoire d'une âme,* the autobiography of Soeur Thérèse of Lisieux. Appearing during the year 1899, it at once took by storm our twentieth century. As a book of significance and power it therefore easily ranks first. Yet for our present purpose the mention of it must suffice.

It is with the literary world alone that our volume is concerned, with its men and women of letters, its books composed by them as works of literature, in a word, with what its title indicates, CATHOLIC LITERARY FRANCE. Through no lack of recognition, therefore, have other writers been excluded whose works may incidentally possess the highest literary qualities, but who nevertheless are classed as citizens of other realms — of science, history, philosophy, or perhaps religion. That parallel developments have taken place in such instances also is merely a further establishment of the truth of a Catholic awakening.

As for the book itself, special attention should be called to the two brief bibliographies that are appended at the end of the various chapters, listing respectively the works *by* the author dealt with and those *about* him. The first list includes such of the writer's books as have received widest recognition, his "principal" works as they are called, without implying thereby that they are actually commendable. The fact is that from the viewpoint of morals and right thinking they at times may even be reprehensible. Their real value must be learned by consulting the chapter to which they are attached. Moreover it is not the author's purpose to enumerate all the books of any writer. Thus, out of the approximately seventy works by Paul Bourget, forty only are listed. In addition a general bibliography has been placed at the end of the entire volume. The works included there have served for consultation in writing this book and most of them are referred to in the text.

The present volume renders available for the first time a judicious and scholarly study, written in pleasant English style, and acquainting us with the unique and often brilliant literary work of Catholic writers in contemporary France, beginning with the years immediately preceding our century. Knowledge of French language or French literature is not necessary for an understanding of its pages. The book can be read with enjoyment and profit by all. On the other hand, literary and modern language departments in our colleges and universities will wisely turn to it as a reliable text or reference book in their classes. With the copious aids supplied here it can be made the starting point for ampler study and research, always prudently guided along correct lines of thinking by the sane, constructive criticism of the author. A fine sense of discrimination is invariably preserved throughout the work and may in fact be pointed to as the characteristic merit of this book.

JOSEPH HUSSLEIN, S.J., PH.D.
General Editor, Science and Culture Series

St. Louis University,
November 16, 1937

Contents

Catholic Literary France

CHAPTER I

Survey of the Field

THERE IS ONLY ONE COUNTRY THAT CAN boast of being "the eldest daughter of the Church," and that country is France. So great was her devotion to the Holy See during the Middle Ages that her kings received the title of "Most Christian Majesty," retained until the time of the French Revolution. At heart she is still Catholic, for even in this age of unbelief and materialism, by far the largest part of her population continues to claim the Church as a mother.

From the beginning French literature reflected the deep-seated faith of the people. The greatest masterpieces of the Middle Ages, of the Renaissance period, and of the classical age are Catholic in thought and tone. A change set in with the eighteenth century, which witnessed a notable decline of the religious element in the realm of letters. The discussion of philosophical, social, and scientific questions held first place. It was an epoch of free-thinking incredulity and of rationalistic optimism, anti-Christian and antimonarchical. Still it can claim the remarkable sermons of Fénelon, Massillon, and Malebranche, and the spiritual poems of Louis Racine, Lefranc de Pompignan, and Jean-Baptiste Rousseau. Chateaubriand, at the head of the Romanticists of the nineteenth century, again found inspiration in the poetry of religion, and celebrated the genius of Christianity. In spite of the fact that Lamartine's Catholicism is often tinged with pantheism, there are passages in *Jocelyn, La Chute d'un ange*, and *Méditations* that are full of faith. Likewise Victor Hugo's *Ecce Homo, La Rédemption*, and parts of *La Légende des siècles* are marked by deep religious sentiment,

I

while the works of Joseph de Maistre and Lacordaire are openly and vehemently Catholic.

Toward the end of the nineteenth century and the beginning of the twentieth, the intensity of the Catholic current seems to increase, and a group of writers appear who are animated by a love for the spiritual life and a belief in the supernatural. It is the age of Verlaine, Jammes, Claudel, Maritain, and Bourget. An era of mystery has set in, followed by a return to Thomistic philosophy and scholasticism, and the systematic study of Catholic doctrine. Never before has such an interest in the interior life or appreciation of unseen values been manifest, as may be proved by the numerous well-written lives of the saints which have appeared during recent years.

This revival is doubtless due to many causes, some of which are evident while others are invisible to human eyes. If it is true that St. Teresa did more than anyone else to keep the Protestant Reformation out of Spain in the sixteenth century, may we not believe that in the nineteenth the miracles at Lourdes which began in 1858, the zeal and sanctity of the Curé of Ars who died in 1859, and the prayers of the Little Flower of Lisieux who was canonized in 1925, were secret forces which fostered the ·Catholic renaissance? It has taken place not only in France, but also in England, America, Norway, Germany, Austria, and Italy.[1]

Cunliffe[2] shows that the return to the orthodox faith was due in great measure to the influence of Bergson, who, though he does not himself profess Catholicity and is looked at askance by the Church, certainly helped to restore a healthier, more elevated tone to French life and thought. The previous generation was weighed down by discouragement and pessimism, by the worship of science which disappointed their hopes, by the positivism of Auguste Comte and Hippolyte Taine. Bergson undoubtedly was a guide toward a more optimistic view of life which expressed itself in a desire for action, and he did much to encourage a natural and inevitable rebound from the ultrascientific spirit of Renan. Calvet credits Baudelaire with having created *le frisson religieux et la nostalgie du divin.*[3] Baudelaire was far from possessing the true faith, but in his poems there is a shade of mysticism and a power of suggestion which had a great influence over his contemporaries.

French literature of the twentieth century is, on the whole, marked by a saner, more energetic view of life, by faith in God, in self, and in France, and by a search for something more desirable and lasting than science alone can give. Too often, unfortunately, it also reflects the sensualism and desire for the bizarre that is characteristic of much present-day writing, though both of these tendencies are opposed to the true Catholic tradition which stands for sobriety and moderation.

In poetry there is great anarchy and confusion. Among the numerous groups and schools, some adhere strictly to classical tradition, while others wish to break away completely from the past and disregard all the time-honored standards of French composition, both in thought and in form. There are evidences of rare talent, even of real genius among the Catholic poets, from Verlaine who died at the end of the nineteenth century, to Claudel who is still singing his sublime spiritual canticles to a world too immersed in material interests to comprehend.

In both the drama and the novel there is a noticeable trend toward a more altruistic, social conception of life, owing to the fact that in France as elsewhere, social problems are becoming more and more important. There is also an ever-increasing interest in psychological studies, with a pronounced tendency to reveal the inmost thoughts and hidden motives of the characters. By means of journals, diaries, letters, confessions, and the like, the protagonists lay bare the most intimate secrets of their hearts. Very often the hero of the novel is none other than the author himself, who, under the veil of fiction, recounts the (not always edifying) story of his life.

Many American readers will be surprised at the frankness with which French authors treat subjects that are scarcely mentioned among us. There is a vast difference between the temperament and character of the two nations, with the result that a Frenchman takes as a matter of course much that an Englishman would veil or conceal. C. Kegan Paul, in his introduction to the translation of one of Huysmans' novels, remarks: "That can be said in French openly, which English *men* would not say to each other in private."[4] The Naturalists, headed by Zola, are in a great measure responsible for this excessively realistic treatment of sex problems in contemporary French literature. They insisted on describing man with decided emphasis on his weakness and depravity, and they used language that is brutally plain and exact. Catholic authors have developed like topics in similar language. But they advocate what Baumann calls a *surnaturalism,* which presents not only man's baseness but also his sublimity, and shows not only the effects of original sin but also the power of divine grace. Many of the characters in Catholic novels are slaves of sensuality, but even in their degradation they retain a realization of their guilt and long for purification. Or if, indeed, they have completely fallen, the author does not defend them, but makes it clear that their spiritual ruin has come about because they did not make use of the aids and remedies that religion offers. We are inclined to regret, however, that so many of these Catholic writers expend their best powers on the portrayal of physical passion and sensual experiences. Even though the motive and end is good, the means seem questionable, and the books are apt to prove dangerous for many a reader.

It is difficult to discuss our contemporaries, because we see them at so close a range that the picture lacks perspective, and we cannot always correctly prophesy which names will remain on the tablets of time and which will be effaced. The present volume is a study of a few representative Catholic writers who seem to tower over a multitude of lesser lights, and who have all done their best work during the past fifty years, most of them since 1900. Some authors are left out who perhaps should have been included. For instance, there are several precursors of the movement who might have been mentioned, such as the vigorous and original Barbey d'Aurevilly, and the idealistic Villiers de l'Isle Adam. In point of time, Paul Verlaine really belongs to this group, as his best religious poems were written before 1890, but he is so definitely a *chef de file* that he could not well be omitted. On the other hand, François Coppée was not included, in spite of his *La Bonne souffrance* which relates his conversion in 1898, since most of his writing was done before that date. Neither was a chapter given to any writers whose work is not primarily literature, as, for example, the historians Georges Goyau, Henri Bremond, and Pierre Batiffol, and the philosophers Étienne Gilson and Jacques Maritain. Maritain has, nevertheless, probably done more than anyone else in France to promote the Catholic revival. Owing to his striking and attractive personality and his profoundly religious outlook, his influence has been widespread and lasting.

With regard to Catholic critics, there are a great many of excellent ability (Paul Archambault, René Johannet, Jean Calvet, Louis Bethleem, Armand Praviel, Fortunat Strowski), but none who seem to have exceptional genius. Only posterity can decide if any or all of them will be remembered in literary history. Abbé Ernest Dimnet, well-known in the United States on account of his lectures here and because he has done his best writing in English, won spectacular success in 1928 with his *Art of Thinking*. His latest work, *My Old World* (1935), contains interesting biographical reminiscences told in a charming manner.

There is a group of lesser novelists worthy of particular study, though they are not as widely read as Bourget, Bazin, and Mauriac. Léon Bloy, an ardent and belligerent Catholic, Pierre Lhande, who studied religious life among the workers in the suburbs, Pierre L'Ermite, a very successful short-story writer, have all made valuable contributions to contemporary fiction. Georges Bernanos, who first attained fame with the publication of *Sous le soleil de satan* (1926), and has again come into the limelight with his *Journal d'un curé de campagne* (1936), deserves special mention. There are also a number of recent converts (Max Jacob, Jean Cocteau, Jacques Rivière) whose work is attracting attention, and who are devoting their talents to the dissemination of Catholicism.

The number of Catholic writers seems to be ever increasing. Paul Claudel wrote in 1911: "When I was converted, I was almost the only Christian poet of my generation. Today I see on all sides the light of Christ reappearing in noble souls. Everywhere, as in the darkest days of barbarism, religion appears as the only assured refuge of those who live for other things than the body."[5] Volumes could be devoted to the long list of writers who, conscious of the spiritual riches they possess, are endeavoring to exteriorize their faith by their pen. The *Manuel illustré de la littérature catholique en France de 1870 à nos jours* mentions several hundred names, and then at the end the editors apologize for omitting so many!

The following chapters are born of the desire to make better known a few of our outstanding Catholic writers. We sometimes complain that they are not appreciated at their worth, but is not this in a measure our own fault? By examining them ourselves and discussing their merits more intelligently, we might eliminate many of the causes of complaint. We trust that the studies contributed here will lead to a better understanding of the beauty of the Church in her literature, as the liturgical movement has revealed her treasures of art and music. They are not intended to be a blind plea for a pet thesis, but an impartial exposition of facts about contemporary French literature viewed from the Catholic angle. The fact that a writer is a Catholic does not, it is true, make his work any better from the artistic point of view, but since we believe that the Christian ideal is the only correct one, that beauty is truth and truth the heritage of the Church, it is only logical to conclude that Catholic literature should surpass in sincerity, depth, and emotion that of writers who do not possess the faith, and who cannot possibly understand the secrets that are written in the aeons of eternity.

CHAPTER II

Paul Verlaine

(*1844-1896*)

PAUL VERLAINE HAS WRITTEN SOME OF THE
best Catholic poetry ever produced by a Frenchman. His
two volumes *Sagesse* and *Amour* reveal a humble, genuine
Catholicity that is far removed from the vague religiosity
and "literary" Christianity of many of his more reputable
contemporaries. Yet his life was a scandal. Symons hardly
exaggerates when he calls it "a disaster, more sordid perhaps
than the life of any other poet."[1] Even Lepelletier, Verlaine's steadfast friend and defender, must confess that his
career was full of "faults, follies, and weaknesses."[2] But
his poetic genius overcame the handicap of his moral lapses,
and his faith remained unquestionably sincere, however
little on occasion his conduct or writings reflected its teachings. His besetting sin, the curse that brought about all his
misfortunes and caused his physical and moral deterioration,
was intemperance.

The main facts of his life are familiar. He was born at
Metz on March 30, 1844. His father, Captain Nicholas
Verlaine, was a worthy member of an ancient Ardennaise
family, while his mother was a pious, thrifty, highly respect-
able woman from French Flanders. Both adored their son,
an only child and consequently hopelessly spoiled. Paul was
sent first to a little school in the Rue Hélène and then to
the Institution Landry, from which the pupils were taken
twice a day to the Lycée Bonaparte. He received his Bachelier ès Lettres in 1862. After his school days were over, he
became an employee in a Paris insurance company, and

then a Government clerk in the Hôtel de Ville. He joined
the group of young Parnassian poets who frequented
Lemerre's bookshop, and the salons of the Marquise de
Ricard and Nina de Callias, and, when twenty-two, he
produced his first book of verse, *Poèmes saturniens,* published in 1866 with money provided by his cousin Elise,
an orphan whom his parents had educated as their own
child.[3] These early poems show the influence of Baudelaire,
and an effort at Parnassian impassibility and pessimism.
Still, they are not wholly imitative, and they breathe already
the tenderness which flowered so exquisitely later on.
Consider, for instance, *Chanson d'automne:*

> *Les sanglots longs*
> *Des violons*
> > *De l'automne*
> *Blessent mon coeur*
> *D'une langueur*
> > *Monotone.*
>
> *Tout suffocant*
> *Et blême, quand*
> > *Sonne l'heure,*
> *Je me souviens*
> *Des jours anciens*
> > *Et je pleure.*
>
> *Et je m'en vais*
> *Au vent mauvais*
> > *Qui m'emporte*
> *Deçà, delà,*
> *Pareil à la*
> > *Feuille morte.**

This poem and *Mon rêve familier* are among the best that

---

* The drawn-out sobbings of the violins of autumn, wound my heart with
a dull langour.
Pale and deeply affected, when the hour strikes, I remember past years
and weep over them.
And I go on driven by a capricious wind, which carries me hither and
thither, like a dead leaf.

he ever wrote. *Poèmes saturniens* were passed over by critics, though Verlaine received many flattering eulogies from his friends, Leconte de Lisle, Théodore de Banville, Victor Hugo, François Coppée, and Sainte-Beuve. The last encouraged him to continue writing descriptive poems, such as his *César Borgia* and *Philippe II*.

Verlaine followed this advice to some extent in his next volume, *Fêtes galantes* (1869), which is still more objective and artistic than *Poèmes saturniens*. Its inspiration was drawn from reading the Goncourts, who had just published some excellent historical studies. His attempt to picture the eighteenth century presents its manners and conversations accurately enough, but lacks atmosphere and life. The volume, however, contains some exquisite gems, such as *Clair de lune, Colloque sentimental,* and *Colombine.*

Verlaine had begun to drink in 1862, during his vacation at Fampoux, after the close of his college career, and the habit grew on him until it bordered on dipsomania. His father died in 1865 and his cousin Elise in 1866. Thus he was deprived of two influences for good which might have been powerful enough to save him. Two other misfortunes followed soon after, his unhappy marriage and his friendship with the poet and adventurer Jean Arthur Rimbaud.

One day while at the home of his friend Charles de Sivry, the musician and composer, a young girl scarcely sixteen years of age appeared in the doorway. It was Mathilde Mauté, stepsister of Sivry, and Verlaine seems to have fallen in love at first sight. He describes her in his *Mémoires d'un veuf* as a pretty young girl with chestnut hair, dressed in gray and green.[4] This picture of Mathilde, as she appeared to him for the first time, seems to have remained with him always, for he mentions it in two poems:

> *En robe grise et verte avec des ruches,*
> *Un jour de juin que j'étais soucieux*

Elle apparut souriante à mes yeux
Qui l'admiraient sans redouter d'embûches.[*]

Simple elle était comme au temps de ma cour,
En robe grise et verte et voilà tout.
J'aimai toujours les femmes dans ce goût.^{**}

He married her in the spring of 1870, and the same year
he published *La Bonne Chanson,* a volume of tender love-
songs, which Victor Hugo called *"une fleur dans un obus."*
The twenty-one poems which make up the volume are, for
the most part, taken from letters written to his fiancée
during her visits to Normandy. He breaks away from the
objectivity of the Parnassians, and expresses freely his hopes
and fears, his dreams of conjugal happiness and his resolutions to reform. We find no philosophic considerations or
abstract declamations on the excellence and grandeur of
love. The poems are simple and sincere, for Verlaine
idolized Mathilde, and 1870 was probably the brightest
year of his life.

Trouble began all too soon. When the Franco-German
War broke out, the poet joined the National Guards
(though he was exempt from military service), came home
drunk one night, and the first domestic quarrel followed.
After the fall of the Commune, to which he adhered, he
gave up his duties as a clerk, went with his wife to live in
his father-in-law's house in the Rue Nicolet, and continued
to drink. Then Jean Arthur Rimbaud, a pale, eccentric
youth, reputed a prodigy, appeared in Paris, and Verlaine
invited him to stay at the Mautés. But Madame Mauté, on
account of his crudity and boorishness, soon dismissed him,
and Verlaine, abandoning his wife for this dubious friend,

---

* In a gray and green dress trimmed with frills, on a June day when
I was troubled, she appeared smiling to me, who admired her without fearing
her charms.
** She was dressed simply as in the days of our courtship, in a gray and
green dress unadorned. I always liked women in these colors.

went with him first to Belgium and later to England. He seems never to have realized the gravity of his behavior (his son was born soon after), and he was indignant at Mathilde for refusing to take him back. It is true that his little wife could have shown more patience with him, been more forgiving, and made greater efforts to influence him for good. He still loved her ardently and she might have saved him, but she was only a child, incapable of mature forbearance, and she did not understand her husband at all.

Verlaine lived with Rimbaud in England for some time, giving lessons in French for their mutual support. When funds ran low, as they frequently did, his mother was always ready to come to the rescue. He returned to France in 1872, but went back to London and Rimbaud the following year. Then in July, 1873, he left for Brussels, where occurred their quarrel and the attempted crime. Verlaine, in a fit of drunkenness, fired at his friend and wounded him. He was tried and condemned to eighteen months of imprisonment. It is amazing what a disastrous influence this boy (he was eighteen at the time of the quarrel) had on Verlaine, eleven years his senior. He encouraged him in his ruinous habit of drink, which he said was the mother of genius, he was the chief occasion of his separation from his wife and of his long imprisonment. Mornet says that he induced Verlaine to "scorn a prudent life, prudent art, old traditions."[8] His poetic gifts were undoubted. His *Bateau ivre* rightly appears in most anthologies of French poetry, but as a man he was a moral wreck, and he brought about the ruin of a greater than himself.

Verlaine accepted his punishment without bitterness, and a complete moral revolution took place in him during the following months. He had, of course, been baptized a Catholic, and he tells us that his First Communion was "good," and that his general confession had been scrupulous,[9] but, like so many of his class and time, he had never received the sacraments again. Solitude, and the grief and despair which overcame him when he received official notice of his wife's legal separation, resulted in a return to the Faith, a deep repentance for his past life, and a sincere determination to amend. He wrote to his friend Lepelletier: "If anyone asks news of me, say that you know that I am well, and that I am absolutely converted to the Catholic religion after mature reflection, being in full possession of my moral liberty and good sense."[10] His sincerity is confirmed by the tone of the poems that he wrote at this time, and by the fact that he abstained from drink and kept straight for six years.

He had completed *Romance sans paroles,* but could not find a publisher, so Lepelletier published it for him in 1873. This volume, with its twenty-three poems, contains excellent examples of both his manners, Parnassian and Romantic. *Paysages Belges,* for instance, is entirely objective, while *Il pleure dans mon coeur* and *O triste, triste était mon âme,* as well as *Birds in the Night,* are very personal. This last is addressed to Mathilde, and begins:

Vous n'avez pas eu toute patience.*

Many of the poems in this volume were composed during his stay in London, and have English titles (*A Poor Young Shepherd, Spleen, Streets, Child Wife,* etc.).

Romance sans paroles and *Sagesse,* which followed it in 1881, contain the best work of Verlaine. Lemaître says that *Sagesse* is perhaps the only book of French Catholic poetry that he knows, the first to express truly the love of God.[11] Charles Morice also maintains, surely with some exaggeration, that it is "the greatest of Catholic poems since that of Dante."[12] Huysmans, in his preface to the *Poésies religieuses de Paul Verlaine,* says: "Alone, indeed, through the centuries, he has found again those accents of humility and candor, those mournful and penetrating prayers, those

---

* You have not been very patient.

childlike joys, forgotten since this return to the pride of paganism, which we call the Renaissance." His simple faith is expressed in musical verse, the like of which was hitherto unknown in French. The first poem in *Sagesse* is *Bon chevalier masqué,* an allegorical explanation of the author's conversion. This is followed by others naïve, and at the same time sublime, with nothing hypocritical or puritanical in them. One of the most beautiful is a long dialogue between the poet's soul and God, which begins:

> O mon Dieu, vous m'avez blessé d'amour
> Et la blessure est encore vibrante,
> O mon Dieu, vous m'avez blessé d'amour.*

In the second part he addresses our Lady:

> Je ne veux plus aimer que ma mère Marie.**

Sometimes there is a touching note of sadness and regret for an irreparable past:

> Qu'as-tu fait, ô toi que voilà
> Pleurant sans cesse,
> Dis, qu'as-tu fait, toi que voilà
> De ta jeunesse?†

In another poem he speaks of having seen "our only child," but this is probably the utterance of a desire, the imagined fulfillment of a dream, rather than the statement of an actual fact, for Donos assures us that Verlaine never saw his little son George,[13] though he made several desperate attempts to do so.

The volume *Amour* was written about the same time as *Sagesse* and expresses similar sentiments, but it was not published until 1888. It contains beautiful prayers, memories

---

* O my God you have wounded me with love, and the wound is still quivering, O my God, you have wounded me with love.

** Henceforth I will love only my mother Mary.

† What have you done, you who are ceaselessly weeping, tell me, what have you done with your youth?

of his brief conjugal happiness, and of the grief and heart-break that followed it.

Verlaine left prison in 1875 and thought himself another man. He tried to approach his wife and see if there was any possibility of a reconciliation, but she repulsed him. He made a retreat at La Trappe, and even wanted to enter there, but was refused.[14] Shortly after, he left for England, where he taught French, Latin, and drawing in a certain Mr. Andrew's scholastic establishment at Stickney in Lincolnshire. The following year his friend, Ernest Delahaye, resigned his position as professor in the College of Notre Dame at Rethel, in the department of the Ardennes, and Verlaine took his place. This was one of the most peaceful periods in his troubled life, where, in an atmosphere of studious leisure, with the temptation to drink removed to a great extent, he kept the good resolutions he had made in prison, taught, and wrote many of the poems that appeared in later volumes. One of the boys in his class at Rethel was Lucien Létinois, and a pure and deep affection grew up between master and pupil. Verlaine conceived the idea of buying a farm and living on it in peace and contentment with his young friend, so in 1879 they left Rethel to carry out the fantastic plan. As neither had any practical knowledge of farming, the scheme completely failed, and the farm at Juniville (bought with his mother's money) was forfeited. Not long after, Lucien died of typhoid fever, and Verlaine poured out his grief in some of his most touching poems. Possibly he was thinking of his own son George also, when he wrote the long poem beginning:

*Mon fils est mort. J'adore, ô mon Dieu, votre loi!**

From the death of Lucien in 1881, we can trace Verlaine's physical, mental, and moral decline.[15] He tried to drown his sorrows in absinthe, and thus wasted what was left of his

---

* My son is dead. I adore, O my God, Your law!

own and his mother's fortune. His health continued to grow worse, until in his last years he was pitifully crippled up with arthritis, gout, and rheumatism.

In 1883 he tried agriculture again at Coulommes, but this attempt was even more unsuccessful than the first one. He quarreled with the neighbors, had a disagreement with his mother, was accused of violence toward her and imprisoned for a month at Vouziers. He regretted his rashness bitterly, and the poor old lady readily forgave him. She died in Paris three years later. Verlaine, alone, sick, a drunkard, spent his last years at charity hospitals, or with one of the two abandoned women who shared his loose affections. He wrote much and became a sort of god to the younger generation of writers, who, on the death of Leconte de Lisle in 1894, acclaimed him "Prince of Poets." But his later works[16] are, with rare exceptions, much inferior to those of his earlier years. He died on January 8, 1896, in poverty and loneliness, for though the priest and his friends had been summoned, they arrived too late. The mourners were headed by his brother-in-law, Charles de Sivry, and funeral orations were spoken by Maurice Barrès, François Coppée, Catulle Mendès, Stéphane Mallarmé, Jean Moréas, Gustave Kahn, and Edmond Lepelletier.[17] We may sympathize with Verlaine, divorced by his wife, forgotten by his friends, condemned by society, but we realize that he wove for himself his destiny. During the last ten years of his life, he published nine volumes of verse, much of it very gross (perhaps no other style could win a public) and little that shows high inspiration.

Verlaine's prose is, on the whole, very inferior to his poetry. Gregh condemns it as too "invertebrate."[18] Much of it is autobiographical, for the author seems to delight in revealing his innermost secrets and in exaggerating his wickedness. *Mes hôpitaux* is an account of his sojourns in poorhouses, *Mes prisons,* his experiences in jails, *Confessions,* his life up to 1871, *Quinze Jours en Hollande,* letters written thence to a friend in 1892 when Verlaine was giving a series of lectures. Then there are several collections of short stories, *Louise Leclerc, Histoires comme ça,* and *Contes,* most of them rather indecent and rather dull. *Les Poètes maudits, Les Hommes d'aujourd'hui,* and *Charles Baudelaire* are literary studies written in a gossipy style, all showing a just judgment and critical estimate of his contemporaries which posterity has in general ratified. *Les Poètes maudits* includes a sketch about himself under the anagram *"Pauvre Lélian,"* in which he seeks to justify, in the name of art, his "dualism" which permitted him to write poems as sublime as those in *Sagesse* and to follow them with obscenity such as is exhibited elsewhere. Aside from the Catholic point of view, which knows no compromise between vice and virtue, most readers would agree that little would be lost if the whole bulk of his lascivious verse were condemned to oblivion.

Even at his best, Verlaine has marked faults. He has often been compared to Villon and La Fontaine. Though he shares the bohemian instincts and the bad reputation of the first, and the lackadaisical character of the second, he does not equal either of them in imagination or originality. Too often his poetry lacks vitality, color, vigor, and passion. It sounds a melancholy, plaintive note which is apt to degenerate into sentimentality or worse. Frequently his ideas are obscure, owing to the fact that he suggests rather than defines. The idea no doubt is clear to himself. The poet sees visions hid from others, but he merely hints at the resulting impressions, dreams, and sensations, and fails to convey their entirety.

In his youth Verlaine was one of the "Parnassians," and schooled himself to write impassible, objective, descriptive poems, of which the oft-quoted verse

Est-elle en marbre ou non, la Vénus de Milo?[*19]

is an excellent example. Later, his romantic temperament
and his admiration of Victor Hugo caused him to abandon
this school. After his first two volumes, he reacts against
perfection of form, and takes many liberties with grammar,
style, and prosody. He introduces foreign words and archaisms, ends sentences with adverbs, abuses assonance and al-
literation, and violates metrical technique. His only rule
seems to be his poetic instinct and intuition, which fortunately rarely fail him.

His best work combines the artistic beauty that characterized his early manner, and the tender personal touch of his
later style. If color is lacking, melody is abundant. He
follows his own theory of "Music before all else," and has
drawn delightful harmony out of the French language.
This language was his servant and obeyed the least will of
the master. Even when the meaning of the poem is doubtful, we can enjoy its exquisite rhythm. All his volumes could
be entitled *Romance sans paroles,* for they are beautiful to
the ear, elusive lyric songs of love or sorrow with an occasional humorous strain or caustic note. Symons says that
"Verlaine is the first to write poetry without rhetoric,"[20] and
Anatole France ventures somewhat rashly to predict that
future generations will call him the greatest poet of his
time.[21] His poems reveal a man deeply in love with life even
though it treated him badly, and they breathe a profound
sincerity. This sincerity is the secret of his *don d'émouvoir.*[22]
He sings with a humble naïveté, with a refreshing simplicity, which arouses a corresponding tremor of emotion
in our hearts.

There are many authentic portraits and accurate descriptions of Verlaine. Bénéteau insists on his "apelike ugliness."[23]
At first glance, the bald head, the unkempt beard, the flat

* Is it marble or not, the Venus of Milo?

nose, the small slanting eyes, and the ambiguous smile are apt to shock us, but his childlike, yet inspired, expression belies the sensuousness of his face, "a face devoured by dreams, feverish, and somnolent."[24] A "poor devil who made verses like an angel," according to Deschamps.[25] Let us hope that what is angelic in his output God, in His infinite mercy, may hold to outweigh what is devilish.

PRINCIPAL WORKS OF PAUL VERLAINE

1866 *Poèmes saturniens*
1868 *Les Amies*
1869 *Fêtes galantes*
1870 *La Bonne Chanson*
1874 *Romance sans paroles*
1881 *Sagesse*
1884 *Les Poètes maudits*
1886 *Louise Leclerq*
1886 *Mémoires d'un veuf*
1888 *Amour*
1889 *Parallèlement*
1890 *Dédicaces*
1891 *Bonheur*
1891 *Chansons pour elle*
1891 *Les Uns et les autres*
1891 *Mes hôpitaux*
1892 *Liturgies intimes*
1893 *Mes prisons*
1893 *Élégies*
1893 *Quinze Jours en Hollande*
1894 *Dans les Limbes*
1894 *Épigrammes*
1896 *Invectives*
1898–1906 *Oeuvres complètes* (6 vol.)

REFERENCES

Bénéteau, André, *Étude sur l'inspiration et l'influence de Paul Verlaine,* Washington, 1930.
Cazals, F. A., *Les Derniers Jours de Paul Verlaine,* Paris, 1911.

Coulon, M., *Verlaine poète saturnien*, Paris, 1929.

Delahaye, Ernest, *Verlaine, Étude biographique*, Paris, 1919.

Donos, Charles, *Verlaine intime*, Paris, 1898.

Fontainas, André, *Verlaine-Rimbaud*, Paris, 1932.

Lepelletier, Edmond, *Paul Verlaine, sa vie, son oeuvre*, Paris, 1907.

Martino, Pierre, *Paul Verlaine*, Paris, 1924.

Montel, François, *Bibliographie de Paul Verlaine*, Paris, 1925.

Morice, Charles, *Paul Verlaine*, Paris, 1888.

Nicolson, Harold, *Paul Verlaine*, Paris, 1921.

Pacheu, Jules, *De Dante à Verlaine*, Paris, 1897.

Porché, François, *Verlaine tel qu'il fut*, Paris, 1933.

Séché, Alphonse, *Paul Verlaine*, Paris, 1925.

Thorley, Wilfrid, *Paul Verlaine*, London, 1914.

Tournoux, Georges, *Bibliographie verlainienne*, Leipzig, 1911.

CHAPTER III

Joris-Karl Huysmans

(*1848–1907*)

BARBEY D'AUREVILLY WROTE, AFTER READING *À Rebours* ("Against the Grain"), that there was nothing left for the author of such a book but the muzzle of a pistol or the foot of the Cross.[1] Huysmans chose the foot of the Cross. Huysmans, the naturalist, the materialist, the sensualist, was converted in 1892, and became one of the great figures in contemporary French literature. With Verlaine, Coppée, Bourget, Jammes, Péguy, Psichari, and Claudel, who all either turned from unbelief, or from neglect and forgetfulness of God, he inaugurated a period of real intellectual and spiritual efflorescence in France. Among these writers he stands out as the Catholic naturalist, retaining all the freshness, vigor, and picturesqueness of his early manner, but making the truth and beauty of religion the sole, absorbing interest in his life. His novels have very little plot and few incidents. Still they fascinate us on account of their penetrating psychology, their supernatural realism, their brilliant satire, and their original though eccentric style.

Huysmans was born at Paris on February 5, 1848. His father, Victor Godefroy Jean Huysmans, belonged to a family which came from Holland, while his mother, Elizabeth Malvina Badin, was of Burgundian descent. It is interesting to note, in the light of Huysmans' later works, that there were sculptors and painters among his ancestors on both sides of the family. One forebear, a Cornelius Huysmans from Mechlin, had some paintings in the Louvre. The child was baptized at the church of Saint-Severin and given the names, Charles Marie Georges. His father died when he was nine years old and his mother married again. The boy was sent to the Lycée St. Louis and later had private tutors. He proved to be a fair student, though not at all brilliant, and received his Bachelier ès Lettres on May 7, 1866. The few souvenirs of childhood and youth scattered through his books are not at all pleasant. For example, in *En Ménage* he describes his wretched life at college, and concludes by exclaiming: "And to think that there are people who pretend that later they recall with pleasure their college days!"[2]

For a time he contemplated law, but in 1868 he entered the Ministry of the Interior. The story of his next years is related in *Sac au dos.* Having been sent to camp at Chalons, he became ill like the would-be hero in the tale, and obtained leave for convalescence. From early years he had been troubled by a malady of the stomach, which army life did not improve. To this fact is due in part his restless disposition, and the continual exasperation and irritability which are reflected in his early works. Only in later life was his forceful intellect able to control this sensitive nervous system.

He re-entered the Interior in June, 1871, and remained there until 1897 as a model official. His mother died in May, 1876, and shortly after this he went to Holland to visit an uncle. Here he was called Karl Joris, which he himself changed to the more euphonious Joris-Karl. The same year *Marthe* was printed in Brussels. Thenceforth he devoted his time to duties in the office, to study, and to writing, as one after another his great works appeared. In July, 1892, counseled by Abbé Mugnier, he went to make a retreat at La Trappe d'Igny, and he spent 1894–96 at Saint-Wandrille and at Solesmes. He even thought of joining the Benedictines there, but Dom Delatte, the superior, advised him not to enter, partly because of his frail health, partly because he did not show signs of a true vocation.

In 1897 he was elected first president of the Goncourt Academy, and soon after he retired from public service on a pension of 2,880 francs. He spent two years at Ligugé in Villa Notre-Dame, occupying two rooms on a second floor, and living the life of a Benedictine oblate, half monk, half littérateur. When the Benedictines were driven from Ligugé to Moerbeke in Belgium, he returned to Paris, where he remained (with short absences) until his death. He journeyed to Schiedam while writing his *Sainte-Lydwine* ("Saint Lydwine of Schiedam"), and each year at Christmas he paid a visit to our Lady at Chartres. He had been decorated in 1893, and in 1905 he was nominated Chevalier of the Legion of Honor. The same year he was afflicted with a zona of the eyes, and his eyelids were sewed up for a time. He recovered his sight in an extraordinary, if not miraculous manner, on Easter Sunday, 1906, and speaks of his cure as *une guérison liturgique*.[3] Having long known the agony of neuralgia, dyspepsia, stomach trouble, and toothache, he was finally attacked by cancer of the throat. He suffered greatly, but refused to take anesthetics to relieve the pain. He died on May 12, 1907, and was buried in the Benedictine habit in Montparnasse cemetery.

Arthur Symons, who knew Huysmans personally, describes him thus: "The face is gray, wearily alert with a look of benevolent malice. At first sight it is commonplace, the features are ordinary, one seems to have seen it at the Bourse or Stock Exchange."[4] Havelock Ellis says that he had sensitive, luminous eyes, and he adds that Huysmans talked in low and even tones, without emphasis or gesture, not addressing any special person. "Human imbecility was the burden of nearly all that he said, while a faint twinkle of amused wonderment lit up his eyes."[5] Huneker speaks of the

Semitic contour of his head, and Dom Besse of his friendly smile. Bachelin tells us that he was very modest, and that he blushed like a girl when he was complimented.

This is the picture of the exterior life of Huysmans. Many of the characters in his novels are likenesses of himself, and reveal much about the author that his biographers omit. This is particularly true of his later books which give us a more or less exact history of his soul, while his early works are rather objective and impersonal. *Le Drageoir aux épices* (1874), his first effort, is indeed a real little box of spices. Symons well describes it as "a pasticcio of prose poems done after Baudelaire, of little sketches done after Dutch artists, together with a few studies of Parisian landscape done after nature."[6] *Marthe,* published two years later, is the story of a woman of the lowest type and was speedily suppressed in France. It is the least personal of his novels, one of the dullest and most repulsive with scarcely a touch of pity. In *Les Soeurs Vatard,* dedicated to Zola, he meticulously describes his neighborhood. We get realistic pictures of life in close, smelly sewing shops, filled with cheap, vulgar women and boorish men. It is truly a "frame without a picture," for there is no beginning and no end, simply the prosaic account of the love affairs of two working girls, Céline and Désirée Vatard. Céline is an out-and-out *fille,* while Désirée is supposed to be *honnête,* and marries her overseer's nephew, but the moral standard of both is deplorably below par.

Huysmans was one of the five admirers of Zola who gathered around him at Médan, and in 1880 he contributed to the collection of short stories entitled *Les Soirées de Médan,* his *Sac au dos.* This, as we have said, relates under the guise of fiction, his own personal experiences in the Franco-Prussian War, and is brutal and cynic in tone. The same year he published *Croquis Parisiens,* a description of Paris, which, he said, was fast becoming a "sinister Chicago." It contains excellent word sketches of people and places in the great capital, chosen apparently at random, of the washerwoman, the policeman, the music halls, the landscape, etc.

En Ménage (1881) records the weariness and dreariness of life, the intolerable monotony of daily annoyances. André, a novelist, marries Berthe. He finds out that she is unfaithful to him and leaves her. His life as a bachelor is so unbearable, however, that he finally takes Berthe back. His friend Cyprien, a painter, is a confirmed woman-hater, but in the end lives with a concubine, Mélie. The latter sums up the pessimistic Huysmansian philosophy of the book when she says: "Provided that I do not suffer too much misery with a man and that he does not beat me, I esteem myself happy. That is the only thing worth while after all."[7]

À Vau-l'eau ("Down Stream") (1882) is the tale of M. Folantin, a government employee with a poor stomach, who spends his life looking for a good restaurant. It has been well called "an Odyssey of a dyspeptic."[8] *Un Dilemme,* the story of an abandoned girl, is published in the same volume. Neither it nor *En Rade* which followed in 1887, occupies an important place in Huysmans' works. The latter tells of Jacques Marles and his wife, who find that life in the city is too expensive, and so move to the country in order to subsist more cheaply. They are quickly disillusioned with regard to bucolic joys, and suffer a perpetual boredom. The nervous state of the couple is increased instead of soothed. *L'Art moderne* (1883) and *Certains* (1890) are both criticisms of modernity in art. Among those "discovered" by Huysmans are Degas, Rops, and Raffaelli.

In all these early works, the author's chief concern seems to be to present to us the picture of universal ugliness, to focus on the sordidness of human existence. He has an extraordinary gift for precise and detailed description, but the quickening breath of hope is wanting to his pictures, as well as the saving touch of human tenderness. His gloomy cynicism is an indirect reflection of Schopenhauer's materialistic philosophy and of Zola's odious naturalism.

The change came in 1884 with *À Rebours*. In the introduction to this book, written twenty years later, Huysmans says: "The strange thing was that without suspecting it at the beginning, I was led by the very nature of my task to study the Church under many aspects."[9] He was not actually converted until 1895, but the seed had been cast into good soil and was trying hard to die, so that it might bring forth the hundredfold. The closing words of the novel clearly indicate this: "Lord, take pity on the Christian who doubts, on the agnostic who wishes to believe, on the outcast from life who sets sail alone during the night, under a sky no longer lit by the consoling beacons of ancient Hope."[10] Des Esseintes, the hero, is an example of a neurotic pervert. He is the last descendant of a family of decadents, and his blood is tainted by the excesses of his ancestors. A frail young man of thirty, anemic and nervous, he retires to his country home at Fontenay where he hopes to gratify his thirst for rare sensations and his passion for silent musing. He imagines that if he takes life *à rebours* ("against' the grain"), he will find in it new satisfaction and a sure escape from the vulgarity and irksomeness of society. It is an original idea, and the extravagant unreality of the book is the first thing that strikes the reader. Des Esseintes turns day into night and night into day; all the floors are covered with a heavy carpeting, and the two old servants wear thick felt shoes; the doors swing on well-oiled hinges; the private study is done in bright blue and orange. He specializes in unusual jewels, perfumes, and flowers, in Latin literature and plain chant. There are some terrible chapters in the book (VI and IX) and also some excellent incidents. Perhaps the attempted trip to London is the finest episode and the most characteristic of the imaginative life led by one of an artistic temperament. This is the hero's only excursion into the exterior world, but when he returns to Fontenay his nervous malady increases so rapidly that the doctor sternly orders him back to a normal mode of living. It is a choice between obedience and madness, so he reluctantly obeys. He had sought by artificial means to gain new interest in life, but the experiment had failed and he wearily packs his trunks for Paris.

À Rebours is more personal and more artistic than any of Huysmans' previous works and it is written in exquisite French prose. The author says that all the romances he wrote after this one are contained in embryo in it. Chapter III on Latin literature of the Decadence and Chapter XV on plain chant are developed in *En Route* and *L'Oblat* ("The Oblate"). Chapter IV on precious stones and Chapter VIII on flowers are recapitulated in *La Cathédrale* ("The Cathedral"), while parts of Chapters VI and XII forecast *Là-bas* ("Down There").

This last work (1891), a compound of magic and occultism, contains many passages overcharged with sensuality and nastiness. Durtal, the principal personage, is writing the life of Gilles de Rais (the traditional Blue-Beard) and in order to understand better the sadism of the protagonist, he undertakes a study of satanism as it was practiced by his contemporaries. Madame de Chantelouve, whom Huneker calls "quite the vilest character in French fiction,"[11] is probably introduced to illustrate a case of sadism in a woman. The monstrous picture of the Black Mass in Chapter XIX, with its obscene and sacrilegious rites, is both repulsive and powerful. Huysmans' principal source of information in writing his book was a bad priest who had experienced all the horrors of the black art. When this unfortunate man wanted to return to the Church, Rome exacted of him a written account of his offenses, and Huysmans possessed a copy of this document. "Do not imagine," says Dom Besse, "that Huysmans was personally associated with these odious mysteries of occultism, the scenes of which he has evoked with such startling force. Satanism piqued his curiosity, but only for a short time. He studied it just enough to convince himself of the existence of spirits superior to man. This conviction led him to the thought of God and marked the first stage of his conversion."[12] Huysmans himself writes: "As for that book *Là-bas* which frightened so many people, neither should I write it in the same manner, now that I am become a Catholic once more."[13]

In *En Route** (1895) Durtal, become a Catholic, is again the hero. His conversion was, first of all, a miracle of grace. He says: "All I know is that having been for years an unbeliever, I suddenly believe."[14] He admits later on, however, that there were three secondary causes, the atavism of an old and pious family, his disgust for life, and his love for art and liturgy.[15] But though his faith is strong, his will is weak and vacillating, and the book relates his struggle between habits of sin and a desire for holiness. He becomes acquainted with Abbé Gévresin, who persuades him to go to Notre Dame de l'Âtre, a small Trappist monastery a few miles from Paris, to make a retreat. The story is autobiographical, a minute psychological study of a man's soul at a crucial moment in its existence. Durtal is amazingly frank, and relates the experiences of his inner life in minute detail. There are numerous digressions, consisting mainly of essays on plain chant, liturgical art, monasticism and mysticism, lives of the saints, devotion to the Blessed Virgin, etc. The book is an odd mixture of medieval earnestness and modern levity. For example, just before Durtal attends Compline with an extraordinary fervor and appreciation of the Divine Office, he sneaks out into the garden to smoke a forbidden cigarette.[16] *En Route* is also an excellent defense of monastic

---

* Translated into English under the same title.

orders, and a sympathetic picture of the life they lead. Henry Thurston Peck says of it: "To those of us who are Protestants the book is full of deep instruction in revealing with startling force the secret of the power of that wonderful religious organization which has made provision for the needs of every human soul, whether it requires for its comfort active service or the mystical life of contemplation."[17]

After Durtal's return from La Trappe he spends the following year at Chartres in the shadow of the old cathedral. Two motives urge him to this decision. First, he wishes to escape from Paris for which he has long felt a profound distaste, and secondly, he longs for a quiet, peaceful refuge where he can retire alone with his thoughts and his books. With Abbé Gévresin for a director and Abbé Plomb for a guide, he studies the cathedral as an exponent of medieval theology. It is indeed not so much architecture and archeology which interest him as their symbolic interpretation. His book is a prayerful hymn to the Virgin of Chartres, in which he celebrates with pious emotion the glories of his Queen, as well as the faith, love, and genius of those who built her temple. There is little action, exterior or interior, and only four characters — Durtal, two priests, and the housekeeper. On the other hand, the story is overloaded with a mass of tiresome details and lengthy digressions. Huysmans in his enthusiasm forgets that most readers are not as vitally interested in ecclesiastical art and music as he is. Still, as we close the book, most of us will say with Mrs. Crawford: "For my own part, I am filled with a sense of gratitude toward M. Huysmans for having given us *La Cathédrale*. It is full of beautiful writing, of wonderful descriptive pages, of delicate appreciations, of spiritual insight into Christian symbolism."[18]

Durtal becomes restless once more. There is at the bottom of his soul a vague "homesickness for the medieval cloister," and in *L'Oblat* we find him at *Val des Saints,* living in a house near the monastery, attending the office and studying the liturgy. He is a novice for a year, and then with impressive ceremonies he becomes an oblate of St. Benedict. His duties and obligations are not very well defined, but he binds himself by promise to follow, as exactly as his state of life permits, the rule of St. Benedict, and to be faithful above all to the *Opus Dei*. In *En Route* Durtal was a sorry hero, continually wavering between evil propensities and the workings of grace. Even in *La Cathédrale*, though he is steadier in the pursuit of good, he is often aweary of well-doing and bored by virtue. But here at last in *L'Oblat* we find that his face is steadily set toward God with his thoughts turned more and more toward medieval mysticism. *L'Oblat* did not appeal to the general public as strongly as did some of his former works (particularly *À Rebours* and *En Route*), nor is it as artistic, but there is a sincerity in its realistic presentation enhanced by a maturity of judgment, that attracts many readers. Huysmans knew how to be pious without becoming saccharine either in sentiment or expression, and his absolute honesty saved him from any shade of hypocrisy. To a medievalist, an artist, a liturgist, a lover of monastic life, a Benedictine, the book is a garden of delights.

Huysmans produced three other works worthy of special mention. While at Ligugé he wrote the life of St. Lydwine of Schiedam. In this he sets forth the doctrine of mystic substitution. Saints, by their voluntary sufferings united to the Passion of Christ, can, in view of the Communion of Saints, satisfy for the sins of the wicked on earth, and also aid the souls in purgatory. Such was St. Lydwine's mission, and Huysmans tells her fascinating story in his strong, colorful style. *Les Foules de Lourdes* ("The Crowds of Lourdes") (1905) is a final tribute to the Virgin, so faithfully loved and honored. Huysmans pays it in his own blunt, outspoken way, but withal it is meant to be a wholehearted offering to our Lady. He relates with childlike faith the wonders he witnessed at Lourdes, and judges correctly that the greatest miracle of all is not the cures, but the depths of hidden charity which one always finds there. His last work was *Trois églises et trois primitifs*. It is an analysis of the art and symbolism of three churches and of three paintings that the author especially admired.

In spite of the evident Catholicity of his later works, Huysmans' conversion, so graphically related in *En Route,* was viewed with suspicion by many. They thought he was merely striking a new attitude. His open censure of Church practices of which he did not approve, scandalized them. We are not surprised at this when we read certain passages. For example, he describes the so-called pious folk who frequented the churches, thus: "Almost all had a side-long look, an oily voice, downcast eyes, immovable spectacles, clothes like sacristans as if of black wood; almost all told their beads ostentatiously, and with more strategy and more knavery than the wicked, took toll of their neighbors on leaving God. The devout women were still less reassuring. They invaded the church, walking about as if quite at home, disturbing everybody, upsetting chairs, knocking against you without begging pardon; then they knelt down with much ado, in the attitude of contrite angels, murmured interminable pater-nosters, and left the church more arrogant and sour than before."[19] In speaking of the Madeleine, one of the most loved and admired churches of Paris, he says: "The clergy make Jesus like a tourist, when they invite Him daily to come down into that church whose exterior is surmounted by no cross, and whose interior is like the grand reception room of a hotel."[20] He found secular priests "so mediocre, so lukewarm, above all, so hostile to mysticism,"[21] that his conclusion is: "Perhaps the secular clergy are only the leavings, for the contemplative orders and the missionary army carry away every year the pick of the spiritual basket . . . so when the cream is off, the rest of the clergy are plainly but the skim milk, the scourings of the seminaries."[22] He declares that bishops are intriguing and servile, that they "have no longer either talent or manners. Caught in part in the fishpond of bad priests, they show themselves ready for everything, and turn out to be souls of old usurers, low jobbers, beggars, when you press them."[23]

Notwithstanding the obvious exaggeration and injustice in these caustic censures, it must be admitted that in some cases there is possibly a grain of truth in them. Most Catholics, however, refrain from expressing adverse criticisms so bluntly, and are exceedingly jarred when they hear others do so. Their respect for the Church, even on its human side, is so great that they cover with the mantle of charity any inessential weaknesses they may discover. But Huysmans had been trained in the Naturalistic school and called a spade a spade with no apologies. When he came into the Church, he brought with him the habit of picking out ugly, nauseous details even when the whole is beautiful and lovely. This practice, applied to spiritual and religious matters, was bound to startle and offend many of his readers. Yet there can be no doubt about the soundness of his Catholicity. He says in *À Rebours:* "I was not brought up in the schools of any religious order but just in a lycée. I was never a pious boy, and the influences of childish associations, of first Communion, of religious teaching, which often loom so large in conversion, never had any effect on me. What still further complicates the difficulty and defies analysis is this: in the days when I wrote *À Rebours* I never set foot in a church. I did not know a single practical Catholic layman nor priest. . . . *À Rebours* appeared in 1884 and I set off to be converted at a Trappist house in 1892."[24] He goes on to tell that Providence was merciful to him and the Blessed Virgin kind, so he awoke one morning with his difficulties solved, and prayed for the first time. His fidelity to the Church during his last years of suffering proves conclusively the genuineness of his conversion. He destroyed letters, notes, manuscripts, which he thought contained anything offensive to religion, thus sacrificing his vanity and offering in satisfaction his sufferings, "those that it may please God to send me here below and also those which His justice has reserved for me in the other world."[25] Abbé Mugnier, who was his personal friend and director, testifies that his was a most thorough conversion, though hardly the classic kind. When Huysmans first came to him repentant, he said: "I wish to clean my soul. Have you any lye?"[26] Ellis's contention that his conversion was merely an "emotional phenomenon" which occurs "especially in those who have undergone long and torturing disquietude"[27] is nonsense. It is true that Huysmans was mightily stirred by the chant, the liturgy, and the sacred art of the Church. But only a deep faith and the grace of God could have made him purify his soul with such a terrible sincerity, and guard its whiteness to the very end.

Critics find it hard to decide whether or not Huysmans should be called a *mystic*. They disagree not so much because their opinions of the man differ, as because their definitions of mysticism vary. Mysticism comes from the Greek word μύειν, to initiate, and its philosophical and religious significance is a desire and tendency of the human soul toward an intimate union with the Divinity, based on a direct and immediate intuition of the Infinite. The term is often used loosely, to denote that which is allegorical and symbolical, or even vague and elusive. Sometimes it is applied to scientific theories alleged to involve the assumption of occult qualities or mysterious agencies of which no rational account can be given. Huysmans' passion for Catholic liturgy, music, and art, his cult of the Middle Ages, his touching devotion to the Blessed Virgin, and finally his heroic patience during the agonies of his last illness, may all be taken as indications of a strong leaning toward mysticism in its true sense. His fondness for allegory and symbol, evinced particularly in *La Cathédrale,* justify his being called a mystic in the second sense also, and *Là-bas* is an excellent example of the third definition of mysticism. But Huysmans is certainly a very prosaic, matter-of-fact mystic. He never becomes sentimental or mawkish in speaking of religion or religious practices. Still less is he inclined to get emotional over himself. His prayer before setting out for La Trappe is characteristic: "My soul is an evil place, sordid and infamous; till now it has loved only perverse ways; it has exacted from my wretched body the tithe of illicit pleasures and unholy joys; it is worth little, it is worth nothing; and yet down there near Thee, if Thou wilt succour me, I think that I shall subdue it. But if my body be sick, I cannot force it to obey me; this is worse than all, I am disarmed if Thou dost not come to my aid. Take count of this, O Lord; I know by experience that when I am ill-fed, I have neuralgia; humanly, logically speaking, I am certain to be horribly ill at Notre Dame de l'Âtre; nevertheless, if I can get about at all, the day after tomorrow, I will go all the same."[28]

His piety is, however, deep and true, and his appreciation of genuine sanctity shows itself continually. He exclaims in *L'Oblat:* "Priests and monks devoid of mysticism! What flocks of dead souls that would mean! The monks will then be mere curators of a museum of old traditions and old formulae; and the priests will be clerks, as it were, in a sort of Heavenly Company, officials under a Board of Sacraments."[29] In his life of St. Lydwine he recounts how God began "to cultivate her, to root out all thoughts which could displease Him, to hoe her soul, to rake it till the blood flowed."[30] In *Les Foules de Lourdes* he insists that we ought not to be praying for the healing of our ills but for their increase: "We should be offering ourselves as holocausts in expiation of the sins of all men."[31]

Huysmans' philosophy is pessimistic. He suffered a bad attack of the *mal du siècle* in early years when he was a disciple of Zola, and he never entirely recovered from it. His characters betray an incurable ennui which annoys the reader. Most of them are weak, spineless, selfish creatures, continually grumbling about food, the victims of irritated nerves. He blames and ridicules without mercy, displaying a keen sense of the absurdity of human affairs which often makes his laughter cruel. For instance, he calls the young ladies' choir "a troop of young and old geese, who make our Lady run around on her litanies as on hobby-horses to the music of a fair."[32] He gets more kindly as he grows older, but even in *Les Foules de Lourdes* he scolds about the vulgarity of the crowds at the Grotto, the poor taste of the artists, the greed of the guardians, and the jabbering of the women. Those poor women! Throughout his books Huysmans treats them either as stupid, brainless nonentities (Céline and Désirée Vatard, Marthe, Berthe, etc.) or as base, vicious creatures of the Madame de Chantelouve type. Even Madame Bavoil, the housekeeper, though a good pious soul, becomes a talkative nuisance at times. This attitude is all the more strange in the light of his chivalrous devotion to the Blessed Virgin.   1503977

Huysmans is also exceedingly plain-spoken. Reference has already been made elsewhere to the observation of C. Kegan Paul that what English *men* would not say to each other privately can be said in French openly without causing consternation.[33] Especially in his early works Huysmans has described indecent and shocking scenes with astonishing nonchalance. In *En Route,* the candor with which he relates his temptations against purity and gives an account of his general confession[34] amazes most Catholics, who are accustomed to regard the secret of the confessional (even on the part of the penitent) as something too sacred to be retailed in a novel. Still his frankness and naturalness is refreshing. Huysmans hates everything that savors of hypocrisy, and says exactly what he means in strong, terse language. He has a remarkable acuteness of vision and sees remote resemblances which suggest an abundance of unusual metaphors and daring epithets. Symons expresses it epigrammatically when he says that "Huysmans is a brain all eye."[35] He often sacrifices rhythm to color, using discordant syntactical inversions and bizarre words[36] with a freedom that is rash. The result is that his style is sometimes harsh and awkward, though always sincere and expressive.

His descriptions are incomparable, and prove him to be a born word-painter. Even in his first story *Le Drageoir aux épices,* his sketch of the carcass of a cow hanging outside the butcher's shop arrests our attention, for with one skillful stroke he brings before us a complete picture. Of a desolate, ugly landscape he says: "It was nature's scab, the leprosy of the earth";[37] of the statue of a queen: "she stands magnificently arrayed in a stiff-pleated robe channelled lengthwise, like a stick of celery."[38] Someone's complexion reminded him of a ripe apricot, another had eyes of a tired blue; an old man at Lourdes displayed a huge pear-shaped goiter. He speaks of "gravies of prayer, concentrated sauces of ideas,"[39] of the afternoon "wearing its colors of bronze and blue."[40] At one time the Church singers "throw up like ditchers their shovelfuls of verses"[41] and again they "churn up a margarine of rancid tones."[42] After listening to the *De Profundis,* he concludes that no music is superior to the old plain chant, "that even and naked melody, at once ethereal and of the tomb, the solemn cry of sadness and lofty shout of joy, those grandiose hymns of human faith, which seem to gush up in the cathedrals like irresistible geysers, at the very foot of the Romanesque pillars."[43]

Huysmans is an egoist and an idealist. He is an egoist because he himself is the center of all his works, because he is so sure that he is right and the rest of the world is wrong; only his keen sense of humor and his absolute honesty save him from being a snob. He is an idealist because he is never satisfied but always seeking something better and higher. He craves the invisible, being thoroughly tired of our dreary, sordid old world. As Dom Besse says: "He is a man from out the Middle Ages strayed into our times."[44] He would have all men live as monks, chanting the psalms, attending the Church offices, praising God by song and brush. And many a monk might well strike his breast and confess that Huysmans has a far greater appreciation of ecclesiastical art and music than he!

PRINCIPAL WORKS OF JORIS-KARL HUYSMANS

1874	*Le Drageoir aux épices*
1876	*Marthe*
1879	*Les Soeurs Vatard*
1880	*Sac au dos*
1880	*Croquis Parisiens*
1881	*En Ménage*
1882	*À Vau-l'eau*
1884	*À Rebours*
1887	*En Rade*
1891	*Là-bas*
1895	*En Route*
1897	*Là-haut*
1898	*La Cathédrale*
1901	*Sainte-Lydwine de Schiedam*
1903	*L'Oblat*
1906	*Les Foules de Lourdes*
1908	*Trois églises et trois primitifs*
1930	*Oeuvres complètes* (12 vol.)

REFERENCES

Besse, Dom Jean, *Joris-Karl Huysmans*, Paris, 1917.

Blandin, Henri, *Joris-Karl Huysmans, l'homme, l'écrivain, l'apologiste*, Paris, 1912.

Céard, Henry, *Joris-Karl Huysmans intime, l'artiste et le chrétien*, Paris, 1907.

Colluci, Frank, *Joris-Karl Huysmans' Art Criticism,* Ithaca, N. Y., 1934.

Coquiot, Gustave, *Le vrai Joris-Karl Huysmans,* Paris, 1912.

Deffoux, Léon, *Joris-Karl Huysmans sous divers aspects,* Paris, 1927.

Du Bourg, Antoine, *Huysmans intime. Lettres et souvenirs,* Paris, 1908.

Harry, Miriam, *Trois ombres, J. K. Huysmans, Jules Lemaître, Anatole France,* Paris, 1932.

Jörgensen, Joh., *Joris-Karl Huysmans,* Munich, 1908.

Seillière, Ernest, *Joris-Karl Huysmans,* Paris, 1931.

Valéry, Paul, *Huysmans,* Paris, 1927.

CHAPTER IV

Paul Bourget

(1852-1935)

JULES LEMAÎTRE, IN HIS ESSAY ON PAUL
Bourget written in 1886, hails him as "a young sage, prince
of the youth of a very old century."[1] Bourget lived to be a
gray-haired man of eighty-three, but it is curious to note
that in one of his last novels, *Le Diamant de la reine,* written
in 1932, he states that he still hopes to remain the laborious
worker that he was in those early days "up until that last
deleatur of the page of life, so well expressed in the old
adage *Mors ultima linea rerum est.*"[2] For over half a century he has courageously worked ahead, publishing some
seventy books in spite of all that he has suffered at the
hands of critics, and bravely clinging to his spiritual convictions in an age when Science is the supreme idol before
which writers worship. In the twilight glory of his long life,
the world laid at his feet the tribute of its homage, and
recognized in him one of the outstanding figures in the
literary history of modern France.

Dimnet believes that Bourget's biography as a human tale
will never be written, for he is a voice rather than a man.[3]
He always sought seclusion, shrunk from everything
that savored of advertisement, and viewed life more as a
spectator and adviser than as an actor. We know him principally from his books, but here again he usually reveals
himself as a thinker and psychologist, seldom as a personal
friend.

Paul Charles Joseph Bourget was born at Amiens on September 2, 1852. His paternal ancestors had come from

central France, his great-grandfather having been a farmer, and his grandfather a civil engineer. His father, Justin Bourget, was a professor of mathematics, and as he moved from one lycée to another, his family had to go with him. Thus Paul began his education at Strasburg, continued it at Clermont-Ferrand, and at fifteen entered Sainte-Barbe in Paris. He attributes the conflicts in his own character to his wandering youth, and to the diverse heredity of his parents. We know little about his mother excepting that she was of German descent and from Lorraine. From her he claims his poetic and philosophic bent, and from his Latin father his aptitude for clarity and analysis.[4]

From early years Bourget was a good student. He read Shakespeare in French translation at the age of six, and devoured Musset, Balzac, Stendhal, and Baudelaire a few years later.[5] At Sainte-Barbe he specialized in philosophy, Greek philology, and Latin, and won a prize in Latin composition in 1870. From August to November, 1871, he followed the clinic at Hôtel-Dieu in Paris. This smattering of medicine proved helpful to him in his psychological dissections later on. He was not much interested in politics, nor did the Franco-Prussian War affect him very deeply. In 1872 he took his licentiate's degree and began teaching at the École Bossuet. The following year he traveled in Italy and Greece, and on his return he contributed to several reviews and papers.

His allowance was stopped when he was twenty-one, because, studious though he was, he did not wish to follow his father's profession. For ten years he struggled on in poverty and obscurity, barely able to support himself by his pen. He lived in an attic, spent a couple of hours a day teaching backward students, and wrote poetry and magazine articles. In 1875 he published *La Vie inquiète,* and in 1878, *Édel.* The first is a volume of verse, artistic and musical, but lacking in depth and vigor. The second is a narrative poem which tells the story of the love of a poor poet for a rich and beautiful girl. The hero, who wishes to awaken and find himself famous, reminds one of Bourget himself, who was nursing the same Byronic ambition. But he soon realized that he would never gain celebrity by his poems, and with the publication of *Les Aveux* in 1882, he bade adieu to verse and turned to prose.

He had written articles for the *Revue des deux mondes, Journal des débats,* and *Nouvelle revue.* He was a friend of Dumas fils, of Taine, and of Leconte de Lisle. He had read omnivorously, and he possessed an extraordinary power of assimilating and retaining what he read. It is no wonder then, that one so well fitted to be a critic should gain applause by his *Essais de psychologie contemporaine.* The first volume, published in 1883, contains psychological expositions of five authors: Baudelaire, Renan, Flaubert, Taine, and Stendhal. One feels that the writer, though only a young man of thirty, has the soundness of judgment and clarity of vision of the mature critic. The same impression is given by the second volume of *Essais* (1885) containing studies of Dumas fils, Leconte de Lisle, the Goncourts, Turgenev, and Amiel. In the revised edition of these essays, issued in 1900, Bourget says in the preface, "I reprint today, under a definitive form, restoring to them the unity of their title, the ten literary studies which I had published in 1883 and in 1885, and distributed in two distinct series, under the titles of *Essays* and *New Essays of Contemporary Psychology.*" It is noteworthy that he chose as subjects of his studies men of his own day, most of whom he knew personally. As a critic, he is formal and at the same time personal. To him, as to Taine and to Sainte-Beuve, the author is of much more importance than the book. Renard notes that, in studying men, he asks himself two questions: "Of what causes is this man the effect?" and "Of what effects is he the cause?," putting the greater stress on the

second question.[6] He passes over external features and tries
to penetrate into thoughts and motives. Henceforth he is
the anatomist of the human soul, and so he attempts to
paint a moral picture of his generation through the books
that affected him most. Sometimes he projects too much
of himself into those he is studying, but he is always honest
in his investigations. The *Essais* were followed in 1888 by
Études et portraits, a collection of articles on very diverse
subjects (writers, aesthetics, travels, nature, art, etc.), and
in 1890 by *Pastels* (ten portraits of women) and *Nouveaux
pastels* ("Pastels of Men"). His first story, *L'Irréparable,* was
begun in 1883, in a little room at Oxford near the old Wor-
cester College, haunted by the ghost of Thomas de Quincey.
It was published in 1884, and *Cruelle énigme* ("Love's
Cruel Enigma") followed in 1885.

There are few other events in his exterior life to be recorded. In 1880 he gave up teaching in order to devote
himself entirely to writing, and in 1890 he married Mlle
David of Antwerp. He visited the United States from
August, 1893, until April, 1894, and published an account
of his impressions of our country under the title of *Outre-
mer* ("Outre-mer: Impressions of America") in 1895. He
was received into the French Academy on June 13, 1895,
occupying the twelfth *fauteuil.* From then until his death,
which occurred on Christmas day, 1935, he lived more or
less in retirement, publishing on an average a novel a year.
In 1922 he was appointed Curator of the Palace of Chantilly,
and in 1923 he was made a Commander of the Legion of
Honor. During his last years he spent most of his time in
Paris in his elegant apartment on the Rue Barbet-de-Jouy, or
in his summer home at Le Plantier de Costàbelle near
Hyères.

Bourget's literary production consists of poetry, criticism,
novels, short stories, and dramas. We have spoken very
briefly of his débuts in the first two classes. We shall now

take up the third and discuss it more at length, for it is as a novelist that Bourget won fame and that he is known to the reading public of today. Moreover what we say of his novels is in general true of his work in other fields, poetry excepted. They are a conscious and normal development of his psychological essays, as he himself tells us in his *Lettre autobiographique*: "I began to write my first novel with the same pen which had just finished the preface of the *Essays*. I have published since then about fifteen volumes: novels, short stories, accounts of travels, composed according to this same method of interior analysis."[7] Most of his short stories are really novelettes, and his plays are in many cases dramatized novels, more fitted for reading than for acting. In all his works the main interest is the psychological study.

Even in his earliest novels Bourget shows his genius for analysis. *L'Irréparable* is an excellent study of woman's character, and both *Cruelle énigme* and *Crime d'amour* ("A Love Crime") portray the disorders of the passions and the contrast between the apparent happiness they offer and the tragic misery which the abuse of them actually brings. He himself calls *André Cornélis* ("The Son") *une simple planche d'anatomie morale*.[8] *Mensonges* ("Lies") tells the story of a handsome Parisian woman who dupes her gullible husband while accepting the attentions and money of a dissolute rascal. An idealistic young poet falls in love with her and for a moment one thinks that, stung by remorse, she will reform. But instead of that, she drags him down to despair and attempted suicide.

Bourget began then by accepting the ideas of his time, Tainian relativity and agnosticism. But in 1889 came *Le Disciple* ("The Disciple"), and with it his so-called conversion. Much has been written of this book and of the change it indicates in the author's views. Briefly it is the story of Robert Greslou, the intelligent but vain disciple of Adrian Sixte, a materialistic philosopher. He enters as tutor

into the family Jussat-Randon, and decides to seduce the
daughter, Charlotte, with the avowed purpose of trying on
her a psychological experiment, namely, to study the mech-
anism of love and to prove the exactness of his own theories.
Another motive is his grudge against the elder brother,
André, whose principal crime is that he is an aristocrat,
while Greslou is a bourgeois. The two young people actually fall in love with each other, and knowing marriage
to be impossible, they decide to die together. But love of life
and a slowness to action characteristic of speculative minds,
causes Greslou to regret his promise and Charlotte indignantly takes the poison alone, after having written a request
to André to avenge her. Greslou is tried for murder, and
from prison he sends to Adrian Sixte a detailed confession,
showing that his moral life ending in crime has been but
the logical carrying out of his master's teaching. Sixte is
horrified and intends to speak in court to save Greslou, but
André, after a terrific struggle, decides to tell the judge the
truth of the case. Immediately after doing this, he shoots
Greslou.

The plot of the novel is slight, and the principal interest
is not in it, but in the study of the soul-states of Greslou,
and in the question of the moral responsibility of the master.
Was Sixte really accountable for the crime of his pupil? Yes,
to a great extent, for he had given him a wrong philosophy
of life and a false conscience. He had made him believe that
it is quite lawful to use a human soul as an instrument in a
psychological experiment, even though the experiment bring
ruin to that soul. So Greslou closes his letter of confession to
Sixte: "Write to me, my dear master, direct me. Strengthen
me in the doctrine which was, which is still mine, in this
conviction of universal necessity which wills that even our
most detestable, our most disastrous actions, even this cold
enterprise of seduction, even my weakness before the pact
of death, be bound up with the whole body of laws of this

immense universe. Tell me that I am not a monster, that there is no such thing as a monster, that you will be there still, if I come out of this supreme crisis, to accept me as a disciple, as a friend."[9] The earlier novels are more entertaining, but not so strong or powerful as this one. It is free from affectation, and Bourget reveals in it a subtle psychology and an astounding knowledge of the secrets of the human soul.

As to his "conversion,"[10] he himself declares that he was not converted. In the preface to the definitive edition of his works (1900) he says: "One is converted from a negation, but not from a purely expectant attitude," and he goes on to show that though there was development in his thought, there was no contradiction. Nevertheless, it is evident from his novels that there was a decided transformation in his views, and that this transformation dates in general from *Le Disciple,* which Brunetière calls "not only one of the best novels of Bourget, but one of his best actions."[11] Probably the germ of faith was never lost, but his early works reveal unwholesome torments of soul. Lalou expresses it thus: "Frightened himself by the consequences to which the positivism which he had described could lead . . . Bourget saw certain succour only in a return to the Christian religion, which he already associates with ideas of order and hierarchy."[12] Henceforth his novels show more religious morality, and are nourished with Catholic principles. Henceforth he will not only present the evil, but will suggest a remedy. Deschamps[13] says that there were two men in him, the dilettante and the mystic, the psychologist and the moralist, the dandy and the preacher; the first of these disappears and the second predominates.

In several of the novels which follow *Le Disciple,* however, Bourget seems to go back to his first manner, to study social problems without offering any sort of redress. For instance, *Un Coeur de femme* (1890) is the story of Juliette de Tillières, a beautiful young widow, the mistress of Henri de Poyanne. She meets Raymond de Casal, and, after the usual feeble struggle, she yields to her sensual love for him. Poyanne discovers her change of sentiment, and with a broken heart, sails for America, while she lives in voluntary retirement, first with her mother and later in a convent. The chief interest in the story is the study of Juliette's heart. There is much moralizing throughout, as, for example, in the last chapter, where after having discussed the enigmatic love of Juliette for two men of such different character as Poyanne and Casal, the author expatiates on the mystery of woman in general. *La Duchesse bleue* ("The Blue Duchess") is much the same type of story. The principal character is a young actress whose moral life is ruined by a heartless dramatist.

But in *Un Saint* (1891), *La Terre promise* (1892), and *Cosmopolis* (1893) there is a tone of deeper seriousness, a more avowed purpose to teach a moral lesson, and less of dilettantism. *Un Saint* ("A Saint"), with its exquisite Italian setting, is one of the most beautiful of Bourget's stories. The scene is laid at Monte-Chiaro, formerly a Benedictine convent, whose custodian is a kind old monk, filled with God's own spirit. He shows some guests a collection of rare coins and medals, and when they explain to him the enormous value of his treasure, he is delighted as he hopes that it will enable him to buy back lands formerly belonging to the monastery, which can be used (when his dreams come true) for the convalescent monks. Early next morning Philippe Dubois, one of the guests, a cynical young man embittered toward life, steals two of the most valuable of the coins. The good monk finds it out, but instead of reproaching Philippe, he offers him the treasure box, telling him that he may have his choice of the coins. Philippe, overcome with shame and remorse, confesses his theft, and immediately there shines in his face "the dawn of another soul."

In the preface of *La Terre promise* ("The Land of Promise") Bourget says: "If such a title would not have appeared too ambitious, this book should be called *The Right of the Child.*" It is in fact an examination of the obligation of a father toward his illegitimate child. Of greater importance than this sociological study, however, is the portrayal of the mental struggle of the principal character, Francis Nayrac. He is torn between his love for a beautiful, pure, young girl, Henriette Scilly, and his duty to Adèle, his child by another man's wife. When Henriette learns the truth, she refuses to marry him, and tries to expiate by sacrifice the sin of her former fiancé. Again in *Cosmopolis,** the lives of the two most admirable characters are ruined: Alba Steno commits suicide, and Fanny Hafner retires to a country estate, and the reader feels that the disaster is the logical result of the dilettantism of Julien Dorsenne and the jealousy of Lydia Maitland. Dorsenne is, in fact, the typical cosmopolite. He passes successively from one locality to another, "lending himself to all, but giving himself to none." The other persons in the story are ethnical types, each one showing the characteristics of his race. The idea of heredity is emphasized still more in the greater novels of the next period, in which pure psychology gives place to sociology: *L'Étape* (1902), *Un Divorce* (1904), *L'Émigré* (1906), and the plays *La Barricade* (1910) and *Le Tribun* (1912). In point of time, these follow closely on the Dreyfus affair, and the characteristic feature of all of them is that they treat social problems, containing political and religious teaching for the group, as well as moral lessons for the individual.

In *L'Étape,* we have Joseph Monneron, the overeducated son of a peasant, become through his intelligent and persevering energy a professor at the lycée. The transition is too sudden and his family cannot adjust itself to the new life

---

* Translated into English under the same title.

of the bourgeois class. Misfortunes fall upon them. The eldest son is a forger, the youngest a street waif, and the daughter is seduced and shoots her faithless lover. The second boy, Jean, an upright young man, is in love with a Catholic girl, Brigitte Ferrand, whose father will not permit her to marry the son of an unbeliever. Jean is converted and the marriage takes place, though Joseph Monneron grieves over it and considers his life a wretched failure. Jean decides to found a family, not according to the principles of his free-thinking Dreyfusard father, but rather built on the solid foundation of Catholic faith professed by his wife and father-in-law. The story, which suggests *Les Déracinés* of Barrès, is profoundly religious, though severe in tone. It urges the slower development of the family, which, in France at least, cannot *brûler l'étape,* that is, hasten from one stage to another.

Un Divorce ("A Divorce"), too, has a touch of harshness mingled with the justice of its teaching. Gabrielle Darras divorces her first husband, a drunkard, and marries an atheist. Her son by her first husband falls in love with a girl who has lived in free love with a man who had abandoned her and her child. When Lucien wishes to marry her, his stepfather objects to such a disgraceful affair, but the son insists that he sees no difference between his union with this girl and that of his stepfather with his divorced mother. The son leaves home and the mother is miserable. Thus the book condemns divorce and upholds the Catholic doctrine of the indissolubility of marriage.

L'Émigré sets forth the thesis repeated in so many of Bourget's subsequent novels, that children have to suffer for the sins of parents. Landri de Claviers discovers that he is an illegitimate son, that the Marquis de Claviers is not his real father. This great lord, belonging to a class fast disappearing in France, is the outstanding character in the book. The picture is sad, for it gives the impression of the loss of something noble and fine. We admire the marquis and sympathize with him, for we realize that his extravagance, his idleness, and his weakness are due, not to any fault of his own, but rather to changes in social conditions.

Two plays, *La Barricade* (1910) and *Le Tribun* (1912) followed closely on these novels, and like them, are studies of social problems. In the preface of *La Barricade,* Bourget says that this is really his first drama, since it is the only one that was not based on a previous novel.[14] He also insists that it does not belong to *littérature à thèse,* but to *littérature à idées,* between which he makes a rather subtle distinction. The import is that he did not construct his play to prove the truth of some principle, nor does he wish general conclusions to be drawn from this particular case; rather he is simply stating the fact that there is war between classes. Almost unconsciously, however, he shows himself on the side of the capitalist, though he declares that he is neutral and in sympathy with both parties. He thinks the problem practically insoluble, though he suggests that a better understanding of the duties as well as of the rights of the class to which we belong, would result in a greater sympathy for other classes. *La Barricade* was criticized severely as a pamphlet against workers and an appeal to brutal suppression, in spite of Bourget's protests that it was merely a picture of things as they actually were in the industrial world. *Le Tribun* shows the greatness of a father's love, which causes him to abandon a brilliant political career for the sake of his son.

The drama by its nature excludes long psychological analyses, and therefore Bourget felt more attracted to the novel, to which he returned in 1914. The next group, *Le Démon de midi* (1914), *Le Sens de la mort* (1915), *Lazarine* (1917), *Némésis* (1918), and *Un Drame dans le monde* (1921) emphasize the religious side of social life rather than the political. All the novels of this period point out clearly one of Bourget's deepest convictions: the only thing that can save modern France is Catholicism. He is not a dreamer nor a visionary, but a clairvoyant doctor, who, seeing the evil increase each day, carefully diagnoses his case, and concludes that only the Church, which had saved the world for nineteen hundred years, could direct the rebuilding of a wholesome society, based on solid principles of religion and morality.

Le Démon de midi is, according to Lalou, the best work of Bourget after *Le Disciple.*[15] It really contains two stories, that of Louis Savignan's unlawful love for Geneviève Soléac, wife of the industrial king Calvières, and secondly that of a priest, Abbé Fauchon, misguided and tainted with Modernism. Both are tempted by the noonday devil, the *daemonium meridianum* of the Latin Vulgate, interpreted in Bourget's own way, and both yield. Savignan's sin is impure love and Fauchon's is pride. Both are converted in the end through Jacques Savignan, noble son of Louis, who offers his life for his beloved father and for his idolized teacher. According to Dom Bayle, who represents orthodox wisdom, Savignan is the more guilty: "These two men were tempted . . . by this aberration of middle life which I call the noonday devil. Only the first one [Fauchon] did not know that he was being tempted, and the other [Savignan] has always known it."[16] The Catholic doctrine of vicarious suffering is presented in this novel as well as in those that followed.

Le Sens de la mort ("The Night Cometh") is one of the finest and most inspiring of Bourget's works. The chief interest is in the study of the materialistic conception of death expressed in the character of Dr. Michel Ortègue, as opposed to the Christian idea shown forth in Captain Le Gallic. *Lazarine* is still more religious, almost idealistic in tone. Like *Le Sens de la mort,* this story reveals the better side of the World War, its power to act as an agent of reparation and purification. Edgar Bowman misunderstands the novel and proves that he is ignorant of Catholic teaching, when he says that *Lazarine* "presents Church confession as a complete covering for murder."[17] The protagonist, Robert Graffeteau, in an impulse of indignant anger, shoots his divorced wife, who had really fallen very low. When he realizes the greatness of his crime, he despairs and is on the point of committing suicide, but he is saved by the pure, selfless love of Lazarine. She makes him realize that by heartfelt repentance, combined with true conversion, he can obtain pardon for his sin. She sends him back to war, and he proves the sincerity of his sorrow by the courage with which he sacrifices his life for his country. He dies after having received the sacraments of penance and Holy Communion. Confession is then not a covering for murder, but a means of obtaining pardon for one who truly repents and makes satisfaction. In *Némésis* the hero struggles successfully against his passion for a free-thinking woman, and in *Un Drame dans le monde,* religion transforms both the man and the woman. From the strictly Catholic point of view, this last novel is a masterpiece.

La Geôle ("The Gaol") and *Le Roman des quatre,* following in 1923, are both worthy of special mention. They are not so decidedly religious as the preceding group, but the general tone is Catholic. Jean Vialis, victim of an unjust accusation, commits suicide. His wife intends to follow his example, but is persuaded by an old friend, Dr. Vernat, that it is her duty to live for the sake of her son Jean-Marie. Vernat attributes the suicide to heredity, and thinks that the best means to prevent the son from following the instinct is to keep him in ignorance of its existence. Jean-Marie grows up and marries unhappily. When his wife leaves him, he is on the point of shooting himself, but his mother intervenes, tells him of the manner of his father's death, and that the whole purpose of her life has been to prevent him, her only son, from doing the act he now intends to perform. Jean-Marie insists that it would have been better to have warned him, so that he might have guarded against the tendency, for, according to him, "To conquer an obsession, one must foresee it, and to foresee it, one must know it."[18] This is the policy which he intends to follow with regard to his own son. But the boy is killed in war at eighteen, and the question, whether or not heredity is a *jail* from which we may hardly escape, remains unsettled. *Le Roman des quatre* is peculiar in its form. It is an exchange of letters by Bourget, Gérard d'Houville, Pierre Benoît, and Henri Duvernois. Its sequel, *Micheline et l'amour* (1926), was also written in collaboration with the same authors.

The more recent novels of Bourget, *Nos actes nous suivent* (1927), *La Vengeance de la vie* and *Agnès Délas* (bound in one volume, 1930), *La Rechute* (1931), and *Le Diamant de la reine* (1932) are less arbitrary in their psychology and more dramatic in their presentation. The analyses are less detailed, the action more rapid. *Nos actes nous suivent* must be classed among the greatest and best of Bourget's novels, with *Le Disciple, L'Étape,* and *Le Démon de midi.* The problem it studies, our responsibility for our acts, has been treated by the author in several other stories, but not so directly as in this one. Here he points out in unmistakable terms the far-reaching consequences of our sins, for which even our most sincere and humble penance is a very inadequate satisfaction. Patrick Müller undertakes to expiate the crime of his father. This father, nearly a half century before, had, through physical fear, allowed another man (mistaken for himself) to be stoned and thrown into the Seine. Patrick, after reading the written confession of his father, takes up the work of reparation which the latter had neglected. He succeeds in finding the Croissy family who had been wronged, and falls in love with Marie-Jeanne, the granddaughter of the man who was drowned. She, swayed by the bolshevistic ideas of the radicals who gather in her grandmother's shop, kills a lawyer Dréard, through whose influence the socialistic leader has been condemned. She had hoped to be a second Charlotte Corday, and realizes too late the greatness of her sin. In her remorse she confesses her guilt to Patrick, who in turn, asks her to marry him, but the father's crime looms up between them, and Patrick returns to America, while Marie-Jeanne becomes a Sister and devotes her life to charity. The plot is excellent, the situation dramatic, and the lesson evident: "Our acts pursue us. They are prolonged in time and in space with the rigor of a scientific law, and it is not the poor human will which can stay them and say to them, 'You will go no further!' "[19]

In *La Rechute* the same theory is emphasized: the punishment of the sins of guilty parents falls on innocent children. Marriage between Pierre Thérade and Cilette Rémonde (both excellent young people) is made impossible by the fact that Cilette's mother was formerly the mistress of Pierre's father, and, worse still, is on the point of relapsing into her guilty liaison, when the daughter discovers it. In *La Vengeance de la vie* the theme is also the chastisement of sin, but here the husband is punished for robbing his wife of her faith. After she leaves him and marries another, he is stricken with remorse and repents, but he confesses to Père Charles de Foucauld that he cannot overcome a desire of revenge. The saintly Father tells him to leave vengeance to the Lord. "Ah, the vengeances of life!" he exclaims, "How hard they are at times, so hard that our most bitter hatreds would not have desired them!"[20] The penitent realizes that this is true, when he sees his former wife, thin and nervous, with her second husband, who was once so handsome, become, through paralysis, a living corpse.

In *Le Diamant de la reine* (1932) the scene is laid in Venice, where Felix de Stravène is loved by two young women, Antonia Malvano, a beautiful Italian, pious, emotional, sincere, and by Mrs. Daisy Warner, a fascinating American widow, gracious but imperious. Felix is divorced, so the Catholic Antonia is tormented by her unlawful love for him, while no such scruples trouble the Protestant Daisy. The latter, who has a mania for collecting, has bought a diamond supposed to have belonged to Marie Antoinette. One evening at a soirée she discovers that it has been stolen from her mantilla. She accuses Stravène of the theft, basing her suspicions on two facts: first, he was a heavy gambler, and second, the pin was found in his overcoat. Antonia never for a moment believes that the one she loves (against her conscience) could steal. Overcoming a very human feeling of satisfaction which arises over the break between Felix and Daisy, she successfully proves that the guilty one was Frida, Daisy's maid. Antonia, struggling against her love for Felix and also against her jealousy of Daisy, is by far the most interesting character in the story.

Besides his novels, Bourget has written many excellent short stories, though his talent scarcely submits to the precision of form and rapidity of narration necessary for this class of literature. *Le Tapin* (1928) is typical and an analysis of it will show, that in these as in his novels, the plot develops in the minds of the characters rather than in exterior circumstances. There is a rather detailed introduction, explaining how schools under the second empire differed from those of 1927. The story centers around Jacques Bussières and has well-defined crises, climax, and dénouement. Jacques, the best Latin pupil in the class, tries to escape from school to plead with Adèle, his first love, about to be married to another. He is expelled and works in a confection shop, until one day his professor, M. Ferreyroles, comes in and finds him reading Vergil's *Georgics* during pauses between customers. Jacques is taken back into school on condition that he will be *tapin,* that is, beater of the drum by which the pupils march to class, recreation, meals, etc. This is considered a rather menial task, and its acceptance proves the sincerity of the culprit's repentance. Soon after this, a great Latin scholar visits Ferreyroles' class, and is amazed at the excellence of Jacques' Latin verses. As a reward, he asks that the boy be freed from his humiliating duties as *tapin*. But Jacques proudly refuses the release and the delighted old master whispers, *"C'est un petit Romain!"* The dénouement sums up the history of Jacques' later life. He was killed in the War of 1870 and on his person was found a slip containing Horace's *Dulce et decorum est pro patria mori*. Bourget has several other well-constructed short stories of this type, but more often they are really novelettes, as *Le Luxe des autres, Drames de famille, Deux soeurs*, etc.

Dimnet complained in 1913 that Bourget wrote the same book twenty times over.[21] Now we might truly say that he wrote it fifty times, and cite countless repetitions that occur both in plot and in character. At least a dozen of his novels relate how children are punished for the sins of their parents. This is the principal theme in some (*Nos actes nous suivent, La Rechute, Le Démon de midi, L'Échéance, Un Homme d'affaires*), while in others (*L'Émigré, La Terre promise, L'Étape, Un Divorce, Cosmopolis*, etc.) it is rather a minor point. Very often, in order to make the story seem more probable, and also to make his long psychological analyses possible, Bourget has it narrated by an interested third person, as in *La Duchesse bleue, La Confidante, Cosmopolis, Un Saint, Le Sens de la mort*, etc. At other times, to accomplish the same end, he makes his characters keep a diary or journal in which they recount their most secret thoughts, as does Cilette in *La Rechute,* and the father of Patrick Müller in *Nos actes nous suivent.* In *Le Disciple,* Robert Greslou writes his life history to his old master Sixte, and in *Lazarine,* the younger sister sends intimate confidential letters to her older sister Madeleine Journiac. Malclerc's journal, in *Le Fantôme,* is used to explain his attempted suicide a few days before the birth of his son. As has already been mentioned, both *Le Roman des quatre* and its sequel *Micheline et l'amour* are in the form of letters. In several novels the would-be hero leads a double life, as Louis Savignan in *Le Démon de midi,* and the father of Patrick Müller in *Nos actes nous suivent.* The majority of Bourget's stories are triangles, though there are some notable exceptions. Most readers breathe a sigh of relief when they pick up *Un Saint, Nos actes nous suivent, Le Sens de la mort,* or *Le Luxe des autres,* and are convinced that, all previous evidence to the contrary, Bourget can write a novel in which the hero does not fall in love with some other man's wife, or vice versa.

This brings us to the second complaint against Bourget's novels — that they are immoral. In one sense they are, for, as Doumic says, "the morality of a book depends less on the precepts there formulated than on the image of life therein contained."[22] His avowed undertaking, to paint for us the maladies of the soul, is both difficult and dangerous, for in spite of good intentions on the part of both the writer and the reader, such novels will inevitably stir up the evil depths of human nature. Too often they leave the reader with the feeling that the struggle is hopeless. They picture so vividly the strength of temptations, the weakness of human nature, the seduction of vice, that sin seems unavoidable. Moreover in reading about these soul-sick characters, we are apt to imagine that their diseases are ours, and that cure is either extremely difficult or totally impossible. In his essay on Dumas fils, Bourget attempts to defend himself against this foreseen criticism. He says that his aim is to present the human soul in its strength and its weakness, to show the growth and development of its passions, and he makes the very doubtful assertion that "All other appetites are more or less restrained by social barriers; love alone, like death, has remained irreducible to social conventions."[23] In his *Lettre autobiographique* he also says, "As I had to encounter in the course of these analyses many maladies of the will, I have been accused of propagating discouragement and pessimism. As I have consecrated many pages to the study of the passions of love in their contemporary shades because it is they which expose best the truth of the heart which they ravage, I have had the sorrow of seeing my intentions calumniated and certain of my books attacked as corrupting."[24] Nevertheless the fact remains that there are numerous voluptuous scenes and an undue stressing of unlawful love,[25] against which Anglo-Saxon readers especially will protest. This is particularly true of his early novels (*André Cornélis, La Duchesse bleue, Un Coeur de femme, Cruelle énigme*) but even in some of the later ones (*Le Disciple, L'Étape, Un Divorce, Le Démon de midi*) there are sensuous scenes, dangerous especially for high-strung, emotional readers and for adolescents. Still, as Bourget grew old, his pessimism disappeared more and more, and his stories revealed a healthier vigor with less of pain and more of faith and hope. In fact, the man who in the nineties was looked upon as "the dangerously seductive incarnation of dilettantism"[26] became during the first decade of the twentieth century "one of the mouthpieces of uncompromising conservatism."[27] Compare the cynical depressing tone of *La Duchesse bleue* with the noble Christian seriousness of *Le Sens de la mort*. The great difference is that the first shows the evil without suggesting a remedy, while the second proves that honesty and uprightness joined to religion make all things possible.

Bourget has likewise been reproached for the detailed analyses and moral reflections which retard the action in his novels and make them slow and heavy. There are two reasons for this. First, Bourget's experience as a professor inclined him to say all that there is to be said on a subject, to insist on essentials, repeat, and illustrate. Second, he is a profound thinker, and his grave cogitations are a vital part of his work. For example, in *Le Disciple,* if we omit Greslou's careful examination of his emotional life, what have we left? In *La Rechute,* the omission of Cilette's exposition of her mental torture when she is torn by well-grounded suspicions of her idolized mother, would certainly ruin the story. We find less moralizing in the more recent novels than in the earlier ones. *La Vengeance de la vie* and *Le Diamant de la reine* are almost wholly free from it.

Again, critics say that the characters in Bourget's novels are, for the most part, too abstract and too much alike. They resemble specimens out of a psychological laboratory more than normal, warm-blooded human beings. André Cornélis, Jean Monneron, Patrick Müller, Gabrielle Darras, Henriette Scilly are all men and women whom we have watched, admired, or blamed, but whom we would scarcely wish to call personal friends. Most of them belong to the higher classes, and Bourget delights in giving minute descriptions of the niceties of their dress and of the elegant milieu in which they live. Perhaps this was an unconscious reaction against the crude realism of the Naturalist school. He says in his *Lettre autobiographique:* "As I have placed several of these studies in the world of the idle in order to have more complete *cases,* since that is the class in which people can think more leisurely of their sentiments, I have had to undergo in turn the reproach of frivolity, of snobbishness, and even of disdain for the poor!"[28]

Lastly, Bourget has been criticized for his style. According to Fäy, it is deplorable, his sentences are discordant, his vocabulary ugly, his images commonplace, his descriptions lacking in color.[29] Victor Giraud's verdict is exactly the opposite: "As is the case with all those who have written much verse . . . he has learned to write well in prose; he has made his instrument flexible; he has made himself master

of all his modes of expression; in chiseling his verses, he
has acquired the habit and kept the taste for sentences skil-
fully rimed, happy combinations of words, fine verbal dis-
coveries, ingenious concise original formulas, striking
images, in short, for all that which is the life of style, and
gives to the true writer his proper value."[30] Both criticisms
are exaggerated. His style deserves neither the severe censure
of Fäy, nor the excessive praise of Giraud. Anyone who has
read the first chapter of *La Terre promise* will agree that it
is one of the finest passages of description in French literature. But usually Bourget does not attain this lyric quality.
He speaks rather the unadorned language of the scientist
or philosopher than the dreams of the poet. There is very
little humor in his books, and when it does occur, it is the
staid joke of the savant, rather than the clever quip of the
Frenchman. True, all his novels are tragedies, and one
hardly expects an atmosphere of frivolous gaiety. But he
could have learned from our Will Shakespeare that even in
a drama as solemn as *Macbeth,* there is place for a drunken
porter.

Considering all these adverse criticisms, one would imagine that Bourget's audience would be limited, that his novels
would be read only by the few, by psychologists and moralists, or at most by very serious, deep-thinking people. Quite
the contrary is the case. Bourget's success is universal and
has been so for practically fifty years. Even those who do
not approve of his ideas and principles, read his books faithfully, as the numerous editions and translations of his
novels prove. These facts lead us to two conclusions: First,
that modern France, in spite of its levity and proverbial
gaiety, likes serious, thought-provoking literature. Second,
that Bourget is, after all, something of a genius. His principal talent lies in plot construction, and in soul analysis, and
usually he succeeds in creating in his stories an atmosphere
suitable to the theme. For example, there is a dreamy air

of mystery in the opening chapters of *La Terre promise,* mingled with a strange touch of restlessness, which forebodes the tragedy that the following chapters disclose. For character study he cannot be surpassed. Le Goffic calls him "our best analyst since Stendhal."[31] The psychological novel, begun in the seventeenth century with *La Princesse de Clèves,* seems to culminate in the seventy volumes of Bourget. His peculiar gift for the dissection of modern types has brought psychology back into fashion and recalled the French people to the study of the interior life. He has strongly reminded them that, in spite of the materialistic trend of the age, they have souls to save. Turquet-Milnes says: "We must be grateful to a novelist who descends into the actual present, and who never wearies of preaching that all the evils of the present time are the outcome of the false and selfish aims of man, and that their remedy lies in honesty and Christianity."[32]

Catholics should be particularly grateful to this illustrious convert for having so successfully shown in his novels that the only remedy for the positivism of Comte and the nihilism of Kant is a return to Christ through faith, and submission to His Church. The words he puts into the mouth of Le Gallic in *Le Sens de la mort* seem to epitomize his philosophy, at least that of his later years: "Since everything in life ends in suffering and in death, if suffering and death have not this sense of a redemption, what meaning have they, and what meaning has life?" And Ortègue answers, "None."[33]

PRINCIPAL WORKS OF PAUL BOURGET

1875   *La Vie inquiète*
1878   *Édel*
1882   *Les Aveux*
1883   *Essais de psychologie contemporaine*

1884 *L'Irréparable*
1885 *Cruelle énigme*
1886 *Un Crime d'amour*
1887 *André Cornélis*
1887 *Mensonges*
1888 *Études et portraits*
1889 *Le Disciple*
1889 *Pastels, Dix Portraits de femmes*
1890 *Physiologie de l'amour moderne*
1890 *Un Coeur de femme*
1891 *Nouveaux Pastels, Dix Portraits d'hommes*
1891 *Un Saint*
1892 *Cosmopolis*
1892 *La Terre promise*
1895 *Outre-mer*
1898 *La Duchesse bleue*
1900 *Drames de famille*
1902 *L'Étape*
1904 *Un Divorce*
1906 *L'Émigré*
1910 *La Barricade*
1912 *Le Tribun*
1912 *Pages de critique et de doctrine*
1914 *Le Démon de midi*
1915 *Le Sens de la mort*
1917 *Lazarine*
1920–28 *Oeuvres* (34 vols.)
1921 *Un Drame dans le monde*
1923 *La Geôle*
1923 *Le Luxe des autres*
1923 *Le Roman des quatre*
1927 *Nos actes nous suivent*
1928 *Le Tapin*
1928 *Quelques Témoignages*
1929 *Agnès Délas*
1929 *La Vengeance de la vie*
1931 *La Rechute*
1932 *Le Diamant de la reine*
1933 *L'Honneur du nom*
1934 *Une Laborantine*

REFERENCES

Baussan, Charles, *De Frédéric Le Play à Paul Bourget*, Paris, 1935.

Bonne, Joseph de, *La Pensée de Paul Bourget*, Paris, 1913.

Bowman, Edgar, *Early Novels of Paul Bourget*, New York, 1925.

Dimnet, Ernest, *Paul Bourget*, Boston, 1913.

Grappe, Georges, *Paul Bourget*, Paris, 1904.

Jean-Desthieux, François, *Paul Bourget, son oeuvre*, Paris, 1922.

Lardeur, F. J., *La Vérité psychologique et morale dans les romans de M. Paul Bourget*, Paris, 1912.

Maurras, Charles, *Triptyque de Paul Bourget, 1895-1900-1923*, Paris, 1931.

Schäfer, Josef, *Paul Bourget als Philosoph*, Munich, 1920.

Visan, Tancrède de, *Paul Bourget sociologue*, Paris, 1908.

CHAPTER V

René Bazin

(1853-1932)

RENÉ BAZIN WAS BORN AT ANGERS ON December 26, 1853, of an old Catholic bourgeois family. His father was an Angevin and his mother a Parisian. In his *Souvenirs d'enfant* and *Contes de bonne Perrette* he tells us a great deal about his childhood. Much of it was spent in the country near Legré, in the fields and woods of that same Anjou which his compatriot Du Bellay had loved and sung three centuries before. He says that he was a rather indifferent student of *De Viris Illustribus,* but zealous in learning from nature. Because of his frail health, his education was less formal than that of most of his companions.

Instead of having for horizon the walls of a classroom or of a courtyard, I had the woods, the meadows, the sky which changes with the hours, and the water of a shallow stream which changed with it. My friends were the mist, the sun, the twilight, when fear creeps along in your shadow; the flowers whose dynasties I knew better than those of the Egyptian kings; the birds whose names are written in the zigzag of their flight; the people of the earth, silent, full of secrets. I recall that on certain days my soul was overflowing with joy, and so ethereal that it seemed to me ready to escape and to dissolve into space. I was preparing my harvest without knowing it.[1]

He and his brother delighted in precarious adventures, pillaging birds' nests and setting traps. They spent the long evenings in reading hair-raising stories of bears and bison and lions and peccaries, and other strange four-footed things that dwell in storybooks.[2] He became a law student at the Catholic University of his home town, and later at the University of Paris. In 1878 he was appointed professor of

law at the University of Angers, in which position he continued until his death.

His literary career began in 1883 with the publication of
Stephanette. This novelette as well as *Ma Tante Giron*
("Aunt Giron") (1886) passed almost unnoticed from the
press. One reader however, Ludovic Halévy, realized the
possibilities of the author, and advised the editor of the
Journal des Débats to secure the young Bazin as a con-
tributor. For many years this Journal published most of his
works before they appeared in book form. One can easily
surmise why *Ma Tante Giron* attracted the attention of the
author of *L'Abbé Constantin*. The stories have a striking
resemblance in plot and even in style. Both relate the com-
plications that arise when an admirable but poor young
man is on the point of proposing to an ideal young lady,
who unexpectedly turns out to be a rich heiress. The modest
hero correctly flees in despair. In Halévy's story the old priest
acts as the kind providence which brings him back, and in
Bazin's, "Ma tante Giron" is the humorous mediatrix.

His *Une Tache d'encre* ("A Blot of Ink") of 1888 was
crowned by the French Academy, and after that he brought
out an average of a novel a year. He also published accounts
and impressions of his travels in France, Spain, Italy, Sicily,
and the East, and several books of short stories. In 1904 he
was elected to the French Academy to replace Ernest Le-
gouvé. He was president of the *Corporation des Publicistes
Chrétiens* and a Knight Commander of St. Gregory the
Great.

He died on July 20, 1932, in Paris, at 6 Rue Saint-Philippe-
du-Roule, but according to his own desire, he was buried at
Saint-Barthélemy d'Anjou (Maine-et-Loire) near the spot
where he wrote the greater part of his works. He was the
father of seven children[3] and his life, full of calmness and
dignity, is mirrored in his writings.

There are two aspects under which the novels of Bazin

may be viewed. First, he is a literary artist, who paints delightful pictures on every page of his books. Second, in treating the social problems of the present day, he is a stanch supporter of tradition. About the first, all the critics agree. They recognize that he has good stories to tell, and that he knows how to tell them. He has been called the landscape painter, and his name joined with that of Millet, the artist of Barbizon. Des Granges says: "He often attains to poetry and eloquence without effort and by the very nature of his subject."[4] Edmund Gosse speaks of his "smoothness of execution, the grace and adroitness of his narrative," "the purity, freshness, and simplicity of his style,"[5] and Henri Chantavoine praises his instinct for "clear, delicate composition, for happy arrangement, for harmony between the setting and the characters."[6] Cunliffe calls him "the charming painter of country life"[7] and René Doumic admires his unerring taste.[8]

He possesses a rare love of nature and understanding of its secrets, associating it with our dreams, our joys, and our sorrows. The setting is always appropriate to the theme. The first page of Le Blé qui lève ("The Coming Harvest") gives us the tone of the whole story. The picture of the sun setting on the ancient forest of Fontenelles, with its one-hundred-and-sixty-year-old oaks about to be destroyed, produces an impression of discordance, a realization that "the times are out of joint." So the story goes on to reveal the singular life and untimely death of Michel de Meximien, victim of the selfishness of a frivolous mother and an extravagant father. Une Tache d'encre is a more cheery story, and so it begins with the first love of a youth of twenty-three. The tragedy in Les Noëllet ("This, My Son") is reflected in the opening description of an October evening, "sad as they always are"; in the boy Pierre dreaming of the stars in Orion, one on his forehead and one at each ear, and thus parading himself magnificently but perilously among the constellations; in Mélie's house, the sunken roof and bulging walls seamed with cracks and held together in places only by the kindly mosses.

Bazin's descriptions of characters show a delicate ability to unravel the skeins of simple souls, and by one word to acquaint us with their secrets. The Abbé Roubioux owed his piety to his mother, who had "the soul of a priest, and bestowed it on her children."[9] The Baron de Clairépée was a chivalrous old gentleman "who bowed to everyone he met within three leagues of the farm."[10] In *L'Isolée* ("The Nun"), when the Mother Superior characterizes Sister Pascale in the words, "Ah, what a reed you are!"[11] we know that the poor girl is going to bend and break in the storms that threaten her when she is driven from the convent by the decrees of an unjust government. Doumic writes of the young girls so frequently to be met in the novels of Bazin, that they are charming with the charm of the old-fashioned girl "who does not ride bicycle" and who loves her own home best, yet they are strong enough to remain unspoiled in the midst of temptations, and to exercise in their modest way a wholesome influence for good on those around them.[12]

Bazin's artistic sense is due in a great measure to his faculty of keen perception which enabled him to be intensely observant of all that passed around him, to note with interest the smallest details in both the visible and the invisible world. His added capacity for sympathy made him put affection as well as curiosity into his gaze at life. Brunetière said in his *Discours de réception* when Bazin was received into the French Academy:[13]

You are a painter and you are a poet: you will remain a painter and a poet. These are the things which will speak for you, in their own language, precise and concrete, living and colorful, sometimes gentler and sometimes sharper, but always eloquent with its peculiar fidelity. And this is why I have confidence, all of us have, that in your hands the social novel will never cease to be a novel and to be artistic.

This brings us to the second aspect of Bazin's work. Practically all his stories treat some social problem, above all the struggle between the old and the new. The ethical purpose is not, however, awkwardly forced upon the reader. As Mornet says, Bazin's novels are not sermons nor even *romans à thèse,* but rather the spontaneous expression of his love of virtue and hatred of vice.[14] In *Donatienne* ("The Penitent"), we have the young wife impelled by poverty to leave her husband and children, and accept a position as nurse in a wealthy family. The luxury and gaiety of city life urges her on, and her lonely, patient husband waits and watches in vain for her return. Their child Noémi finally brings them together again after years of bitter separation. The same theme is treated, though in a somewhat different manner, in *Madame Corentine* ("Those of His Own Household"), in which the lovely daughter Simone reconciles her divorced parents. This novel, with its setting on Jersey island and the Lannion coast, reminds one strongly of Loti's *Pêcheur d'Islande.* In both we have the fascination of the ocean, the pathos of the fisherman's death at sea, the agony of the wives and mothers impatiently awaiting at home the news which they dread to hear. Loti is the greater magician of nature, but Bazin's characters are more lifelike.

Une Tache d'encre depicts the traditional hostility of the provincial bourgeois toward Paris, but the Parisian, by her tact and sweetness, wins in the end. In *De Toute son âme* ("Redemption"), it is the young girl of the people, Henriette Madiot, who exemplifies by her life the glory of sacrifice and of consecration to God in His poor. The subject of *La Terre qui meurt* ("Autumn Glory") is the drain of the villages to fill the cities of France. La Fromentière, an ancient farm, has seen many prosperous days, but one by one the children leave the ancestral home, which is finally saved by the youngest daughter's marriage with Jean Nes-my, a laborer with an inborn love for "the dying land." *Les Noëllet,* also, portrays the disaster that results from the pull of the new life of the city away from the old life of the farm.

L'Isolée is more tragic. It shows in the person of Pascale, a secularized religious, the infamy of the law of proscription. To many, Bazin's last novel *Magnificat* is also a tragedy, for it presents the distress of a young Breton girl in love with one who has already heard the divine call to the priesthood. But the Catholic-hearted reader, like the courageous heroine of the story, appreciates the power of the divine in man, which enables him to sacrifice the human.

There are two stories of patriotism, *Les Oberlé* ("Children of Alsace") and *Les Nouveaux Oberlé* ("Pierre and Joseph"). In both the scene is laid in Alsace, the first during the war of 1870, and the other during the World War. *Les Oberlé* is the better, and gives us a more sympathetic picture of the struggle between love of *patrie* and the interests of money and social position. *Les Nouveaux Oberlé* has very much the same theme, but the only really admirable character in it is Marie de Clairépée, "a being of singular strength and sweetness, whose virtue was not prudery, whose courage had the air of ignorance but was not."[15] According to Pierre, she incarnated the very spirit of France, was France itself.

Gosse speaks of Bazin's strenuous provinciality[16] and links his name with the regional novelists of France. They are legion, and their books give us many interesting details that cannot be found in geographies. One could profitably study Normandy with Maupassant, Brittany with Loti and Charles Le Goffic, Lorraine with Daudet and Barrès, Savoy with Bordeaux, Auvergne with Bourget, La Vendée[17] with Bazin, and so on. In practically all of his works from *Ma Tante Giron* (1886) where the action takes place in Craonais (which is half in Vendée, half in Brittany) to his recent *Magnificat* (which relates the trials of a Breton family during the gloomy days of the World War) his scenes are laid in western France, in ancient Anjou, Brittany, or Poitou.

In his article *Le Roman populaire*,[18] Bazin gives us a sketch of his literary ideals. He expresses regret that the common people, eager for something to read, are served only the sensational *feuilleton* in the daily papers. These too often portray the lowest, basest type of man, ruled by selfish, unworthy motives. He holds that the popular novel should be educative, that it should aim to lighten the burden of life, lead the reader to higher ideals, to self-sacrifice, and to God. Again, he declares that a *popular* novel, to be true to its name, should be imbued with genuine love of the common people. When Bazin began to write, the Naturalist school was at the height of its influence. Many of the novels of this school were filled with bitterness and brutality. He felt that the picture they gave of France and the French people was exaggerated and slanderous, at least with regard to the great mass of the population. Therefore he proposed to set forth the simplicity, loyalty, patriotism, energy, and faith, which are to be found especially in the humbler classes in France. He himself says:[19] "I desire to portray the sweetness, purity, and beauty of French family life and not to perpetuate a gross libel upon it. . . . I am also anxious to dispel the illusion that the French are a godless people."

While Zola and his school are inveterate pessimists and treat with surgical coolness the ills of society, Bazin is an optimistic realist. His optimism does not, however, border as much on unreality as some of his godless critics would have us believe. Much of it is nothing else than practical Catholicism. For example, in *De Toute son âme,* when Henriette gives up wealth, position, friends, and even her love for Etienne to consecrate her life to charity, an atheist will see in this an idealistic creation of the author's imagination.

But a Catholic knows that she is only doing something almost commonplace, something that thousands of Catholic girls are doing all the world over, when they enter one of the many religious orders. In *Donatienne* it is characteristic of Bazin that, instead of focusing on the wife and picturing with vivid realistic details her downfall, he turns to the desolate, deserted husband, and shows his desperate struggle to remain a man and to protect his children. As Doumic remarks:[20] "He inclines toward a realism of which the just, frank, and even distinguished note is new in our literature."

Sometimes his pictures are more realistic, and approach more nearly those of the Naturalists. Take, for example, the terrible scene in *L'Isolée,* where poor fallen Pascale is crouching beneath a lamppost at the mercy of a drunkard, and cowed by the fear of Jules Pradou. Not less dreadful is the final scene of her tragic death, out on the stony road, where she is stabbed by the knife of her tormentor. We also find some very realistic scenes, depicting the horrors of war in *Les Nouveaux Oberlé.* It is worthy of remark that probably the most dramatic of all Bazin's works is not a novel but a biography, *Charles de Foucauld* ("Charles de Foucauld, Hermit and Explorer"). Calvet says of it:[21] "No novelist would have dared to imagine a hero of the stature of this French officer, turned hermit in the Sahara, and apostle of the Touaregs."

His most Utopian characters never go beyond the bounds of possibility, but develop naturally under the influence of circumstances and surroundings. Bazin is first and foremost a Christian and he finds in religion the most adequate explanation of man's mission. In the first chapter of *Fils de l'Église* ("Sons of the Church"), he says that "God wills His creature should be associated with Him in the spiritual government of the world." Like his great contemporary, Paul Bourget, he emphasizes his belief in authority and tradition and the Church, but while Bourget selects his

models from the leisured classes, Bazin invariably writes of
the laborers, peasants, and employees, and of the happiness
to be found among the lowly. Thus we have Pierre Noëllet,
the peasant boy, trying to make of himself a *gentleman* in
Paris, and aspiring to the hand of a *lady;* he fails utterly,
and learns too late that he is always a Breton peasant. In *Le
Blé qui lève,* Gilbert Cloquet's love of justice and devotion
to an unworthy daughter who broke his heart, give him the
nobility of a prince, but he only really learns the value of life
from a retreat made among the humble Picards. In *Questions littéraires et sociales* Bazin explains that his greatest
grudge against the Naturalists is that they emphasize the
brute too much, and show no feeling of brotherhood nor
sympathy for the poor.[22] He, on the contrary, stresses man's
higher powers. His stories are seldom laid in the sickening
atmosphere of vice, of which most modern novelists are so
fond, but in the wide open country which exhales freshness
and vigor and clean bracing life.

This is doubtless why some of the critics speak of Bazin's
work in a rather scornful tone. The *Journal de Jura* (July
26, 1932) says that he passed for a rose-water writer (*un
écrivain à l'eau de roses*), and Calvet quotes a critic who
states that Bazin's novels were written *pour les jeunes filles
par une vieille fille.*[20] Fäy classes him with a group of novelists who are earnest and who have the gift of constructing
plots — rather wearisome ones at that — but to whom all
else is lacking.[24] On the other hand, most readers will agree
with the verdict of T. Greenwood:[25] "As an outstanding
example of the fruitful combination of literary genius with
zeal for the faith, his name deserves to be held in memory
and benediction among us." Edmund Gosse wrote in 1901:[26]

We have spoken of a strong spiritual digestion; but most of the
romances of the latest school require the digestion of a Commissioner
in Lunacy or of the matron in a Lock hospital. Therefore — and not
to be always pointing to the Quaker-coloured stories of M. Edouard

Rod — the joy and surprise of being able to recommend, without the possibility of a blush, the latest of all the novelists of France.

Since then, Bazin has published about twenty-five novels, but Gosse's judgment is as correct now as it was in 1901.

Bazin can hardly be called one of the great forces in modern French literature. He is not a profound thinker, neither is he dynamic. He rarely arouses in us violent passions and intense emotions. It is not surprising that to many of the present generation, surfeited with cheap melodramatic serials, his novels may seem dull and weakly sentimental. It is also true that his peasants are somewhat idealized and a little artificial. We find them philosophizing too much. The life of the farmer is painful, and though he may dimly realize that there is a poetic beauty about it, still he is too crude to make known his feelings. We love Bazin's tillers of the soil, but now and again we become vaguely conscious that it is the author who is speaking through them, formulating their opinions and expressing their sentiments in very elegant French.

These faults are minor ones, however, and we are happy to find a modern novelist who writes an artistic story in excellent French, who gives an honest, interesting picture of life, whose novels are healthy and stimulating, and whose Catholicity is evident without provoking propaganda. What Norah Meade says of the *Magnificat* is more or less true of all Bazin's works.[27] "This is M. Bazin's picture of one of those clear cold streams that subtend and give strength to the muddier main current of confused contemporary thought." Like René Doumic, "we love him for the delicacy of soul and elevation of sentiment in his works, and for the courage he has to remain upright and chaste, while at the same time clearsighted and truthful."[28] We Catholics love him also because he so effectively defended his Faith with his pen in story form, and because he gave the best that was in him to Christ.

PRINCIPAL WORKS OF RENÉ BAZIN

1884 *Stephanette*
1886 *Ma Tante Giron*
1888 *Une Tache d'encre*
1890 *Les Noëllet*
1893 *Madame Corentine*
1897 *De Toute son âme*
1897 *Contes de bonne Perrette*
1899 *La Terre qui meurt*
1901 *Les Oberlé*
1903 *Donatienne*
1905 *L'Isolée*
1906 *Questions littéraires et sociales*
1907 *Le Blé qui lève*
1909 *Le Mariage de Mademoiselle Gimel*
1910 *La Barrière*
1911 *La Douce France*
1912 *Davidée Birot*
1919 *Les Nouveaux Oberlé*
1921 *Charles de Foucauld*
1928 *Pie X*
1931 *Magnificat*

REFERENCES

Baussan, Charles, *René Bazin*, Paris, 1925.

Bersaucourt, Albert de, *René Bazin, Biographie critique*, Paris, 1910.

Catta, Tony, *Un Romancier de vraie France, René Bazin*, Paris, 1936.

Chantavoine, Henri, "M. René Bazin," *Correspondant*, CXCV (1899), pp. 37–54.

Gosse, Edmund, "The Novels of M. René Bazin," *Contemporary Review*, LXXIX (1901), pp. 264–277.

Lecigne, C., *René Bazin*, Paris, 1901.

Mauriac, François, *René Bazin*, Paris, 1931.

Ryan, Mary, "René Bazin," *Studies*, XXI (1932), pp. 627–635.

CHAPTER VI

Henry Bordeaux

(1870-   )

FRENCH NOVELS HAVE A BAD REPUTATION. They usually connote that which is sensational, risqué, or even worse. Clothed in yellow paper without, they too often reek with naturalism, snobbism, and sensualism within. Still, strange to say, none of this is to be found in the works of the best-known living novelist of France, Henry Bordeaux. His novels will scandalize no one. They deal with *honnêtes gens,* who live according to the dictates of honor and duty. But can good people be interesting? Or is it only vulgar, perverse rascals that amuse us and attract our sympathy? The universal popularity of Bordeaux answers this question, for, though there are undoubtedly some who are disappointed to find his novels so wholesome and elevating, the vast majority of readers derive genuine satisfaction from them. La Bruyère wrote in his *Caractères:* "When a book uplifts your mind and inspires you with noble and courageous sentiments, do not seek any other rule by which to judge the work; it is good and done with a master-hand."[1] If this criterion be correct, Bordeaux's greatness is unquestionable. Practically his whole life has been devoted to literature, and he has accomplished with his pen a mission which his talent and energy, combined with training in sound social principles and Catholic doctrine, have made possible.

He was born in 1870 at Thonon on the shore of Lake Geneva in Haute-Savoie, where the scene of many of his stories is laid. His father, "a man of faith and discipline after the manner of Joseph de Maistre,"[2] was an officer in the War of 1870, and then became chief magistrate of his town. Henry's childhood and adolescence, passed among mountains, woods, and waters, under the eye of this stern but loving father, was happy and peaceful. He suffered from illness during his early years, and whiled away many a long day by reading the *Contes de Perrault* and *Anderson's Fairy Tales*. After attending the college in Thonon, he went to the Sorbonne and Faculté de Droit in Paris. He recalls that as a college student he played the part of Berthe in *La Fille de Roland,* that he wrote verses, a volume of which (*Rebecca*) was later crowned by the Academy of Savoy, and that he read classics and moderns, but especially liked Shakespeare, Balzac, and Tolstoi. At twenty, he fulfilled his duty of military service at Annecy, and then practiced law in Savoy. All the time, however, the "literary demon" was tormenting him, and he gave more attention to writing than to his profession. He contributed to several periodicals, articles which in 1894 were collected in a volume, *Âmes modernes.*

This same year he had returned to Paris, but was brusquely recalled to Savoy in 1896 at the death of his father, to fill the post left vacant by him, and to continue the family tradition and name. For four years he practiced law in Thonon, was mayor of the village, and head of the home. At the time this seemed contrary to his interests as a writer, but in the end the experience proved beneficial. He became acquainted with all classes, and acquired a knowledge of character and an insight into human nature that he would never have derived from books. His next work, *Les Écrivains et les moeurs,* begun in 1897 and completed in 1902, bears witness to this transformation in him. In 1900 he abandoned law and gave himself entirely to literature, as home conditions made it possible for him to transfer the responsibilities of the family to a younger brother. He married in 1901, and since then his life has been that of a busy literary man. During the World War he served his country generously as a captain, and was twice decorated for conspicuous bravery. In 1919 he became a member of the French Academy, the youngest of the "Forty Immortals." A number of other distinctions have come to him. He is one of the most prolific of contemporary writers, having produced some hundred volumes, in addition to innumerable articles in periodicals.[3] He spends the winter and spring in the capital, for the Parisian fever stimulates him to work, the summer and autumn in his beloved Savoy, where he does most of his writing.

Bordeaux began his literary career with critical essays, and he has never abandoned that field. Though the bulk of his work consists of novels, he is one of the leading critics of his generation. We have mentioned *Âmes modernes,* a collection of original studies of his contemporaries (Rod, Hérédia, Ibsen, Lemaître, Loti, A. France, Bourget, and Vogué).[4] This was his first book, and it brought him to the attention of the litterati. It lacks maturity, is overrun with neologisms, and suffers from a touch of precocity, but there is in it the charm of youth, of ardent, enthusiastic, confident youth, which, in Byron's phrase, "sucks books like flowers," and is eager to talk about them. *Les Écrivains et les moeurs* (1897–1902) shows an advance, in that Bordeaux exhibits a greater knowledge of social questions, a wider experience of men, and a more natural style. In the preface to *Pèlerinages littéraires* (1906) he says: "I hope that there can be found in *Pèlerinages littéraires* a little of that clearness of analysis which I relish with so much ardor in others." He accomplishes his wish, for intelligibility is one of his striking qualities as a writer. Under the title of *La Vie au théâtre,* Bordeaux published each month from 1907–1921 in *La Revue hebdomadaire,* a dramatic chronicle. His taste is excellent, though he shows a marked preference for the seventeenth-century Classicists, and very decidedly condemns the

Romanticists. He dislikes their lack of order and moderation, and in a letter to Jules Lemaître,[5] he complains that
"we are undergoing in art the weight of more than one
hundred years of political and moral confusion." In addition
to these, Bordeaux published *Portraits de femmes et d'enfants* (1900), and *Portraits d'hommes* (1924), in which he
follows Sainte-Beuve's method of biographical criticism,
Vies intimes (1906), historical and literary evocations of
scenes in the French Alps, and *Visages Français* (1930),
which contains excellent chapters on Maurice Barrès and
René Boylesve.

He has also written biographical essays, such as *La
Vie de Guynemer* ("George Guynemer, Knight of the
Air") (1920), a panegyric of the heroic French aviator who
died during the War, *Le Walter Scott Normand, Barbey
d'Aurevilly* (1925), a study of a writer too often misunderstood and unappreciated, *Saint François de Sales et notre
coeur de chair* ("Saint Francis de Sales, Theologian of
Love") (1924), the edifying life story of his beloved saint
of Savoy, and *Henri de Bournazel* (1935), a sketch of a
French commander in Africa, who helped win Morocco
for France. He usually chooses to write about those whom
he enthusiastically admires. M. Ernest-Charles accuses him
of a lack of perspective in time and space.[6] Indeed, his choice
of subjects is sometimes disconcerting. Run through the
table of contents of *Visages Français* or *Portraits d'hommes,*
and you will probably find that some of the names are quite
unfamiliar. But souls attract him, not on account of their
celebrity, but for their marks of inborn genius, which are
not always apparent at first sight. We may say, in general,
of Bordeaux as a critic, that he follows Taine, Sainte-Beuve,
and Bourget. He is a clear, incisive thinker, fair in his judgments, without sarcasm or indignation toward those whose
work he does not approve. Even in 1901, when he was only
thirty-one years of age, André Hallays welcomed him as

"one of the most penetrating and erudite critics of our time.'"

It is true that Bordeaux's first literary endeavors were in the field of criticism, but fame came to him with the publication of his first novel, *Le Pays natal* (1900). It is the story of a young man, Lucien Halande, who, lured by the garish life of the capital, decides to sell his paternal domain in Savoy and live permanently in Paris. He returns to Annecy to accomplish these plans. Voices of the past awaken in him love of his native soil and an almost unconscious jealousy at seeing another, Jacques Alvard, usurping his place among the people, so he remains there on his estate to continue the family traditions. This novel contains in germ the theses of practically all Bordeaux's future works. He has certain convictions essentially Catholic, which permeate his novels and may be summed up as follows: (1) He is the defender of the family and of tradition. (2) He teaches the value of life and the happiness found in service. (3) He does not palliate sin, but shows that it carries with it its punishment.

BORDEAUX, THE DEFENDER OF FAMILY AND TRADITION

Bordeaux in his novels studies the life of the individual in relation to society. He agrees with Auguste Comte that the family is the social cell of a greater organism, the nation, and that the individual ought to be willing to sacrifice his personal interests for the sake of the larger group. In an article published in the *Atlantic Monthly,* February, 1915, he insists on this principle: "The family is thus considered as the foundation of society and the symbol of government itself. And this is not merely a theory for philosophers to wag their heads over, but a fact proved by experience in the course of those many perilous and glorious centuries throughout which the might of France was revealed." All his novels preach the sacredness of marriage, the strength derived from the family bond, and the power of Christian traditions to maintain the dignity of man and prevent him from following every individual caprice.

Les Roquevillard ("The Will to Live") (1906) tells how a younger son by his misdeeds brings ruin and disgrace to an entire family. François Roquevillard, the father, describes the disaster thus: "A moment of weakness suffices to shatter the effort of so many united generations. Ah, down there in his shameful flight, may he measure the extent of his treason: his sister's engagement broken, the future of his brother jeopardized, his mother's health shaken, our fortune compromised, our name stained and our honor tarnished."[8] It required all the generous loyalty of the other members of that noble family to atone for the sin of this prodigal and to lead to his regeneration.

Again, in La Croisée des chemins ("Parting of the Ways") (1909), a clever young Lyonnais doctor, Pascal Rouvray, is affianced to the daughter of a rich Parisian. He has to choose between life in Paris, where success, wealth, and reputation await him, and a return to Lyons where he must face obscurity, pay the debt left by his grandfather, sustain his mother, raise his brother, and marry off his sister. The struggle is a hard one, but Pascal realizes that, though ambition would lead him to Paris, duty calls him to his native Dauphiné, where he settles down, marries a humble, sensible wife, and founds a family.

In La Maison ("The House") (1912), which is a prudent combination of fiction and autobiography, Bordeaux upholds the rights of the family, when he presents the Christian father fighting for "the most sacred thing he has, the soul of his son, the continuer of his race."[9] The action unfolds in the ancestral home, which the author considers an appropriate setting on account of its customs, traditions, and unwritten moral code.

Les Yeux qui s'ouvrent ("Awakening") (1908) is the
story of a broken home. Madame Dérize is about to sue for
a divorce, and so destroy her own happiness and that of
her husband and children. But her eyes are opened when
she reads her husband's diary and realizes that the estrange-
ment is in great measure due to her own narrow selfishness
and lack of sympathy. Ferchat says that this book might
serve as a "directory for wives,"[10] as it contains valuable
hints on marriage. Ligot, too, would like to see it "among
the wedding presents of all our contemporary brides."[11]

Tuilette (1930), one of Bordeaux's more recent works,
shows the sorrow that results when home conditions are not
as they should be. The poor little girl, unwanted even before
her birth, hungers in vain for a mother's love and tenderness. Her father, who is really very fond of her, though he
dare scarcely show his affection in the presence of his
jealous wife, bids her, "Be brave all your life," and then
goes off to war, to fight and die. Tuilette needs courage, for
she is left with her vain, egotistical, superficial mother, who,
instead of aiding her, thwarts her every chance for happiness.

Bordeaux does not, however, advocate a selfish, unreasonable love of family. In *Le Chemin de Roselande* (1926),
Dr. Bronoy's baby Jean is dying, yet in spite of his own
heartbreak and the reproaches of his wife, he leaves the
sickbed to go to succor and save the child of a peasant who
inopportunely begs his assistance. When he returns, his Jean
is dead, but he realizes that he has done well in placing his
duty as a doctor before his feelings as a father. Thus, Bordeaux teaches that the happiness of the individual as well as
the success of a nation depends to a great extent on fidelity
to duty, to home, and to tradition; that, as he expresses it in
the preface to *Pierres du foyer* (1918): "The family united,
consolidated, protected by institutions, alone guarantees
duration to a nation. If it is reduced to a precarious state, it
presages the extinction of a race" (p. x).

BELIEF IN LIFE AND HAPPINESS IN SERVICE

La Neige sur les pas ("Footprints beneath the Snow") ends
with the counsel to love life "with its need of order and its
natural dislike for all that disturbs this order, its possibilities
of greatness and perfection, its eternal pursuit of peace
through war, its unsatisfied desires, its depth of solitude and
bitterness, life which conducts to God or to nothingness, life
stronger than the love it contains." This novel tells of a man,
Mark Romenay, whose wife leaves him to go mountaineer-
ing with her lover. The tragic death of the latter brings the
woman to her senses, and makes her realize the greatness
of her sin. There is a struggle between despair and hope, but
love of life wins, and she determines to return to her forgiving husband and to strive to reconstruct their broken
happiness.

La Peur de vivre ("The Fear of Living"), which René
Doumic hailed as "one of the best novels that had appeared
for a long time,"[12] was crowned by the French Academy.
Strange as it may seem, the heroine is a tired old lady,
Madame Guibert, who allows her children to depart one by
one when she feels that duty or their own greater happiness
calls them. She is not afraid of life with its trials and sacrifices, and she understands that true affection often bids a
mother rejoice when sickly sentimentalism would make her
weep. She is the valiant woman of the Scriptures, and the
prototype of many of Bordeaux's heroines. Opposed to her
is Alice Dulaurens, who, because she is afraid to face life,
weakly allows herself to be married to a man she does not
love, and lives in misery ever after. Madame Guibert's advice to Alice in the last chapter is: "You have been afraid
of life. Your parents have been afraid of life for you. Life,
Alice, is not the distraction and the unrest of society. To live
is to feel one's soul, one's whole soul. It is to love, to love

with one's whole strength, always, to the very end, and even to sacrifice. One must not fear pain, nor great joys nor great sorrows; they are the revelation of our human nature. One must snatch from days which are passing away the good which does not pass."[13] *La Resurrection de la chair* (1920) and *La Petite Mademoiselle* (1905) also show this mastery of life over death.

The greatest joy and satisfaction that man can experience comes from unselfish service. M. Roquevillard says: "There is grandeur only in servitude. We serve our family, our country, God, art, science, an ideal. Shame on him who serves only himself!"[14] Most of Bordeaux's heroes and heroines are those who have dedicated their lives to generous labor for others. In one of his recent works, *La Revenante* (1932) Isabelle de Foix seeks to regain her lost happiness down in Morocco as a Red Cross nurse, caring for the wretched natives. In *Les Déclassés* (1933) Count Robert d'Ormay, weary of the empty life of Paris, finds satisfaction in turning peasant and working for his living among his former servants. Often it is not the idle rich who are happiest, but the poor who share their mite with those more destitute than themselves. In *La Nouvelle croisade des enfants* ("Annette and Philibert") (1914), a charming story for children, Anthelme gives away to Péronne, who has been deserted by her husband and left with four babies, all the money with which he was to buy the Christmas turkey and some few toys for his own children.

SIN BRINGS ITS PUNISHMENT

Bordeaux does not condone sin or defend the sinner on the plea of the weakness of human nature, as do so many of our modern novelists. He shows that it destroys true happiness and brings in its wake ruin and death. The sinner himself must pay the penalty or it is apt to devolve on some

(1924), *Dieu et Mammon* (1929), *Souffrances et bonheur du Chrétien* (1931), *Commencements d'une vie* (1932), *Le Romancier et ses personnages* (1933). Frédéric Lefèvre tells us that when he interviewed Mauriac in 1923, the young author said: "I believe, indeed, that it is fortunate for a novelist to be a Catholic, but I am also sure that it is very dangerous for a Catholic to be a novelist."[23] The difficulty is not doctrinal — no one has ever questioned Mauriac's faith — but moral. The problem he has tried to solve is this: How far is the Catholic novelist responsible for the harm his books may cause? Must the creative artist avoid writing such novels as would give scandal? He relates that after he had published *Genitrix,* he received a photograph from a boy with this startling message: "To the man who almost made me kill my grandmother."[24] Gillouin paid Mauriac a rather doubtful compliment in 1926, when he said that he was a Catholic "as one is light or dark complexioned, without any more effort and almost without any more merit."[25] Maritain saw in him a Manichean, and Calvet did not give him a chapter in his *Renouveau Catholique* (1930) because he was "a Catholic who wrote novels, but not a Catholic novelist."[26]

In other words, his early works up until about 1928 are an indirect apology for Christianity. They prove the need of faith by showing the lamentable consequences of the lack of it. "Just by presenting beings completely deprived of religious life," he says, "we discover the great void in souls, a void especially felt in women."[27] He realized that there was an element of corruption in his work, "prowling over it as it prowls over cemeteries which are nevertheless dominated by the Cross."[28] It seemed to him that he had to choose one of three courses: change the object of his observation, falsify life, or run the risk of spreading scandal and misery among his fellow creatures.[29]

Charles Du Bos, who has made a study of Mauriac's

attitude toward Catholicity,[30] distinguished *three* stages in his work. The first, until 1922, when he was a devout, melancholy adolescent, is the period of his poems and his earliest novels (*L'Enfant chargé de chaînes, La Robe prétexte, La Chair et le sang, Préséances,* etc.). These reflect his early faith and piety, but it is a piety more or less emotional that had little effect on his life and writings. As he himself said, it all evaporated in fumes of incense, for it was not sufficiently nourished with study and prayer.[31] The second period was from 1922 until 1928, when Mauriac wrote *Le Baiser au lépreux, Genitrix, Le Fleuve de feu, Le Désert de l'amour,* and *Destins.* These novels unite the material and the spiritual, and show that without succor from on high man is a miserable creature, but they make us feel that, though the *novelist* is progressing, the *Catholic* is losing. He kept his faith intact, but he was often far from edifying, and his piety suffered a total eclipse. He persistently set forth sins of the flesh (*Genitrix* is an exception), and painted the baser passions only too well. He often stressed the sufferings of the Christian, but never the joys. "Then," says Du Bos, "six weeks after the publication of *Souffrances du Chrétien,* the conversion of Mauriac was an accomplished fact."[32] It should hardly be called a conversion, but rather a change in his outlook. *Ce qui était perdu* is the novel of transition, and his later works (*Le Noeud de vipères, Le Mystère Frontenac, La Fin de la nuit, Les Anges noirs*) show a definite turn for the better. Grace plays a greater part in the lives of the characters, and though sin and vice are still strongly depicted, they do not triumph in the end, but yield to supernatural influences.

Another mark of Mauriac's change of attitude is the fact that he has published during the past few years a number of books decidedly religious in their subject and tone: *Jeudi saint* (1931), *Pèlerins de Lourdes* (1933), and *La Vie de Jésus* (1936). Pierre Troyon tells us that at Mauriac's reception into the French Academy in November, 1933, the supernatural entered with him. "Never, under the cupola, even in the days when the princes of the Church were received there, had there been so much talk of Newman, St. Paul, St. Catherine of Siena, St. Thomas, St. Augustine, and St. Bonaventure."[33]

From the beginning, there was a Jansenistic shade in Mauriac's writings, but it is probably deepest in *Souffrances du Chrétien.* When he edited this essay again in 1931 with *Bonheur du Chrétien,* he was tempted to delete some of the half-blasphemies that are in it, but decided that it was better to leave it unchanged. Even in his later works there is a black pessimism that is rarely lightened by any streak of hope, for he paints vices of the darkest hue with a fatalism that begets utter despair. In 1933 André Chaumeix gently reproached him thus: "You are the great master of bitterness. . . . Occasionally there is something hallucinating in these harsh pictures where your heroes strike against the walls of their corporal prison, and where you watch the mocking battles of these future corpses over passing earthly goods."[34]

Many have been shocked by the frank and open description of evil in his novels. Mauriac wrote in his essay entitled *Le Roman:* "We have lost . . . the sense of indignation and disgust, we dare to read in the poorest eyes, because nothing offends us, nothing disgusts us if it is human."[35] His own experience, however, should have proved to him that not every scandal can be related in a novel, and his psychological studies might have taught him that, though very often in the modern world sexuality is substituted for love, many readers object to stories which are the candid portrayal of the habits of a decadent society. Even Catalogne, who defends him lustily, and who is not at all squeamish, grants that "Occasionally he suggests images of sensuality too precisely."[36] As Barjon remarks in speaking of this tendency of Mauriac, it is easier to paint vices than virtues, as vice and sin are our own work, while in virtue there is more of God's action, and therefore it is harder to analyze.[37]

The characters in Mauriac's novels suffer from their wickedness, but they often seem quite helpless in overcoming it. They have not enough liberty nor will power. They do not seem to realize that it is possible to say *no* to a temptation, to turn one's back upon it and avoid a fall. Most of the characters, besides bowing too easily to circumstances, are somewhat abnormal. Either they are sick, feeble souls, descendants of René and afflicted with the *mal du siècle* (Bob Lagave, Jean-Paul Johannet, Edward Dupont-Gunther) or they are voluptuaries, avaricious, and cynical (Louis, Daniel Trasis, Hervé de Blénauge, Gabriel Gradère). Bidou says that they wander the earth like damned souls.[38] Mauriac paints them pitilessly, leaving in the greater number neither faith nor happiness. His women are as bad as or worse than his men. He says in the preface of *Thérèse Desqueyroux:* "Many are astonished that I have been able to imagine a creature more odious yet than all my heroes." Some of them travel from novel to novel, improving little with time and change of scene. Nevertheless his portraits are true, and most readers have met people much like them in their own experience. The novel centers around them, for they are the important element in it. They take hold of us and make us think of them, see them, and pity them for days after we have finished the book. None of them are banal or uninteresting, and the psychology with which they are drawn is sure though merciless. Mauriac tells us that "his heroes are born of the marriage that the novelist contracts with reality,"[39] and again, in the introduction to *Trois récits* (1931) he says that when he creates his characters, it is part of his living flesh that he sets forth. He likes to put youth in his stories, youth with its love of glory, its secret sensuality, its hidden aspirations, and its thirst for inde-

pendence. He remembers his own adolescence with its lights
and shadows, its smiles and tears. Many of his young people
are hopelessly degenerate, but one fault they rarely have —
self-complacency. They are restless, dissatisfied with themselves and their milieu, and retain, in spite of their baseness,
an inborn nostalgia for the divine. Usually they belong to
the bourgeois class and a provincial setting lends relief to
their moral struggle. Thus Mauriac ranks with the numerous regional novelists of contemporary France, for he has
celebrated the Landes of Gascony, with their pine forests
and vineyards stretching out to the Pyrenees.

Perhaps the most striking feature of Mauriac's novels is
their style. Victor Poucel confesses: "Their reading has interested me in spite of the horror that I experience on opening a book."[40] Through the sincerity and perfection of his
art, he succeeds in creating an atmosphere that bathes the
story in enchanting beauty. Ramon Fernandez says: "His
voice from page to page never ceases to sing,"[41] and De
Buck declares that "his style consumes the subject."[42] The
plots count little, but the grave lyric note with which they
are told, always in harmony with the tragic lives of the
characters, transforms them into symphonies which remind
François Le Grix of Schumann's music.[43] Mauriac's good
taste and infallible instinct of the pathetic never fail him,
even when he rises to a feverish tension. At times his language is abrupt, vigorous, compact, agitated, and again it is
supple, eloquent, humble and broken like a human wail.
He never sustains a tone too long, but touches only the
essential. By a mere suggestion, a passing allusion, he opens
up vistas to the reader and arouses emotions that pages of
exposition and description could never have evoked. Many
critics have called attention to the importance of odors in
Mauriac's novels. He makes use of all sensory material —
sounds, forms, colors — to enhance his picture of human
emotions, but it is to the sense of smell that he particularly

appeals. Even in his *Vie de Jésus* he cannot resist this tendency. When speaking of the visit of Nicodemus to Christ at night, he says: "When Nicodemus was there, Jesus was already breathing an odor of myrrh and of aloes."[44]

There is an originality about his style peculiar to himself, which tends to reproduce the state of mind and personal traits of his characters. He repeats but he is always new, and the source of his poetic expression seems never to be exhausted. Though there is an ever-present tinge of melancholy, this does not detract from the robustness and vigor of his language. In both Lefèvre's interviews (1923 and 1935), he asked Mauriac *how* he composed, and the answer was the same: "I write in a sort of creative fever. . . . I carry my novels in my mind for a long time, but I write the first version very quickly, without interrupting the flow of thought."[45] The words seem to rush on without any effort, with a spontaneous and expressive art, from a source grave, sincere, melancholy, and, above all, poetic.

Mauriac's work is, we hope, far from complete. He is still a comparatively young man, and he gives promise of fuller development and greater accomplishments during the years to come. He spends his winters in Paris, but he does most of his writing during the summer, at Saint-Maixant, or Arachon, or especially at Malagar, the old family estate where the scene of *Genitrix* is laid. He confided to André Maurois that those who had influenced him most were Barrès, Rimbaud, Jammes, Baudelaire, and Verlaine.[46] This is not surprising, for he himself, even in his novels, is one of France's greatest lyric poets.

PRINCIPAL WORKS OF FRANÇOIS MAURIAC

1909 *Les Mains jointes*
1911 *L'Adieu à l'adolescence*
1913 *L'Enfant chargé de chaînes*

1914 *La Robe prétexte*
1920 *La Chair et le sang*
1920 *Petits essais de psychologie religieuse*
1921 *Préséances*
1922 *Le Baiser au lépreux*
1923 *Le Fleuve de feu*
1924 *Genitrix*
1925 *Le Désert de l'amour*
1925 *Orages*
1926 *Le Jeune homme*
1927 *La Province*
1927 *Thérèse Desqueyroux*
1928 *Coups de couteau*
1928 *La Vie de Jean Racine*
1928 *Destins*
1928 *Le Roman*
1929 *Dieu et Mammon*
1929 *Mes plus lointains souvenirs*
1930 *Ce qui était perdu*
1931 *Blaise Pascal et sa soeur Jacqueline*
1931 *Jeudi saint*
1931 *René Bazin*
1931 *Souffrances et bonheur du Chrétien*
1932 *Le Noeud de vipères*
1933 *Le Mystère Frontenac*
1933 *Pèlerins de Lourdes*
1935 *La Fin de la nuit*
1936 *Les Anges noirs*
1936 *Vie de Jésus*

REFERENCES

Barjon, Louis, "M. François Mauriac et le mystère de Thérèse," *Études religieuses*, CCXXII (1935), pp. 459–475.

De Buck, J. M., "Le Pessimisme religieux de Mauriac," *Revue générale*, CXXIX (1933), pp. 316–327.

Doumic, René, "M. François Mauriac," *Revue des deux mondes*, July, 1926, pp. 461–469.

Du Bos, Charles, *François Mauriac et le problème du romancier catholique*, Paris, 1933.

Lefèvre, Frédéric, "Une Heure avec François Mauriac," *Nouvelles littéraires,* May 26, 1923.

Luppé, A. de, "François Mauriac romancier," *Correspondant,* CCCII (1926), pp. 694–707.

Maurois, André, "François Mauriac," *Annales politiques et littéraires,* C (1933), pp. 632–635.

Poucel, Victor, "Scrupules de M. François Mauriac," *Études religieuses,* CXCIX (1929), pp. 672–696.

Shuster, George, "François Mauriac," *Bookman,* LXXII (1931), pp. 466–475.

CHAPTER IX

Francis Jammes

(1868–)

THE YEAR 1935 SAW THE PUBLICATION OF *De tout temps à jamais,* by a poet who had been for a time silent. Though Francis Jammes is an old man now, we find in this latest volume of poems all the charming freshness and artless beauty of his early work. He ever remains the simple, humble poet of country life, who lives and writes far from Paris, in his beloved country of the Hautes-Pyrénées. He belongs to an old Creole family and many of the traits of his ancestors appear in his books which emit a perfume of exoticism, a fragrance of bygone days.

In his three volumes of memoirs,[1] he tells us the story of his life up to his thirty-eighth year. *Ma Fille Bernadette* and *Le Testament de l'auteur,*[2] also contain autobiographical material. In fact, all of Jammes' works reveal much about himself, external and internal. He was born on December 2, 1868, at Tournay, where his father was receiver of records, and he lived there six years and six months. His mother, nee Anna Bellot, was from the Basses-Alpes of a family of merchants and nobles. His only sister, Marguerite, three years his elder, went to live at Pau with the maternal grandparents, who took care of her education.

Jammes has an astonishing memory[3] and relates many interesting incidents of his childhood. He recalls distinctly that the water of his favorite stream was *sucrée,*[4] that his first illness made him realize the devotion of the "tenderest of mothers,"[5] that Marie, the servant, used to save him cream from the fresh milk,[6] and that his aristocratic grandfather showed some annoyance when he saw his grandson getting off the train like "Jeannot-lapin, or the country rat."⁷

In 1875 his father was transferred to Sauve-terre-de Gironde, and he left his wife and two children with the grandparents at Pau. While here, Francis often visited Orthez, where his two great-aunts, Clémence and Célinaire, dwelt in the old home. At night he slept on an ancient trunk of camphor wood brought from the Indies, and during the day he attended the school of three old maids. On occasion he would visit his rich uncle from Mexico in his sumptuous villa. In 1876 the family was reunited at Saint-Palais, an agreeable little city watered by the Bidouze and the Joyeuse, and not yet spoiled by railroads. Here Francis' teacher was M. l'Abbé Duc, and a distrust of schools and schoolmasters, which was to last many years, took birth. It is true that the boy was sometimes misunderstood, and consequently treated with apparent injustice both by professors and students,⁸ but Jammes himself acknowledges that he was often lazy and rebellious, neglecting everything but botany and poetry.

It was at the primary school of M. Sabre that his "poetic initiation," as he calls it, began. It came quite unexpectedly; "A book is open before me. Suddenly, without any warning, I see and realize that the lines are living. . . . I had just received from Heaven this reed, shrill and dull, humble and sublime, sad and joyful, sharper than the dart of a savage, sweeter than honey. I exercised it a few days after. My father was astonished at my attempts, and showed me more tenderness than he had ever before evinced."⁹ Later Francis stayed with his grandparents and attended the lycée at Pau, but he was no more successful than before, so his father undertook to give him private instruction in his office, and obtained better results than any of the schoolmasters.

In 1871, owing to a disagreeable change of situation imposed upon him, M. Jammes resigned his position, and the family went to Orthez to live with the Huguenot aunts, one of whom (Clémence) was "thin and long, and could have been one of the Sisters of the primitive Church who followed Paul of Tarsus."[10] The other (Célinaire), though angular, was quite different from her sister, without mysticism, but with housewifely instincts well developed. The family moved to Bordeaux in 1880, and they would have wished to see Francis enter the polytechnical school there, but unfortunately, it was his sister and not he, who manifested talent for mathematics. He had developed at thirteen or fourteen, what he calls a "malady, odious especially for the associates of the one who is attacked by it, and which becomes more manifest in early adolescence, *l'âge ingrat.*"[11] Nevertheless the boy was doing more satisfactory work in school. He was delighted with his discovery of Jules Verne and charmed with his studies in natural history under M. Dabas. Another teacher, "who belonged to that class of professors who displeased him least,"[12] was Professor Ducasse. Francis studied botany with him, and was even punished because he was caught examining flowers during history class! In fact, he failed in his examinations and left the lycée at seventeen without his degree.

Early in 1888 the family made a sojourn at Béarn with the Mexican uncle and his wife, but soon returned to Bordeaux. The father's health had been poor for some time, and on December 3, 1888, at the age of fifty years, he died and was buried at Orthez. Francis, his mother, and sister decided to live in this city with one of the aunts. He was spared military service, being the only son of a widow and in poor health, the result of a state of nervous depression. He went into the office of a notary for a time, but hated it and abandoned it to become a poet. Stéphane Mallarmé, Henri de Régnier, and André Gide, who had read some of his verses, encouraged him to publish them, and *Un Jour* appeared shortly after. He says of it: "It was in the heart of April, 1895, that I was *invaded* — I can find no other word to express my meaning. A simultaneous outburst of all my lyrical powers took place in me. I do not know why I did not die from the breath, as it were, of a violent wing which seemed to strike me, and of which my poem *Un Jour* was born."[13] Alfred Vallette edited it and Raymond Bonheur set it to music.

In March, 1896, a friend invited him to accompany her to Algeria, where she was to visit André Gide. Jammes made quite an extensive trip, going on from Touggourt through the desert to Biskra. Later he describes his journey in his *Notes sur des oasis et sur Alger*.[14] He begins his third book of Memoirs (*Les Caprices du poète*) with the words: "*Mon Dieu,* how young I was at that time [1897] when I was nearly thirty!" He and his mother were living in a cottage near the road between Bayonne and Pau. Jammes loved this house, of which Charles Guérin wrote: "O Jammes, your home resembles your face."[15] He was still much disturbed mentally and spiritually, and continuously speaks of his *mal*. Nature always had power to soothe him, however, and a trip to Normandy, which he took in the autumn of 1898, ameliorated sensibly the crisis of sadness in which he was plunged.

About this time he published *De l'Angelus de l'aube à l'Angelus du soir,* which drew from Hérédia this comment: "It is certain that this fellow is a poet."[16] *Clara d'Ellébeuse* followed in March, 1899. Jammes calls this novelette a *folie de pureté* and says that Claudel wrote him an admirable letter about it. The following summer he and his mother visited the Basses-Alpes where she had been born, and on their way saw the country where Jean Jacques Rousseau passed his adolescence. His poem to Madame de Warens, one of the best Jammes ever wrote, was composed at this time.[17] It begins:

Madame de Warens, vous regardiez l'orage
plisser les arbres obscurs des tristes Charmettes,
ou bien vous jouiez aigrement de l'épinette,
*ô femme de raison que sermonnait Jean Jacques.**

In 1900 he spent several days at Paris on his way to Belgium, where he gave a series of lectures. From there he went on to Holland, and during the return trip he made the personal acquaintance of Paul Claudel. M. Schwob had written to Jammes: "This poet [Claudel] is the only one besides you who moves me."[18] *Almaïde d'Etremont* appeared in 1900, and not long after, that strange poem, *Existences*. Jammes himself says it is "burlesque and satiric, an act of madness,"[19] in which he maliciously ridiculed the Orthezians. Soon after he wrote *Jean de Noarrieu*, an idyll full of paganism. Later these two long poems were united in one volume entitled *Le Triomphe de la vie*. The next years were troubled ones for Jammes, and he gave expression to his dejection in a volume, *Tristesses*. This is an "interior drama in three acts and in three years." It was followed in 1903 by a more normal and readable book *Le Roman du lièvre*.

His life glided by peacefully at Orthez, with occasional visits to Bordeaux where he had many literary friends, or to Estang where his married sister was living. He and his mother passed the evenings reading favorite authors, among whom he numbers Homer, Vergil, Cervantes, La Fontaine, Rousseau, Victor Hugo, and Eugénie de Guérin. In 1905 Claudel came to Orthez to visit Jammes. The latter was going through a moral and religious crisis at the time, and though very unlike Claudel in every way, he was greatly impressed by the rugged Catholicity of his illustrious contemporary. The following year he returned to the faith of his childhood and recovered peace of mind and heart.

---

* Madame de Warens, you used to watch the storm bend the dark trees of dreary Charmettes, or in a sour mood you played the spinet, O woman of sense, whom Jean Jacques used to lecture!

Jammes tells us nothing of his marriage, but in his book *Ma Fille Bernadette,* he relates the story of the babyhood of his little girl, who was born at Orthez in August, 1908. Her first smile, her first tear, her first Christmas, her first illness, are all of paramount importance to the loving parents. He gives a portrait of the child's father (himself at forty years), and describes his bushy eyebrows, his strong curved nose and sensual mouth. He declares that his only beauty is in his hair turning gray, and in his green, catlike eyes, sometimes hard in expression and again very gentle. He makes no mention of his beard "big and black like that of Robinson Crusoe,"[20] which he may have grown later. He gives us a glimpse of his wife at twenty-six with well-formed features and beautiful teeth, singing the baby to sleep in true motherly fashion. In a poem entitled *La Vie* he tells Bernadette,

> You will understand how dear is the little house;
> The house on the path in which there is nothing extraordinary,
> But where four hearts live: your father, your mother, your
> grandmother and you.[21]

From *Le Testament de l'auteur* we learn that Jammes had four other daughters (Emmanuèle, Marie, Anne, and Frances) and two sons (Paul and Michel). This last testament was drawn up and signed in March, 1928, at Hasparren, where Jammes moved about 1919. Here, far from the capital, which attracts him no more than does literary fame, he still lives in the midst of his family, presiding over his humble hearth "more sonorous with crickets than with gold pieces,"[22] praying much, writing occasionally, dreaming always, surrounded by his beloved flowers and animals.

Critics usually stress the difference between Jammes' earlier and later manner, making 1905 the point of division. Before this date, his work is more pagan and lyric, and he writes in free verse. After 1905, the date of his conversion (or reversion) to the faith of his early years, his poems are more religious and didactic, and he uses regular verse. As he grows older, we notice that his poetry is somewhat less original, more mature and studied.

His first publication *Vers,* which appeared in 1893, created quite a sensation. It was a volume of poems about the common things of everyday life, written in a simple, direct style, without pretension to poetic diction. He says in the preface to this volume: "I have written irregular verses, disdaining or nearly so, all rules of form and meter. My style stammers, but I have spoken according to my own truth." *Un Jour,* mentioned previously, followed in 1895. This outlines a typical day in the life of a poet, with three scenes, morning, afternoon, and evening, and seven characters, the Poet, his Soul, his fiancée, his mother, his father, his servant, and his dog. Later this was printed in the same volume with *De l'Angelus de l'aube à l'Angelus du soir* (1898), a collection of poems, humorous, sensual, descriptive, romantic, malicious, sad, or gay, according to the mood of the author. He writes of the blue mountains, of the shepherd with his big umbrella and dirty sheep, of his favorite animals (the donkey, dog, and cat), of his house full of roses and of wasps. The lines[23]

> . . . *je pleurais, ô mon Dieu! sans savoir pourquoi,*
> *et sans savoir sur qui, et sans savoir de quoi**

remind us of the more famous *Il pleure dans mon coeur* of Verlaine.

Quatorze prières (1898), *La jeune fille nue* (1899), *Le Poète et l'oiseau* (1899) and *Élégies* were published in one volume with *Le Deuil des primavères* in 1901. The fourteen prayers are interesting, in fact astonishing at times, but not very pious. In one the author begs God for a star, in another

---

* I was weeping, my God, without knowing why, and without knowing for whom, or wherefore.

for a simple wife; again, he prays to go to Paradise with the donkeys; in another[24] he asks to love sorrow:

Je n'ai que ma douleur et je ne veux plus qu'elle.＊

La Jeune fille nue is a poetic drama with three characters and three scenes in which the poet relates a dream and gives full play to the caprices of his imagination. *Le Poète et l'oiseau* is a dialogue between the Poet and a very philosophic bird, which displays more wisdom than do most men.

Le Triomphe de la vie, including the two narrative poems mentioned before (*Jean de Noarrieu* and *Existences*), also belongs to his first manner. The former is a Hesiodic poem, divided into four cantos. The hero is a gentleman farmer of thirty years, who is enamored of his servant, the peasant, Lucie. She, however, has lost her heart to Martin, the shepherd. At first Jean is jealous, but finally plays the part of the magnanimous master and marries the two. A hint at the end gives us to understand that he did not die of a broken heart, but immediately turned his eyes toward Jeanne, a lass "with red and laughing lips." More important than the love story is the picture of country life — the harvest, vintage, fishing, and hunting. *Existences* chronicles everyday happenings in a village, and has no plot, but is merely a series of incidents. They are entertaining and realistic, but vulgar and salacious at times. The keynote is given at the beginning: *Et c'est ce qui s'appelle la vie.*

Besides these books of verse, Jammes published four volumes of prose before 1905: *Clara d'Ellébeuse* (1899) *Almaïde d'Etremont* (1901) *Le Roman du lièvre* (1903) and *Pomme d'Anis* (1904). Three of them are stories of young girls, lovely, graceful, and unreal, but fascinating just the same. Clara d'Ellébeuse is a pious, scrupulous, convent girl, who worries so much over a slight fault which her ignorance

---

＊I have only my grief and I wish nothing more.

exaggerates, that she commits suicide. Almaïde d'Etremont is an orphan of much the same type, and would probably have ended her life like Clara, a victim of her shame and remorse, had she not been saved by the sound advice of a kind old gentleman, a friend of the family. Pomme d'Anis is more mature and worldly-wise than her two antecedents. She is a cripple, and realizes too late that it is rather pity than love which has attracted Johannes to her. *Le Roman du lièvre* stands out alone in Jammes' work. It pictures as no other French story does, the frail animal protecting itself from man. Jammes catches La Fontaine's manner, especially in the opening pages of the book:

> Between the thyme and the dew of Jean de La Fontaine, Lièvre listened to the hunters, and climbed to the path of soft clay, and he was afraid of his own shadow, and the heather fled behind him, and the blue belfries arose from valley to valley, and he redescended and mounted, and his leaps bent the grass where hung dewdrops, and he became the brother of the larks in his rapid flight, and he crossed the high-ways and hesitated at the finger-post before following the connecting road, which, pale with sun and sonorous at the cross-roads, is lost in the dark and silent moss.

The hare is a living person, and never once does Jammes lose the sense of proportion and balance so vital in this attempt to merge the human and animalistic.

It is usually granted that the prose of Jammes in these early works is superior to his poetry. The probable reason for this is that the simplicity and naïveté of his verse is apt to degenerate into triviality or affectation. It is extremely difficult for a writer to treat at any length the humble things of life in a familiar and natural manner, especially in poetry where the form is more or less arbitrary. When Jammes writes spontaneously the freshness and originality of the verse delight us. But as soon as the creative impulse seems forced, when preciosity mingles with candor, we can pick out verses which either repel us by their banality or amuse us by their ingenuous affectation. The last lines of *La Salle à manger*[25] exemplify this:

> *Il est venu chez moi des hommes et des femmes*
> *Qui n'ont pas cru à ces petites âmes.*
> *Et je souris que l'on me pense seul vivant*
> *Quand un visiteur me dit en entrant —*
> *Comment allez-vous, monsieur Jammes?**

The principal volumes of poetry published by Jammes since his conversion are *Clairières dans le ciel* (1906), *Les Géorgiques chrétiennes* (1912), *La Vierge et les sonnets* (1919), *Le Tombeau de Jean de la Fontaine* (1921), *Les Livres des quatrains* (4 books, 1923–25), *Brindilles pour allumer la foi* (1925). With the exception of the first-named, all of these are inspired by faith and piety and are written in classic prosody. They contain beautiful verses, full of "sweetness and light" and if they are more restrained and at times more monotonous than his earlier ones, still there is an added charm which comes from religious fervor. We agree with Amy Lowell that "his Catholicity is a very sweet and lovable thing."[26] His attraction to nature is as strong as before, but now he turns more quickly to the God of nature. *Clairières dans le ciel* contains *En Dieu* (a poem on the death of Eugénie de Guérin), the pessimistic *Tristesses,* the poetic drama *Le Poète et sa femme, Poésies diverses,* and the long poem *l'Église habillée de Feuilles.* This last is an allegory which relates the author's return to Catholicity. Pilon remarks that the church Jammes describes is not the cathedral of Huysmans but a little rustic chapel.[27] *Les Géorgiques chrétiennes* is a lengthy, bucolic poem, giving a series of kaleidoscopic pictures of rural life, and treating nature from the Christian point of view. Critics judge the

---

* Men and women came to my house, who did not believe in these little souls. And I smile because they think I am living alone, when a visitor says to me on entering, "How are you, M. Jammes?"

poem differently. Some praise it highly while others speak of it as a long accident to be deplored.[28] It is true that the Alexandrine doublets are rather monotonous, but they are well suited to convey the idea of the peace and calm of country life.

La Vierge et les sonnets is fresher and more buoyant. For instance, Sonnet VII relates how, when out walking with an old servant, he caught a gay and gaudy butterfly and brought it home in a box. But it did not seem nearly so pretty in its cage as it did flitting through the air, and the poet ends:

> . . . *O mes frères en poésie!*
> *Il n'avait plus autour des ailes la prairie*
> *Qui me l'avait fait croire aussi grand que le ciel.**

Clouard says that the sonnets contain "incomparable harmonies, worthy of the beautiful evening of life of an inspired poet."[29] *Le Tombeau de Jean de la Fontaine* is a collection of short, clever poems, in which the different animals in La Fontaine's fables appear to lodge complaints against the author for the way in which he misrepresents them. *Brindilles pour allumer la foi* is, as the title indicates, and the preface explains, a small collection of devout thoughts, simple explanations of Catholic doctrines, short meditations, and bits of pious admonition with no pretense at style or art.

The principal volumes of prose written after his conversion are: *Feuilles dans le vent* (1914), *Pensées des jardins* (1906), *Ma Fille Bernadette* (1910), *Le Rosaire au soleil* (1916), *M. le Curé d'Ozeron* (1918), *Le Poète rustique* (1920), *De l'âge divin à l'âge ingrat* (1921), *Le Livre de Saint Joseph* (1921), *L'Amour, les Muses, et la chasse* (1922), *Les Caprices du poète* (1923), *Le Mariage Basque* (1926), *Trente-six Femmes, La Divine Douleur* (1929), *La*

---

* O my brothers in poetry! It had around it no longer the wings of the prairie, which had made me believe that it was as large as the sky.

Vie de Guy de Fontgalland, L'Arc-en-ciel des amours
(1930), *L'École buissonière* (1931). His three volumes of
memoirs have already been mentioned, as also *Ma Fille
Bernadette*. In this latter book, the dedication to "Mary of
Nazareth, Mother of God," and the passage in which the
watchful care given to Bernadette by her guardian angel is
described, are exquisite. *Le Poète rustique,* the tale of a poor
poet and his family living in a small village, also contains
much autobiographical material, though not avowedly so.
Le Rosaire au soleil and *M. le Curé d'Ozeron* are both idealistic novels. The first is divided into fifteen chapters, each
representing a mystery of the rosary. This rather artificial
framework does not help a novel which is almost too nice
in itself, and in which the heroine, Dominica, is a beautiful
but bloodless character. *M. le Curé d'Ozeron* is somewhat
better, for the curé is a living, lovable old priest. In both,
however, the mixture of fiction and piety is rather labored
and displeasing. Calvet calls them "paradisiac novels, the
color of angels' wings."[30] *Pensées des jardins* is a book in
both poetry and prose, full of insects and animals, of flowers
and vegetables, of snow and wind, and of humble folk. It
was written during the period between the old and the new
manner of Jammes. *Feuilles dans le vent* contains twenty
meditations (many of them on Scripture texts), *Quelques
hommes* (biographical notes on friends of Jammes), *Pomme
d'Anis,* and *La Brebis égarée.* This last is a prose drama
which relates how Françoise, wife of Paul, goes off with
Pierre Denis, a friend of her husband. They are punished
and brought to a sense of duty by poverty and misfortune.
La Divine douleur is an exposition of all types of human
suffering which result from death, mourning, separation,
injustice, poverty, sickness, and humiliation. *L'Arc-en-ciel
des amours* is a collection of little love idylls, prose poems
with the verses numbered. *La Declaration d'amour acceptée*
from *L'Idylle de la palombière*[31] may serve to illustrate:

1. *Onze ans après Pierrech a vingt-cinq ans et Kattalin les a auusi;*
2. *Dans la même palombière;*
3. *Dans la même cuisine;*
4. *Seul à seule, de même;*
5. *Avec les réjouissantes escalopes de veau qui, à chaque fois, l'emportent de fort loin, dans le goût du jeune homme, sur le reste de menu.*
6. *Kattalin regarde ce beau garçon de tout son coeur et de tous ses yeux qu'elle a bleus et en amande, d'un bleu sauvage qui n'est que basque, le bleu d'un certain dur calcaire lorsque la pluie a passé dessus.*
7. *Précisément le soleil de l'amour les fait luire.*
8. *Rompant, vis-à-vis d'elle un silence de toute sa vie.**

L'École buissonière contains selections from Jammes' earlier prose works with a few unpublished sketches.

The characteristic that strikes us most in Jammes is his love of nature. The different epithets applied to him by critics indicate this. He has been called *"le fils de Virgile,"* *"Coppée bucolique,"* "the Catholic rustic," "brother of La Fontaine," "the Theocritus of his native Béarn." Though, as we have pointed out, there is some difference between his early and late manners, his devotion to nature remains the same. Humble creatures seem to be full of mystery for him, still he treats them with a familiarity and fraternal love that recalls St. Francis. He loved all animals, and they march through his books in an endless procession: dogs, cats, rabbits, butterflies, wasps, larks, swallows, doves, goats, sheep. . . . He seems to be partial to donkeys, however, as he wrote a whole series of poems to them in *Pensées des*

---

* 1. Eleven years later Pierrech was twenty-five years old and so was Kattalin; 2. In the same dove cot; 3. In the same kitchen; 4. Alone, just the same; 5. With the heartening pieces of veal which, each time, according to the taste of the young man, were by far the best thing on the menu. 6. Kattalin looks at the handsome lad with all her heart and with all her eyes which are blue and almond-shaped, a savage blue which is only basque, the blue of a certain hard limestone when the rain has fallen on it. 7. It is the sun of love that makes them shine. 8. Breaking, opposite her, the silence of a lifetime.

jardins. His descriptions of landscapes, plants, and trees show first-hand knowledge, and prove that he heard the story of Mother Earth from her own lips. Amy Lowell says that "all his books are cool and white like snow, and threaded with the blue of skies, of snow-shadows, of running water."[32] He also writes of those human beings who are close to nature, shepherds, villagers, and peasants. He is especially attracted to young girls, frail, innocent, and graceful like sweet flowers; old-fashioned girls with musical names. Jammes has been compared to Wordsworth for his effort to do in French poetry what the latter did in English (interpret nature's soul), and also to A. E. for his close communion with the lowly beings of earth. But there is more faith and humility in Jammes than in either the British or the Celtic poet, both of whom are tinged with pantheism.

All Jammes' books are full of himself. As Lalou remarks, "Jammes recounts Jammes abundantly."[33] Besides his three books of memoirs, the story of his daughter Bernadette, and his testament, we have *Un Jour, Le Poète et sa femme, La Mort du poète,* and *Le Poète rustique,* in all of which he is the protagonist. He has related his conversion in verse and in prose. In his prefaces he explains his motives and intentions copiously. Often this personal note is pleasing, and lends a flavor of veracity to his work, but at times it jars upon the reader.

The outstanding quality of Jammes' style is its simplicity. His language is pure and sober. He has an extraordinary ability to write of simple things in a simple way, to see poetry in the commonplaces of life, and to transfer his impressions to paper without any flourish of language or straining after effect. Moreover, he has the soul of a child and he speaks like a child in a direct, spontaneous manner, unmindful of form and order. This naïve ingenuousness sometimes degenerates into affectation and absurdity. In fact, the word

Jammisme connotes just this excess of simplicity. But Francis Jammes usually saves himself from this fault, however, by his ability to convey swiftly the humor of the situation. We feel that he writes with a twinkle in his eye and thus he prevents others from laughing at him.

We must admit that, although Jammes is to be admired for his love of nature, his simplicity, and his power of imagination, there is something lacking in his poetry. We read his verses and enjoy them, but we are never profoundly moved. Somehow they fail to awaken thoughts "that do often lie too deep for tears." Jammes is a charming, lovable writer, but the sublimity of Claudel, the tenderness of Verlaine, the psychology of Bourget, and the vigor of Huysmans are unknown to him. He believes that when a poet looks at the sky and says that it is blue, he has said all, and everything else would be vain epithets.[34] There were vaster and more extended literary domains, to be sure, but he consciously avoided them, likening himself to the poor faun. He deliberately chose "the way of spoliation of the primitives, who have not sacrificed sentiment to form."[35] Perhaps this realization of his limitations is one of the greatest proofs of his genius. How many failures there are in life because men neglect what they can do and attempt what they cannot! Jammes caught a glimpse of the hidden beauty in the Creator's work, and he celebrated it in free verse admirable for its rhythmic variety, or in musical prose adapted to the manifold moods of the author. He is an anonymous troubadour, wandering through the twentieth century, content to sing his humble canticles to God and His Virgin Mother.

PRINCIPAL WORKS OF FRANCIS JAMMES

1898 *De l'Angelus de l'aube à l'Angelus du soir*
1898 *Quatorze prières*
1898 *La Naissance du poète*

1899 Clara d'Ellébeuse
1899 Le Poète et l'oiseau
1901 Almaïde d'Etremont
1901 Le Deuil des primavères
1902 Le Triomphe de la vie
1903₁ Le Roman du lièvre
1904 Pomme d'Anis
1906 Clairières dans le ciel
1906 Pensées des jardins
1910 Ma Fille Bernadette
1912 Les Géorgiques chrétiennes
1914 Feuilles dans le vent
1916 Le Rosaire au soleil
1918 M. le Curé d'Ozeron
1919 La Vierge et les sonnets
1920 Le Poète rustique
1921 De l'âge divin à l'âge ingrat
1921 Le Tombeau de Jean de la Fontaine
1922 L'Amour, les Muses, et la chasse
1923 Les Caprices du poète
1923 Les Livres des quatrains (4 books)
1925 Brindilles pour allumer la foi
1928 Le Chemin de la croix
1929 La Divine douleur
1930 L'Arc-en-ciel des amours
1931 L'École buissonière
1933 Pipe, chien. Le rêve franciscain
1935 De tout temps à jamais
1936 Le Pèlerin de Lourdes

REFERENCES

Bersaucourt, Albert de, Francis Jammes, poète chrétien, Paris, 1910.
Guidetti, Augusta, Francis Jammes, Turin, 1931.
Leblond, Marius-Ary, "Francis Jammes," Mercure de France, XLVI (1903), pp. 324-347.
Pilon, Edmond, Francis Jammes et le sentiment de la nature, Paris, 1908.
Rush, Leonard, "Francis Jammes," Catholic World, CXXIII (1926), pp. 162-171.
Schilla, Alfred, Francis Jammes, Konigsberg, 1929.

CHAPTER X

Louis Mercier

(*1870–*)

IN HIS INTRODUCTORY STUDY TO *RELIGIOUS Poems of Richard Crashaw*, R. A. Shepherd states that "there exists a class of persons whose minds are preyed upon night and day by the suspicion that it is easier for Catholics to write poetry than for other people."[1] Now, after all, is not that class of persons to a great extent right? Given the natural genius, a Catholic poet will come by noble inspiration and high argument far more easily than one who is not a Catholic. Both will write good poetry, but the Catholic poet has a larger opportunity for writing great poetry.

Mr. Shepherd also says that in his opinion a convert's poetry is more ecstatic than that of a born Catholic, owing to the fact that the former is so wholly taken up with the glory and magnitude of his discovery. The beauty and grandeur of Catholic truths strike the convert in his maturity for the first time, and he gives vent to a burst of admiration that we rarely hear from one brought up in the Catholic Church. Many of our Catholic poets have been converts, among others Crashaw, Dryden, Faber, Newman, Tabb, Joyce Kilmer, Péguy, Coppée, and Claudel. Mr. Shepherd's view is shared widely, and there is undoubtedly some truth in it. But habit does not always destroy the faculty of wonder in the born Catholic as may be proved by illustrious instances, and surely the latter must have resources of poetic material denied to the convert. We cite in evidence the works of the French poet, Louis Mercier.

True, not many of Mercier's poems are burning songs of

praise, though he has written a few rare gems of this type
(*Le Cantique d'action de grâces, Dic nobis Maria, À Celles
qui brûlent*), but all through them runs a stream of faith
and trustful love, which the reader recognizes immediately
not as a sudden torrent just let loose, but as an ever-abiding
undercurrent in the mind and heart of the author. Often by
a mere hint or suggestion he arouses emotions too deep for
words. Take, for example, this verse from *Coelestis urbs
Jerusalem:*[2]

> *Nous savons qu'un rayon échappé de ta face*
> *Briserait le miroir fragile de nos yeux*
> *Créés pour réfléchir le seul monde qui passe.**

Almost everything that Mercier wrote can be called religious
in the broad sense of the term, for he sees creatures as the
work of the Creator, and their beauty and perfection as a
reflection of the eternal beauty. Many of his poems are distinctly religious, for in them a direct allusion is made to the
supernatural. His early life and training are in a measure
responsible for the subject as well as for the spirit of many
of his poems.

He was born on April 6, 1870, at Coutouvre not far from
the Roanne in the department of the Loire. Here in the
shadow of the Monts de la Madeleine he grew up under the
care of parents deeply religious, but whose piety, especially
that of the father, smacked somewhat of Jansenistic rigor.
In *Hélène Sorbiers,* a novel of which he himself writes,
"without being an autobiography, it is composed of souvenirs of childhood arranged and dramatized,"[3] he gives us a
vivid picture of his father, stern and grave, who in the
evening, used to make the sign of the cross at the beginning
of the prayer; and of his mother, patient and gentle, but
often troubled with headaches, of whom he says in another

---

* We know that a ray escaped from your face, would break the fragile mirror
of our eyes, created to reflect only the passing world.

place, that he did not see her, he felt her. If the little Jean Sorbiers is himself, he was a solitary child of a sensitive nature, and extremely observant. These early years spent on the lonely farm in Forez proved a valuable asset to him later on, for they instilled into him an intimate knowledge and intense love of nature.

The oldest son remained on the home farm, and his sister (perhaps the sweet Hélène Sorbiers) died shortly after entering the Sisters of Charity. Louis commenced his studies with the vicar of Coutouvre, and continued them at the seminary of St.-Jodard, and afterwards he followed the courses of the Faculté Catholique de Lyon. He passed three years in Tunis in military service, where he learned to know the sea — the sea of which he wrote in *Notre-Dame-des-flots:*[4]

> *La grande mer mugit au bas du promontoire,*
> *Et, toujours affamés sous les falaises noires,*
> *Ses monstrueux troupeaux font claquer leurs mâchoires.* *

At the return of the regiment in 1897, he settled at Roanne, and remained there until the outbreak of the World War, during which he gave his services to the defense of his country. At present he edits a local paper, the *Journal de Roanne,* and his life is divided between this work and study. He loves his little city, and cares not at all for the great Paris, in which he has never spent a whole week at one time. As Ferdinand Gohin says of him: "He seems indifferent to success, and he seems to disdain glory. . . . This poet is a sage. He continues to write beautiful poems, and thus his literary career is developing in a simple and harmonious manner; without literary industrialism he has acquired a fine reputation and is showing himself worthy of it."[5]

---

* The great sea roars at the foot of the promontory, and, always famished under the black cliffs, its monstrous herds snap their jaws.

Mercier's published works in prose comprise six volumes: *Hélène Sorbiers* (1911), the novel mentioned above; *Petites géorgiques* (1923), quaint but genuine pictures of the country life of the local peasants; *Les Demoiselles Valéry* (1924), a pathetic story of innocent lives blighted by the malignant persecution of others, followed by sketches similar to those in *Petites géorgiques; Contes de Jean-Pierre* (1907), humorous stories in *patois roannais; Des Contes et des images* (1929), a collection of thoughts and souvenirs most of which are on religious subjects; *Témoignages* (1932), six short addresses and six conferences given on various occasions. But Mercier is pre-eminently a poet. Even in his prose works very often we can say that all that is lacking to make a paragraph a poem more exquisite than many an anthology can boast of, is the prescribed cadence. For instance, in *Sur la naissance des feuilles,* we read: "If the leaves are cords under the bow of the wind, they become, under the fingers of the rain, so many little tambourines which reverberate with a throbbing sound through the country, and fill it with fresh and restful music. There is nothing more delightful than a summer shower which pours down through the woods."[6]

Seven volumes of poems have appeared: *L'Enchantée* (1897), *Voix de la terre et du temps* (1903), *Le Poème de la maison* (1906), *Lazare le ressuscité* (1910), *Les Pierres sacrées suivis des poèmes de la tranchée* (1922), *Les Cinq mystères joyeux* (1924), and *Virginis corona* (1929). René Lalou[7] classes Mercier with the Traditionalists, those who returned to the traditional forms after the enthusiasm for the Romanticists and Symbolists had died out. He commends in particular the two poems *Lazare le ressuscité* and *Ponce Pilate,* on account of their evangelical simplicity. This simplicity is one of Mercier's striking characteristics, both from the standpoint of subject matter and from that of style. Tennyson once said, "Water is the element that I love best of the four." If it had been Mercier speaking, he would surely have given the preference to earth. Whatever belongs to it, comes from it, is near to it—the grass, flowers, trees, stones, birds, animals, the peasant folk — appeals to him, and he sees these humble creatures through the eye of God. In *Pour mon église natale*,[8] he himself gives us his creed:

> *Église, je voudrais te ressembler un peu;*
> *Je voudrais qu'en restant voisine de la terre*
> *Et fraternelle avec les choses dont s'émeut*
> *Le village où s'épand ton ombre salutaire,*
> *Mon oeuvre, à son sommet, se rapprochât de Dieu.**

If he sings of churches, it is of *L'Église des blés, L'Église des bois, L'Église des vignes;* if he composes prayers, it is *Prière pour les soldats paysans, Pour les cuistots, Pour la cagna.* Occasionally he leaves these topics for loftier themes, as for instance, in *Lazare le ressuscité* and *Pilate,* but by far the greater number of his poems have been written about the lowly things of earth.

Nature is for Mercier a vast mirror, in which he beholds reflected dimly but truly the myriad tints of the transcendent beauty of God. The sight of a snowflake, of a grapevine, of ugly flowers even (he has a poem, *Les Fleurs laides*), raises his mind to a higher sphere. The great South American painter Subercaseaux, has in his picture life of St. Francis of Assisi, a striking scene entitled, "Nature disappoints her lover." Francis, having drunk in all the delights of Nature, turns away dissatisfied. Another Francis expresses much the same experience in his *Hound of Heaven:*

> *Nature, poor stepdame, cannot slake my drouth;*
> *Let her, if she would owe me,*
> *Drop yon blue bosom-veil of sky, and show me*
> *The breasts o' her tenderness.*[9]

---

* O Church, I would like to resemble you in a measure; I would wish that while my work remains close to the earth and fraternal in spirit with the things that stir the village lying in your salutary shadow, it may, at your summit, come closer to God.

Mercier is certainly one of Nature's most ardent lovers. We hardly think that she will disappoint him, for, to keep Thompson's figure, he has ever regarded her as but the lovely handmaid of God. In his treatment of nature, he is very exact, noting each little characteristic detail. As a child he had heard Nature's story from her own lips, and he had learned his lesson well. His *Laus herbarum* was one of the very first of his poems to receive public approbation. André Theurier, in his *Journal* of January 12, 1898, wrote of it: "This is true poetry, beautiful in form and in sentiment, adorned with images delightfully suggestive, as limpid, natural, and fresh as springwater."[10]

He combines simplicity with a rare earnestness. There is no straining after effect; he says what he has to say and we feel sure that he has described no place that he has not seen, and expressed no sentiment that he has not felt. Of the church steeples, so numerous in his native Forez, he writes:[11]

> *O clochers paysans, humbles clochers perdus*
> *Dans les pays sans gloire et les bourgs inconnus;*
> *Clochers bleus dont l'ardoise entre les arbres brille,*
> *Et qui cousez le ciel de votre fine aiguille.* *

Such verses prove that Mercier is a painter and a musician as well as a poet. There is a symmetry, grace, and smoothness about them, combined with a rare lightness of touch and pleasing melody. Yet he paints and sings for his idea, not color for color, sound for sound, art for art; not primarily to give us a picture or a tone, but to express his thought. Thus the last verse about the *clochers* expresses their principal beauty: "You do not cease speaking of God."

Winchester, in his book, *Some Principles of Literary Criticism,* says that "to buy illustrated editions of poetry is stupidity,"[12] and he goes on to explain that the poem itself

---

* O peasant steeples, humble steeples hidden in obscure country places and unknown towns; blue steeples, whose slated roofs shine among the trees, and which sew the sky with your fine needle.

should be a picture representing not so much what the poet sees as what he feels. The truth of these observations is attested by *L'Ombre éternelle* of Mercier. It presents a striking scene, all black with splashes of gold for the stars, far-off Danaïdes, striving to vanquish the darkness, but in vain:[13]

> *L'Ombre, patiente en son éternité,*
> *Attend l'heure fatale où, dans la nuit profonde,*
> *Les étoiles ayant épuisé leur clarté,*
> *L'Ombre victorieuse engloutira le monde.**

La Nuit révélatrice is painted in the same colors, but the central figure is the Earth beholding the wonders of the firmament, of which she would never have dreamed if Night had not revealed them to her. *À la neige* contrasts with these, as it is all white with the dazzling purity of the Immaculate Virgin shedding rays of light over it. *Poème du vent* is a magnificent picture, all restless, ceaseless motion. The Wind, "this eternal vagabond of life," rushes over the earth, never tranquil, ever moving, and the poet tries to guess the riddle of its incurable desires:[14]

> *Peut-être que le Vent est frère de la Mort!*
> *Des confins de l'espace et du plus loin des âges,*
> *Unis tous deux dans un indissoluble accord,*
> *Le Vent avec la Mort font le même voyage.*
> . . . .
> *Et le Vent n'est-il pas complice de la Mort,*
> *Le Vent qui s'insinue et siffle dans les portes*
> *Et qui, comme un voleur, pendant que l'homme dort*
> *Sans l'éveiller lui prend sa pauvre âme, et l'emporte?***

---

* Darkness, patient in its eternity, awaits the fatal hour, when, in a profound night, the stars having exhausted their brightness, victorious Darkness will swallow up the world.

** Perhaps the Wind is the brother of Death! From the limits of space and from the most remote ages, Both united in an indissoluble accord, Wind with Death makes the same journey. . . . And is not the Wind the accomplice of Death, the Wind which steals in whistling through the doors, and which, like a thief, while man sleeps, without awakening him, seizes and carries away his poor soul?

To illustrate such a poem would be to attempt to add something to what is already complete, and would spoil it. We
would be imitating the poor artist of whom Rodin says:
"Intending to improve upon nature, he adds green to the
springtime, rose to the sunrise, carmine to young lips; he
creates ugliness because he lies."[15]

Another noticeable characteristic of Mercier's style is its
freshness and originality. Alfred de Musset thinks that a
man must be very ignorant "to flatter himself that he is able
to say a single word that someone here below has not said
before him."[16] But certainly there are many lines in Mercier
that only a genius could have uttered before him. His poems
are rich in new connotations, in metaphors and similes
drawn from nature, and these figures are marked not only
by fidelity to fact and charm of phrase, but also by a subtle
harmony between the figure and the human mood or experience to be illustrated. He sees through the imagination
in broad, bright glimpses, and his descriptions are brief and
vivid. The new church is "like a red rose with petals of
tiles."[17] The oven, in *Poème de la maison*,[18] looks like a
sunset:

> Et, dans les braises qui s'accumulent,
> On voit s'ouvrir de grands jardins
> Où des bûchers de roses brûlent;
> Ou bien, quelque tison s'écroulant soudain,
> Voici s'envoler, innombrables et belles,
> Des étincelles.*

Mercier has two long poems, *Lazare le ressuscité* and
Ponce Pilate, published together in one volume, which deserve special mention. G. K. Chesterton says that usually a
particular piece remains in our minds in connection with an

---

* And in the burning coals which pile up, we see great gardens open, where
funeral piles of roses burn; or perhaps a fire-brand suddenly falls, and we see
innumerable and beautiful sparks flying away.

innocent head. Raymond Cernay, in *La Robe de laine* ("The Woolen Dress") (1910), is one of the most exquisite of Bordeaux's heroines. She is gentle, sweet, pure, and tender, but withal strong and faithful to duty. She is happy in her secluded country home, but when transplanted to the capital and brutally forced to enter the whirl of Parisian society, the angelic girl cannot stand the change. The breath of sin kills her, and her remorseful husband realizes too late her priceless worth. Likewise, Minie, in *Le Mont des anges* (1933), feels at the touch of sin that "the sweetness of life, faith in life, have been suddenly torn from her."[15]

Yamilé, a Maronite Christian, in *Yamilé sous les cèdres* ("Gardens of Omar") (1923), commits the unpardonable crime of loving and marrying a Mohammedan. Her punishment is death. André Bermance, in *La Vie recommence* (1921), in a moment of weakness before departing for the war, yields to temptation. He is killed in battle, but his sin lives after him. His noble mother, Madame Bermance, and Maria Ritzen, his fiancée, must suffer the consequences through many a long hard year. "These two souls, intimately united to each other," says Ligot, "purify the novel of sins of the flesh, which are its whole plot."[16] *La Remplaçante* (1935)[17] tells the terrible tale of an unfaithful priest, whose saintly daughter, Albine, undertakes by a life of sacrifice and renunciation among the Carmelites, to expiate her father's sacrilege. He is converted by her example and prayer, and enters La Trappe. Again in *Valombré* (1929), two other excellent women, the aristocratic Sylvie d'Arnay, and the humble Monique Desclaux, atone for the despicable cowardice of Eynard de Varce. In *L'Écran brisé* (1907) the temporal punishment of sin reaches even beyond the grave. Mathilde has been killed in an accident, and has left a packet of love letters from Pierre Émagny in a secret drawer of her desk. Her sister Marthe learns of this, and, eager at any cost to save her sister's honor, and to prevent her husband from learning of her infidelity, takes upon herself the guilt, saying that the letters were written to her. The lie is inexcusable, but Marthe's generous loyalty and self-forgetfulness win our admiration.

At the beginning of *La Chartreuse du reposoir* (1924), Bordeaux quotes this passage from Pascal: *"Ceux qui croient que le bien de l'homme est en la chair, et le mal en ce qui détourne du plaisir des sens, qu'ils s'en soûlent et qu'ils y meurent."** Twentieth-century moralists laugh at the doctrines of hell and purgatory, and encourage us to eat, drink, and be merry, but Bordeaux clings tenaciously to the Church's teaching on penance and satisfaction, expiation and redemption.

CONCLUSION

In addition to these general characteristics of Bordeaux, there are some other points worthy of mention. The scene of most of his novels is laid in Savoy. We read on the first page of *Promenades en Savoie* (1908): "There is scarcely one of my books in which Savoy does not occupy the principal place." He loves its mountains and valleys, its lakes and forests, its homes and villages, and he paints them with the brush of an artist. He is interested in its history, legends, and institutions. *Le Lac noir* (1904), is a study of the belief in sorcery in Savoy, besides being a very good story with a fascinating plot. He says in the introduction: "In their diversity, the fields of Savoy, in turn charming and pathetic, with their vast pastures, their ancients forests and threatening horizons, suffice as a setting for my tales." His heroes are practically all Savoyards, and his favorite saint is the beloved bishop of Geneva, to whom he dedicated one of his best studies.

His novels present a gallery of noble girls and women, the

---

* "May those who believe that the good of man consists in carnal pleasures, and the evil in abstinence from them, be surfeited with this belief and die in it."

like of which no other modern novelist can boast. Sometimes perhaps they are too ideal, but they are always lovely and beautiful, if not imitable. There are Madame Guibert, Madame Bermance, Madame Dérize, true cornelian heroines, the highest type of Catholic mothers, who, by their noble influence, preach lessons of courage, resignation, and self-sacrifice. There are his gentle fairylike maidens, too good for this world, but emitting around them the perfume of paradise, Raymonde Cernay, Albine Fournel, Pernette Fégère, Minie Pérouze, symphonies of grace and light. There are others less ethereal but perhaps more human and sympathetic, Paule Guibert, Tuilette, Marguerite Roquevillard. These are better able to cope with life, for they accept it as it is, and communicate to others their enthusiasm for virtue. Another class that Bordeaux likes to present is the modern athletic type, with her sane, wholesome outlook on life, such as Dianah Powlys, Ginette, Isabelle de Foix, etc. Of course, not all of Bordeaux's women are saints. He realizes that there are many descendants of Eve who are no improvement on their illustrious ancestor. We have Thérèse Romenay, Sandrine de Loury, Berthe de Cheraus, Andromède, Micheline d'Entrève, Edith Frasne, besides a host of spineless, insignificant women who stand over against the valorous heroines to enhance their virtue. Thus the weakness of the Dulaurens augments the courage of the Guiberts. The worldliness of Elizabeth Dérize's mother, Madame Molay-Norrois, makes the saintliness of her mother-in-law more evident.

Lastly, Bordeaux is a born storyteller. He knows how to construct a plot and to hold the attention of his readers to the very end. According to Émile Faguet, we are always sure of finding his novels "very well composed, very clear, very interesting, and founded on well-made observations."[18] For the delineation of character he has a special gift. Even when different novels treat the same theme, he varies the story by strongly individualizing his characters. His style is classic, with the usual qualities of good French prose — clearness, order, taste. Britsch says that it is always smooth and sustained, and never permits a suspicion of weariness or negligence in the writer, and that "M. Bordeaùx appears a master of form."[19] Though he writes of the provinces, he rarely uses either argot or neologisms. He has been reproached for this very exactness, but most readers appreciate his impeccable prose, which never becomes dull or monotonous.

He is without question a moralist, though he is far from emotional pietism. There is a tonic message in his work, based on Catholic doctrine and principles. All his teachings on marriage, divorce, the family, the punishment of sin, the purpose of life, etc., are impregnated with Catholicism. In his novels religion gives courage, hope, and strength, while the lack of it engenders egoism, cynicism, and despair. In 1922, he expressed his understanding of the duty of the Catholic novelist thus: "The Catholic novelist has first of all the same obligations toward art as his other confreres in the field, obligations too often misunderstood, moreover, by those who believe themselves freed from all responsibility. But he has still others too, or rather, his obligations become complicated for this reason: beauty and truth have for him a sense more formal, a supernatural sense, a divine sense."[20]

The editor of *Blackfriars* says that he is "a great apologist, devoting all his energy, all his superb gifts to the service of the Church," and that his tales consist for the most part "of magnificent expositions of the rightness of Catholic teaching."[21] He seldom preaches, but the serious tone of his work, and the convincing example of his heroes and heroines accomplish more than a sermon. Theodore Roosevelt, in the letter addressed to Bordeaux on the publication of his life of Guynemer, says: "You have written with such power and charm, with such mastery of manner and

matter, that the lessons you taught have been learned unconsciously by your readers — and this is the only way in
which most readers will learn lessons at all."[22]

PRINCIPAL WORKS OF HENRY BORDEAUX

1894   *Âmes modernes*
1900   *Le Pays natal*
1900   *Portraits de femmes et d'enfants*
1902   *Les Écrivains et les moeurs*
1904   *La Peur de vivre*
1904   *Le Lac noir*
1905   *La Petite Mademoiselle*
1906   *Vies intimes*
1906   *Les Roquevillard*
1906   *Pèlerinages littéraires*
1907   *L'Écran brisé*
1908   *Promenades en Savoie*
1908   *Les Yeux qui s'ouvrent*
1909   *La Croisée des chemins*
1910   *La Robe de laine*
1910   *La Vie au théâtre*
1911   *Un Médecin de campagne*
1912   *La Maison*
1912   *La Neige sur les pas*
1913   *La Maison morte*
1914   *La Nouvelle croisade des enfants*
1918   *Le Chevalier de l'air, Vie héroïque de Georges Guynemer*
1918   *Les Pierres du foyer*
1920   *La Resurrection de la chair*
1921   *La Chair et l'esprit, La Vie recommence*
1923   *Yamilé sous les cèdres*
1924   *Portraits d'hommes*
1924   *Saint François de Sales et notre coeur de chair*
1925   *Le Walter Scott Normand, Barbey d'Aurevilly*
1926   *Le Chemin de Roselande*
1926   *Les Jeux dangereux*
1928   *Andromède et le monstre*
1929   *Valombré*
1930   *Visages Français*

1930 *Tuilette*
1931 *Murder Party*
1932 *La Revenante*
1933 *Les Déclassés*
1933 *Le Mont des anges*
1935 *Henri de Bournazel*
1935 *La Remplaçante*

REFERENCES

Britsch, Amédée, *Henry Bordeaux, Biographie critique,* Paris, 1906.

Carrière, Henri, *Une doctrine de vie. Extraits de l'oeuvre d'Henry Bordeaux,* Paris, 1920.

Chaumeix, André, "Les Idées d'Henry Bordeaux," *Revue hebdomadaire,* Feb., 1912, pp. 393–414.

Crawford, Virginia, "Henry Bordeaux," *Studies,* XVI (1927), pp. 306–316.

Ferchat, Joseph, *Le Roman de la famille française, essai sur l'oeuvre de M. Henry Bordeaux,* Paris, 1912.

Héritier, Jean, *L'Amour dans l'oeuvre d'Henry Bordeaux,* Paris, 1930.

Ligot, Maurice, *Le Sens de la vie et l'idée de l'ordre dans l'oeuvre d'Henry Bordeaux,* Paris, 1924.

Pascal, Félicien, "L'Oeuvre de guerre d' Henry Bordeaux," *Revue hebdomadaire,* May, 1920, pp. 482–495.

CHAPTER VII

Émile Baumann

(1868–   )

OF ALL CONTEMPORARY FRENCH NOVELISTS, perhaps the most completely Catholic is Émile Baumann. His religion is not a convention, a pose, nor a literary veneer which he clumsily spreads over the book as an afterthought, but, as Louis Bertrand expresses it, "Catholicism is truly the soul of his soul."[1] He paints life, and his only view of life is that seen with the eyes of faith and from a supernatural vantage. He does not belong to *les grands convertis,* for he was a believer from the beginning.

In his biography of his brother Léon, *Mon Frère le Dominicain,* he tells us that his early ancestors were Lutherans, but his great-grandfather married a Catholic and all his descendants were brought up in the faith. He attributes to this Protestant ancestry, however, his "precocious passion for the Bible, especially the Apocalypse . . . and a certain propensity to rigorism."[2] The love and talent for music, common to all the Baumanns, he traces back to a German progenitor born about 1720. His own father, Henri Baumann, gave lessons on the violincello and was soloist at the Grand Théâtre of Lyons.

Émile was born in the center of Lyons in 1868, and here he and Léon, five years younger, grew up. His latest book, *Lyon et les Lyonnais* (1935), a monograph on his native city, is filled with souvenirs of childhood and youth. He went to the Jesuit school and received a thoroughly religious education, supplemented by the teaching and influence of a devout Catholic mother. He read the Bible, the Fathers of the Church, and the mystics, and from these he derived his extensive knowledge of theology so evident in all his writings. In 1890, we find him a young agrégé at Roanne, and about the same time he married. True to heredity, he was fond of music, and at twenty-four undertook his first work, *Les Grandes formes de la musique, l'Oeuvre de Saint-Saëns,* which was published in 1905.

Baumann has written seven novels, all of them strange, serious, stern illustrations of some thesis that he wants to prove. The first, *L'Immolé* (1908), tells the story of a family of degenerates, in which the last member, Daniel Rovère, attempts to repair not only materially, but also spiritually, the sins of his ancestors, especially those of his father. The latter, cashier in a big bank, committed suicide after having stolen a large amount of money to satisfy the demands of his mistress. Daniel has little of the hero in him, but his saintly mother urges him to offer himself to God to expiate the crime and to save his father's soul: "Do not complain, there is nothing better than the will to suffer in God. You will begin the restoration of a fallen family, you will be the liberator."[3] The sacrifice is accepted, and Madame Rovère dies of tuberculosis, while her son devotes his life to good works. Daniel's prayer in the chapel of the Poor Souls, after the death of his father, sums up the meaning of the novel: "O Jesus, may I be a victim, an *immolé,* and may none of my expiation be wasted by not being united with Thine, but may every part of my life be a part of Thy life."[4] This is the first of Baumann's victims, who continue to appear in his books, accomplishing their share in the Redemption, and filling up what is wanting in the sufferings of Christ.

La Fosse aux lions (1911) shows progress, as it is more dramatic than *L'Immolé,* but it is also more improbable and more brutal. On Good Friday, Madame de Bradieu, while meditating on the wickedness and ingratitude of men, offers herself and her children in reparation for sin. Soon after, she dies without the consolation of the last sacraments, her daughter Claire enters the Carmelites, and the novel recounts how her son Philip returns to the Broux, the old family manor, to find his father, a drunkard, living in sin with the maid Diane. The latter, on account of her master's preference, tyrannizes over the rest of the household. Philip, the opposite of his father, is shocked and pained to see the moral and physical degradation of his parent, and indignantly protests, but he gains nothing. Diane becomes insane and is taken away. Philip marries a pure, noble girl, Alix de la Thébaudrie, whom M. de Bradieu at first appears to welcome, but on whom he swears vengeance when she repulses his too familiar advances. A few months later, half-mad from debauchery, he strangles Alix's first-born son and throws him into a ditch. Too late he is put in an asylum, where he hangs himself. The characters are intensely living in this domestic tragedy, but the plot is rather complicated and the situations are often melodramatic. The thesis is that sins, especially sins of the flesh, bring their own punishment, and satisfaction is demanded in this life or in the next.

Le Baptême de Pauline Ardel (1913) is less harsh and rigid, simpler in plot, and more wholesome in tone. It relates the conversion of a young girl from agnosticism to Catholicism. Pauline's mother is dead and she is living with her father, a professor at Sens and an unbeliever, who really loves his daughter and tries to fashion her to his own likeness. He is the cold, intellectual type, and delights in study, argument, and analysis. "The only true paradise," he assures her, "is that which one creates for oneself, the paradise of labor and of thought."[5] Pauline seems satisfied with this teaching until she becomes acquainted with the Rude family, devout Catholics. First she discovers that they possess an enviable domestic happiness, and then she realizes that it proceeds from a spiritual joy quite unknown to her. She becomes intimate with Edmée Rude, a girl about her own age, and falls deeply in love with Julien, the eldest son and somewhat of a mystic. Her father likes Julien, but he is absolutely opposed to his daughter marrying a Catholic, in fact he declares that "he would rather see her dead than a bigot."[6] Julien, after a short illness, dies, and his private notes reveal the fact that he has offered his life for Pauline's soul. She is baptized, and although her father is not converted, he becomes less prejudiced, and in the end even urges her to marry a Catholic, Gabriel Authelin. The novel would lose nothing if this last chapter were omitted, as it detracts from the idyllic love story of the noble hero and beautiful heroine, who were united by spiritual espousals, though earthly marriage was denied them.

Le Fer sur l'enclume (1920), which Levaux calls "a Catholic *Madame Bovary*,"[7] shows how God *forges* a soul and arouses it to the true meaning of a Christian life. Séverin Lhostis, a retired marine officer, is apparently happily married to an excellent wife, Marie Budéron, but he falls in love with the sympathetic Eliza Lougrée, and only too late understands what shame and sorrow his passion has caused. Marie forgives him and is willing by prayer and sacrifice to help him expiate his crime. Eliza goes away, and the second part of the novel relates his remorse and punishment. The third part (sixteen years later) shows us Séverin purified by suffering, bearing with resignation the painful consequences of his sin, which are particularly evident in the covert hostility between his rightful son Albert, and the illegitimate son Xavier. The father's final and greatest humiliation comes when he is obliged to reveal his past to his own children. The title of the story is explained by the lines: "What is done is done. . . . Words as weighty as the anvil on which is struck the red iron of all expiations."[8]

Job le prédestiné (1922) is probably the best known of the novels of Baumann, owing to the fact that it was awarded the Grand Prix Balzac in 1922. It is not as realistic as those which preceded it, and in the judgment of many critics it is less well written and less interesting. The hero, like Job of old, is tried by God in every conceivable way, but he blesses the Lord in his trials, and accepts them with admirable fortitude. Bernard Dieuzède, an orphan who has inherited a fortune of six hundred thousand francs, retires to his father's house at Portzic to live *à la Des Esseintes,* surrounded by every luxury. Suddenly all is changed. His money is gone, his mistress is drowned before his eyes, and he is obliged to open a bookstore to earn a living for his wife, the selfish Hélène, and his three children. He is more of an idealist than a businessman, and difficulties increase. Hélène follows a lover to Paris and takes one of the children with her, Bernard faces starvation, sickness, and even the loss of sight, but not a murmur or complaint escapes him. Finally the tide turns and his patience and humility are rewarded. He regains moderate wealth, Hélène's lover dies and she returns to him, and the story ends with a picture of their broken happiness patched up as perfectly as possible. The novel recalls Balzac both in its good qualities and in its faults. It is a powerful study in which the characters are vivid and well-defined, but it lacks proportion and drags along in useless details and episodes, when we would wish for more rapidity and condensation.

Le Signe sur les mains (1926) is one of the best written of the novels of Baumann, but the choice of subject is unfortunate. There is some audacity in the attempt to make a priestly vocation the theme of a novel, and few writers could succeed in doing so without being offensive. Baumann presents to us Jérôme Cormier, torn by doubt and indecision with regard to his vocation. His friend Montcalm, who had intended to become a priest to repair the sacrilege of his father (an ex-priest), died on the battlefield after having asked Jérôme to take his place. Jérôme had answered, "If God so wills." He felt little inclination for the sacerdotal

life, and before long found himself in love with Agnès
Duprat, an orphan living with his mother. She returns his
love and he plans to marry her. Meantime, the half promise
to Montcalm, the great need of priests, and the warning of
Dom Estienne, his Benedictine confessor, that God's call is
not to be rejected, all determine him to give up Agnès and
enter the seminary, to receive on his hands "that mysterious
mark, impossible to destroy."⁹ Agnès is heartbroken, and,
refusing to accept another husband, retires to the province
where she lives with her sister Antoinette. The novel is less
complex and monotonous than his others, the tragic and
pathetic are developed with more ease and rapidity, and
from the literary point of view it is one of his best works.
But just what is its purport? Doubtless Baumann wanted
to point out that an exterior vocation may become an interior one, that Jérôme's love for Agnès was mere passion
and t : his decision was a triumph of grace over nature.
But .ost readers will be in sympathy with Agnès, and feel
inclined to agree with her when she says at the end: "I
believe that he became a priest somewhat against his will."¹⁰
If Jérôme felt that his promise to Montcalm was binding
and that God was really calling him to a higher state, he
can hardly be excused for encouraging Agnès to conjugal
hopes. Moreover, usually one of the definite marks of a
vocation is an inclination to the life, while in Jérôme we
find a positive aversion, overcome only by the recollection
of his words to a dying friend, the realization of the gaps
left in the ranks of the French clergy by the World War,
and the encouragement of his confessor. Father Tonquédec,
in his review of the novel, says he would be inclined to fear
for Jérôme's future if he were accepted for Holy Orders.¹¹

The latest novel of Baumann, *Abel et Caïn* (1930), is the
story of two stepbrothers of very different characters. Hubert
Chaptal resembles his father, businesslike, practical, avaricious, and an atheist, while François is like his mother

Christine, dreamy and impulsive, governed by the heart rather than by the head. Madame Chaptal tries to be just and impartial, though her sympathies are naturally with her own son François. The latter becomes infatuated with a young war widow, Odile Egmont, and contrary to his mother's advice, he frequents her home. Hubert also has been looking with favor on Odile, and when repulsed, burns with jealousy and the desire for revenge. One evening he treacherously lures François to Odile's house, where he is awaiting him. A quarrel and struggle ensue in which François is accidentally killed. Hubert gives himself up to the police, is tried and condemned to three years' imprisonment. The mother, by a heroic effort, forgives Hubert, visits him in prison, and treats him with great sweetness and patience. She seems to win him at last, and ennobled and strengthened by suffering, she herself becomes a model Christian woman. As in many of Baumann's novels, there is a superfluous last chapter, and the thesis is evident: Patience hath a perfect work.

Some of the critics have praised Baumann very highly, while others have criticized his novels mercilessly and scoffed at them. Paradoxical as it may seem, both these judgments are in a measure correct, depending on the viewpoint from which his work is judged. First of all, his purpose, as he states it in the dedication of *Abel et Caïn* to Bourget, is commendable: ". . . the cure of the modern world, the defeat of the principles of error which poison it." He set about accomplishing this purpose in no half-hearted, blundering way, but with all the determination and vigor that were born of deep-seated conviction. Sin is a terrible thing, the one great evil in the world, and he paints this evil and the curse that it brings in somber colors. His pictures are sometimes graphic and repulsive in their violence, but more often they are profound and moving. For him life is not a comedy, but a tragedy which he describes with a deep note of Christian seriousness. Yet he does not despair, but shows us fallen souls purified and rising to great heights by prayer and sacrifice. They suffer and weep, but they have confidence that their tears are not shed in vain. This idea of expiation is the key to all his work. It haunts him and we find it everywhere. In *Mon Frère le Dominicain* he relates that even when he was a child "the ruin of our family left us the idea of mysterious faults which had merited it, of an expiation which was extended to us."[12] There is not much variety in his novels, as we have someone atoning for his own sins or those of others in all of them.

This endeavor to return to a belief in God in literature, to write novels permeated with religious faith, was a bold undertaking. Baumann attempts it without making any concessions to public opinion, quite indifferent to the bait of popularity and success which attracts so many writers. He is not a mystic dreamer, but rather a visionary realist, severe and even harsh at times. There are traces of Zola's scientific realism in his books, and even more decided evidences of the influence of Huysmans' "supernatural naturalism." His sinners are great sinners (M. de Bradieu, M. Rovère, Hubert Chaptal, Séverin Lhostis) and their fall is followed by torture and ignominy. Therefore the reparation must be rigorous likewise, and the victims, innocent or guilty, are punished pitilessly. These victims are usually not of the weeping type, but are strong, courageous, resigned souls, who voluntarily accept their share in the work of satisfaction (Bernard Dieuzède, Philippe de Bradieu, Julien Rude, Antoinette Duprat, etc.). All these characters, the good and the bad, are clearly drawn and true to life. Vandérem remarks that Baumann has one trait in common with Balzac, he himself firmly believes in the people he puts into his books and he makes his readers feel that he knew them personally and was intimate with them.[13] This was partly the result of his absolute sincerity and hatred of anything artificial. In an article published in *La Minerve Française* in 1919, he says: "Art, sprung from the real, ought to tend with all its energetic certitude to the real."[14]

Most of Baumann's novels treat of love and show the ravaging and far-reaching effects of illicit passion. He illustrates how a small flame, which seems quite harmless at first, becomes a raging fire if not checked at the outset. Séverin Lhostis was attracted by the intelligent sympathy of Eliza Lougrée, Daniel Rovère by the "delirious music" of Henriette Saint-Albon, and Hélène Dieuzède by the easy, charming maner of Dr. Klenka. But, *On ne badine pas avec l'amour,* and when this proverb is disregarded, spiritual, moral, and physical disaster follow, sometimes through long years of pain and suffering.

Baumann's aim then is admirable, and his effort to accomplish it, highly commendable. His pictures of repentant sinners, of voluntary, generous victims, of young people with apostolic aspirations, desiring to live and act their faith, are an inspiration to his readers. As Calvet remarks, "to appreciate the grandeur of his thought, it suffices to be a man who has an ideal."[15] He is a deep thinker, a philosopher with a large vision, and a theologian whose exegesis of suffering in the world is excellent. But is he a good novelist? Hardly.

First of all, his plots are not well constructed. They are too complex, too long drawn out, and the action is retarded by the relation of unnecessary incidents. For example, Daniel's efforts at social reform in *L'Immolé,* and Philippe's ambitions to be elected mayor in *La Fosse aux lions,* are foreign to the main story. Often, as in *Le Baptême de Pauline Ardel,* the last chapter could well be omitted. *Le Fer sur l'enclume* begins "as a drama, and ends as a biography."[16] *Job le prédestiné,* in spite of the fact that it won the Grand Prix Balzac, is the worst of his novels from the artistic standpoint, on account of its monotonous slowness of plot and the unattractive character of the would-be hero. All his novels are encumbered with useless details about the past history of secondary characters, and with tiresome descriptions of unimportant places. These faults are less noticeable in his two latest novels (*Le Signe sur les mains, Abel et Caïn*) which, from the viewpoint of composition, are better than the four preceding ones.

Secondly, the characters are, as a rule, abnormal, either excessively bad or extremely good. Old Bradieu is a real monster, and Hubert Chaptal is not much better. On the other hand, Philippe de Bradieu, Jules Rudel, Bernard Dieuzède, and Antoinette Duprat are almost too good to be true. Heredity has much to do with their moral stamina, as Madame Rovère explains to Daniel: "When one is of a blood like ours, one must choose either to be damned or to be a saint."[17] Still, as we mentioned above, in spite of their actual improbability, Baumann succeeds in investing these characters with an air of verisimilitude on account of his own faith in them.

Thirdly, Baumann is too severe. He teaches the gospel of fear, not of love, and he never departs from his rigid austerity. Like one of the ancient prophets, he preaches compunction and penance, and his cruelest pages are scarcely softened with a soothing word. Two things might have saved him, a sense of humor which could lighten the heaviness and break the strain with a smile, or a poetic instinct which could give a mystic touch to the sufferings he so lavishly inflicts on his characters. Claudel writes spiritual dramas as deep and as tense as any in French literature, but they are sung with lyric beauty and punctuated with mystic effusions that raise them to the sphere of the sublime. But none of this in Baumann. He is neither a humorist nor a poet. As Levaux says: "In his books no one ever laughs, unless it be with a laughter sadder than tears."[18]

Fourthly, many people, especially Catholics, object to

Baumann's novels, because of the frankness and daring freedom with which he describes sin in all its vulgarity and shamelessness. He handles without gloves passion, villainy, adultery, and baseness of every type with a candidness that is alarming. Louis Bertrand says: "He excels in painting the weaknesses, the pretensions, and sometimes the brutalities of the dechristianized soul."[19] Sin is ugly, and he does not hesitate to show it in its true colors. Barbey d'Aurevilly, in his preface to *Une Vieille maîtresse,* says that Catholicism in no way forbids the representation of sin and passion in literature with this absolute reserve: "that the novel should never be a propaganda of vices or a preaching of errors; that it should never permit it to appear that good is evil and that evil is good." According to this criterion, Baumann is indeed within his rights. Neither can anyone accuse him of lingering over these scenes on account of any secret satisfaction in them. It is quite evident that his sole purpose is to teach the hideousness of sin and the danger of temptation, and he does it boldly and openly in his abrupt, vivid manner, without apology or disguise. Thérive, his most severe critic, finds "under the vulgar weave of material incidents, a mystic woof which is beautiful and noble; for it participates in the poetic grandeur of the dogmas."[20] But not all readers discover this woof, and they feel that he could accomplish his end without using such questionable and offensive means. Levaux draws attention to the fact that the ancients and the classics did not paint evil with all the minute details that the moderns find it necessary to go into.[21]

Lastly, Baumann's style is deplorable. It lacks grace, ease, elegance, and harmony, qualities so essential to good French prose. He uses rare words, neologisms, archaisms, and inversions, and the result is often an impression of bad taste, heaviness, and incoherence. Whether he despises a facile style, or whether he simply lacks the artistic sense, he seems to make no effort to rid his pages of their harshness, rigidity, and dissonances. One cause of these faults is probably an excess of imagination, an inability to choose among an abundance of details, and a lack of equilibrium and proportion. It is true, however, that, at times his strong contrasts, picturesque energy, and forceful epithets please us, and give a semblance of crude veracity to his scenes and characters.

On the whole, then, Baumann may be classed with contemporary writers of evident talent and competence, but not among the great geniuses. In spite of his faults, or perhaps on account of them, he imposes himself and his supernatural view of life upon the reader and forces him to realize that there are powers ruling the earth, above those of scheming little men. If he has accomplished that, the rest scarcely matters to him, for he has never sought to please by his novels, but to deliver his message to the modern world, which hearkens none too eagerly to reproving voices.

Besides his novels, Baumann has written a number of other works, some of which have been mentioned. Among them are meditative descriptions of places and people he knows and loves so well: *Lyon et les Lyonnais* (1935), *Trois villes saintes* (1912), *Pages Vendéennes* (1929); essays in literary criticism, *Intermèdes* (1927); three studies of different types of love — human, misguided, satanic, intellectual, courtly, platonic, holy, and divine: *La Symphonie du désir* (1933), *L'Amour et sagesse* (1934), *Héloïse l'amante et l'abbesse* (1934); a book on the end of the world and the last judgment, *La Paix du septième jour* (1917); and biographies: *Marie Antoinette et Axel Fersen* (1931), *Bossuet* (1929), *Mon Frère le Dominicain* (1927), *L'Anneau d'or des grands mystiques* (1924), *Les Chartreux* (1928), and *Saint Paul* (1925). Of these, his *Saint Paul* (translated into English under the same title) deserves special mention, as it is considered by many his masterpiece. This may be due to the fact that there is a certain likeness of temperament between the author and the generous, rugged, outspoken apostle. At any rate, after having studied the Saint for thirty years and visited the places that were the scenes of his labors, he gives us a complete and convincing picture of him. Perhaps this is where Baumann's true field lies, in hagiography. In fiction all is invented and his great imagination runs riot, but in spiritual biographies he is hemmed in and checked by facts. Moreover, as François Mauriac explains, it is difficult in novels to show the finger of God directing events without seeming arbitrary, but this is not the case in relating the lives of saints. And he adds this parenthetical tribute: "One condition, however, is necessary, which is not common among novelists but which we admire in Baumann: the cult of the interior life, the aspiration to sanctity."[22]

PRINCIPAL WORKS OF ÉMILE BAUMANN

1905 *Les Grandes formes de la musique, l'Oeuvre de Saint-Saëns*
1908 *L'Immolé*
1911 *La Fosse aux lions*
1912 *Trois villes saintes*
1913 *Le Baptême de Pauline Ardel*
1917 *La Paix du septième jour*
1920 *Le Fer sur l'enclume*
1922 *Job le prédestiné*
1924 *L'Anneau d'or des grands mystiques*
1925 *Saint Paul*
1926 *Le Signe sur les mains*
1927 *Intermèdes*
1927 *Mon Frère le Dominicain*
1928 *Les Chartreux*
1929 *Bossuet*
1929 *Pages Vendéennes*
1930 *Abel et Caïn*
1931 *Marie Antoinette et Axel Fersen*
1933 *La Symphonie du désir*
1934 *L'Amour et sagesse*
1934 *Héloïse l'amante et l'abbesse*
1935 *Lyon et les Lyonnais*

REFERENCES

Bertrand, Louis, "Émile Baumann," *Revue bleue,* March 5, 1921, pp. 141–147.

Mandadon, Louis de, "Émile Baumann," *Études religieuses,* CLXVII (1921), pp. 231–244.

—— "Le Grand prix Balzac du roman," *Études religieuses,* CLXXIII (1922), pp. 580–589.

Massis, Henri, "M. Émile Baumann et la querelle de l'art et du roman," *Revue universelle,* XI (1922), pp. 637–646.

Mauriac, François, "Saint Paul d'Émile Baumann," *Revue hebdomadaire,* Sept., 1925, pp. 100–104.

Schiefley, William, "Émile Baumann and His Art," *Catholic World,* CXXII (1926), pp. 644–650.

CHAPTER VIII

François Mauriac

(1885–   )

LIKE MOST TWENTIETH-CENTURY WRITERS, François Mauriac has told us much about himself. He simply cannot keep out of his books, and either consciously or unconsciously enters into every one of them. Even in his recent masterpiece, *Vie de Jésus* ("The Life of Jesus") while we are busy looking upon the impressive vision of Christ that he calls up before us, we cannot forget the author, whose personality is indelibly stamped on every page. He has described his childhood in *Commencements d'une vie*, his youth in *Le Jeune homme*, his early environment in *Bordeaux* and *La Province*, his religious attitude in *Dieu et Mammon* and *Souffrances et bonheur du Chrétien*, and his literary theories in *Le Roman* and *Le Romancier et ses personnages*. Frequently he writes prefaces to his books, explaining how, when, and why he composed them, and interpreting their meaning. He lays the scene of most of his novels in or around his native city, and many of his characters reflect his own qualities of body and mind. But he reveals himself with such a becoming modesty and absolute sincerity that no one can take offense, or accuse him of egoism. We want him to keep right on telling us about this interesting individual named François Mauriac, for we realize that he has much in common with each of us, but that he analyzes his sentiments and expresses them infinitely better than we ever could.

He was born on October 11, 1885, in Bordeaux, the city which he loved so much and of which he later wrote: "The history of Bordeaux is the history of my body and of my soul."[1] When he was but twenty months old, he lost his father, and one of his books of memoirs begins thus: "I have never grown accustomed to the misfortune of not having known my father."[2] His widowed mother, left with five children of whom he was the youngest, sought refuge with the grandmother, and François was brought up by these two pious women in a thoroughly Catholic atmosphere. His youth was passed in the country of the Landes, under the glowing skies and odorous pine forests of the Midi. He tells us that he was "a sad child, easily hurt."[3] Why sad? Probably because he was too sensitive and solitary, too conscious of his inner life, and not very strong physically. He assures us that it was not religion which darkened his childhood, for "it gave him more joy than pain."[4] He attended the school of the Marianites in his native city and later went up to Paris to study. With André Lafon and Vallery-Radot he planned to gather together a group of Catholic artists under the patronage of St. Francis of Assisi and to found a review in which they might freely express their sentiments, but the project was not carried out.

His literary career began with the publication of a collection of verses, *Les Mains jointes* (1909), which attracted the attention of Paul Bourget and Maurice Barrès. The latter wrote of it: "In this book, I like the charming gift of spirituality, joined to youth and the purest taste. I do not find in it (great prodigy for a poet!) a single absurdity."[5] A second book of poems, dedicated to Barrès and reminiscent of Jammes, followed in 1911, *L'Adieu à l'adolescence*. In spite of the flattering reception which these two volumes received, Mauriac definitely left poetry and turned to prose.[6]

L'Enfant chargé de chaînes (1913) and *La Robe prétexte* (1914) were both published before the World War, and though they presage the greatness of Mauriac's later work, they are inferior to it and show signs of immaturity. After

the War, in which he fought, he took up his literary labors
again with *La Chair et le sang* (1920), and from that day
to this his genius has slowly but surely unfolded itself.
Mauriac's novels are so numerous that it would be impossible to analyze them all. Yet it is difficult to choose from
among them, because each one is perfect in its own way,
and is a link in the chain that binds the sensitive, timid
youth who bade farewell to poetry in 1911, to the
mature middle-aged man, one of the greatest living writers
in France, but still humble and diffident, as we may judge
from his preface to the *Vie de Jésus,* when he declares that
such a work "should be written on bended knee, in a sentiment of unworthiness that would make the pen fall from
our hands." As Edmond Jaloux says, "Each new novel . . .
increases our esteem for him, and each one gains in gravity,
in depth, and in intelligence."' We have tried to select those
that more definitely mark a stage in his literary career: *Le
Baiser au lépreux* (1922), *Le Fleuve de feu* (1923), *Genitrix*
(1924), *Le Désert de l'amour* (1925), *Thérèse Desqueyroux*
(1927), *Destins* (1928), *Ce qui était perdu* (1930), *Le Noeud
de vipères* (1932), *Le Mystère Frontenac* (1933), *La Fin de
la nuit* (1935), and *Les Anges noirs* (1936).

   Le Baiser au lépreux ("The Kiss to the Leper"), published in *Les Cahiers verts,* which took the place of the pre-
war *Cahiers de la quinzaine,* established Mauriac's reputation. It is scarcely more than a short story and concentrates
on a single theme, a *mariage de convenance,* which turns
out badly. The setting is in the region of the Landes. Jean
Péloueyre, the son of a rich landowner, grotesquely ugly
and wholly unattractive, is to be married to the charming,
pretty Noémi d'Artiailh. The marriage has been arranged
by her mother and the parish priest, and, though Noémi
scarcely knows Jean, she does not even think of rebellion,
for "one does not refuse a Péloueyre. One does not refuse
farms, fields, flocks of sheep, silver-plate, the linens of ten

generations carefully piled in wide, high, sweet-smelling cupboards; alliance with the best that is to be found in the moors. One does not refuse a Péloueyre."[8] So poor little Noémi silently submits, and in the cure's parlor she looks upon the man with whom she is to pass her life. "The virgin took in with her eyes this larva that was her fate. The handsome lad with multiple face, the dream-companion of all young girls . . . this young man vanished in the twilight of the parish house, melted and faded until he became no more than the invisible cricket she heard in the darkest corner of the room."[9] They are married, and Noémi tries her best to fulfill her duty as a faithful wife, but she simply cannot overcome the physical repugnance she feels toward Jean. He understands this, and, far from complaining, worships her in silence like a whipped dog. Ashamed of his infirmity, he goes to Paris for a long visit in order to rid her for a time of his hated presence, and when he returns, he voluntarily contracts tuberculosis, and patiently awaits death. Noémi, stung with remorse (though she has nothing with which to reproach herself) nurses him faithfully, kissing him "with the lips of those saints who of old kissed lepers."[10] Even after his death she refuses the advances of the handsome young doctor who would gladly have made her happy. "Her fidelity to the dead was to be her humble glory."[11] The novel is sober and brief in form, melancholy and poetic in tone. It proved that the author had talent of a rare quality, and that he could handle a commonplace theme (an unhappy marriage) with perfect art.

Le Fleuve de feu relates an incident that occurs at a watering place in the Pyrenees. Gisèle de Plailly, a young girl who has grown up during the War without a mother, and who has fallen once through weakness, meets at the hotel Daniel Trasis, a Parisian debauchee, who immediately determines to win her. Her friend, Lucile de Villeron, arrives and endeavors to protect her, but Gisèle's desire is greater than

Lucile's power, and she deliberately seeks Daniel. The next day Gisèle returns to her father, and Daniel to Paris. Months later, when he wishes to see her again, he finds her at Mass in the village church, apparently converted and leading the hymns, so he leaves without disturbing her. This unexpected change in Gisèle is partly explained by the fact that in his early years Daniel had been loved by a pure young girl, Marie Ransinangue, who sacrificed her life for him and entered the Carmelites. Her mysterious substitution saved Gisèle from "the river of fire," and had a regenerating effect on Daniel also. From the artistic point of view this novel is not so good as *Le Baiser au lépreux*. There is some artificiality in the sudden conversion of Gisèle, the psychological development of the characters is not well traced, and the structure is awkward. Here, as in the preceding novel, there is a struggle between the spirit and the flesh and the action is all interior, but the triumph of the spirit is not very convincing.

*Genitrix** followed in 1924. It likewise treats of a single passion, maternal egoism, and the note of cruelty is accentuated. The book opens with the last agony of a neglected young wife, whose death resulted from a miscarriage. Her husband, Fernand Cazenave, is the only son of a doting mother, and, though he is fifty-two years old, he allows himself to be tyrannized over by her to such an extent that he can scarcely have an opinion of his own. She cares for him, smooths away all the difficulties in his path, and adores him with a jealous love. The conflict had begun when he married Mathilde, an enterprising young school teacher, who dared to dispute Madame Cazenave's absolute dominion over her son's heart. As long as his wife lived, the mother had the advantage, but after her death Fernand became dimly conscious that it was his mother who had separated him from Mathilde, and that she had died from lack of

---

* Translated into English under the same title.

care. So the living mother engaged in a mighty struggle with the dead wife, but she knew instinctively that she had lost. She found out that "the absent are always right. . . . It has always sufficed that an adored being lives at our side in order that he become less dear. It is those present who are wrong."[12] The mother was completely crushed by Fernand's desertion, and suffered a stroke of apoplexy. After her death, however, he missed her and realized what she meant in his life, so she regained in a measure her empire over him. The novel is grave and somber without a ray of light, but the rapid exposition is excellent, and the style is impersonal and classic. Mauriac shows his originality by opening the story with the death of Mathilde, thus avoiding the banality that would have resulted from scenes of petty bickering between wife and mother-in-law. It is worthy of remark that this is one of the few novels of Mauriac which does not center around sins of the flesh.

Le Désert de l'amour ("The Desert of Love") is the strange tale of two men enamored of the same woman. It is the last love of the old father and the first love of his son, and neither one knows the other's secret. There is nothing particularly attractive about Maria Cross, the twenty-seven-year-old widow, lazy and bourgeoise, without money or good reputation, who returns the love of neither of her suitors. Mauriac, as usual, does not relate events in chronological order, but begins near the end and then goes back to show what led up to this dénouement. Raymond Courrèges meets in a bar this Maria, who, years before, had jilted him. As a youth of eighteen with angelic face, but cynical and caddish, tingling with the desires of adolescence, he had known her and had brutally attempted to win her, but had been brusquely repulsed. In the meantime, his father, Dr. Courrèges, had made professional visits to Maria's home and had also fallen in love with her. But though she respected and reverenced him as a friend, she had no other sentiment for this serious, gray-haired man of fifty. She finally marries her paramour and protector, Victor Larousselle, and when she meets father and son seventeen years later, she scarcely remembers them and gets rid of them as quickly as possible, though they are both eager to renew acquaintance. They all three live in a desert of unrequited love, which is skillfully reflected in the aridity of the landscape. One of the finest things in the book is the picture of the Courrèges family, where to outward appearances all are united in perfect harmony, but where there is really no understanding nor sympathy. It illustrates Mauriac's *idée maîtresse,* that "members of the same family are more strange to each other than men of different continents."[13]

One of the most remarkable creations of Mauriac is Thérèse Desqueyroux in the novel bearing her name. She is a criminal, fundamentally immoral, and yet we cannot refrain from feeling compassion for her. She is guilty of an unsuccessful attempt to poison her husband, and the whole book is an analysis of her crime, showing its causes and results, physical and spiritual. Her husband and his family are stupid and vulgar, and the psychological study of Thérèse's reaction to her surroundings, of her final decision to rid herself of this thick-skulled, egotistical Bernard, a *malade imaginaire* whom she married because he was the brother of her school friend Anne, and because he possessed valuable pine forests, is the theme of the novel. The author begins the story after the trial at which Thérèse was acquitted, and then relates the preceding facts in the case. This is one of the cruelest of Mauriac's books, owing partly to the fact that murder by poison is in itself a cold, heartless act. If a woman kills her husband in an impulse of anger, jealousy, or hatred, the deed can be palliated in some small degree on account of the blindness and heat of passion. But for a wife deliberately to administer daily doses of poison to her husband, who, though he is not particularly lovable, has never really done her any greater harm than to weary and bore her, this is abominable. Why then, do we unwillingly sympathize with this creature? Perhaps because we are penetrated with the significance of the quotation from Baudelaire which Mauriac puts at the beginning of the novel: "Lord, have mercy on the men and women gone mad!"

Thérèse is again the principal character in *La Fin de la nuit*. Mauriac states in the preface to this book that he did not intend it to be a sequel to *Thérèse Desqueyroux* ("Thérèse") but "the portrait of a woman at her decline, whom I had already painted at the time of her criminal youth." We left her alone on the streets of Paris, fifteen years before, and we find her again in a dark little apartment of the same city. She has not changed, she is the same poisoner, though perhaps she is a little more pitiful now that she has lost her youth and health. Her daughter Marie comes to her for aid in winning the man of her choice as a husband, but Thérèse realizes that the only thing she will ever do for her child is "to poison her happiness."[14] Mauriac insists that he wanted to convert Thérèse from her evil ways, and show the *end* of her night, but that he could not find a priest to hear her confession. Later at Rome he discovered this priest that he had been seeking, and he has promised that some day, in a few pages, he may relate "how Thérèse entered into the light of death."[15]

The atmosphere in *Destins* ("Destinies") is both Parisian and provincial. It tells the tale of the typical modern youth, Bob Lagave, the son of peasants, corrupted by the fast life of the capital. His father always felt that this delicate, pretty boy would never amount to anything, and he was totally incapable of directing him into paths that might have led him to intellectual and moral safety. Bob loves Paule de la Sesque, a modern girl somewhat better and more wholesome than most of the crowd of dissolute idlers that make up his circle of friends. He has an attack of pleurisy and his father, glad to get him away from this Parisian set, sends him to the country to stay with his grandmother, Maria Lagave. In the same vicinity lives Elizabeth Gornac, a practical countrywoman past forty and a widow, with her father-in-law and her son Pierre. She understands Bob, sympathizes with him, and, contrary to her better judgment and her conscience, allows him to invite Paule to her home for a visit. Then suddenly there comes to Elizabeth the realization, first, of her loneliness, then of her inordinate love for this boy. She denies it, struggles against it, but cannot overcome it. Pierre finds out that Paule is engaged to Bob, and officiously undertakes to enlighten her as to the character of her lover. Paule half believes him and leaves the next morning. A few days later Bob is killed in an automobile accident, and Elizabeth's grief is immoderate, beyond control. Life has suddenly become empty for her, and she listlessly returns to her duties "one of those dead bodies who are carried along by the current of life."[16] The characters are drawn with sure psychology and their destinies are mingled and intertwined with consummate skill. But the theme is unpleasant, and this time the flesh seems definitely to triumph. The novel aroused much adverse criticism. Even André Gide, after reading it, wrote that Mauriac was striving to pass for a Christian without being obliged to burn his books.[17]

Ce qui était perdu ("Suspicion") is the first of Mauriac's novels in which he has two centers of interest, closely woven together though they be. One gravitates around Marcel Revaux, an unsuccessful writer who marries Tota Forcas, a young girl whom he picked up in the province. Tota had been encouraged by her brother Alain to accept Marcel's offer, not because she loved him, but because he would take her away from the miserable life she was leading at La Hume, where her sick father, half-demented, ruled the household. Marcel was a friend of Hervé de Blénauge, a base, unprincipled individual, who married Irene principally because she had the money he needed for his dissipated life. Irene is an invalid and a freethinker imbued with Nietzschian philosophy, but withal courageous and high-minded. She tries to believe that Hervé really cares for her, but when she is finally persuaded that he does not, she takes an overdose of sedative and dies. The two groups are brought together, first, by the affectionate and respectful admiration that Marcel has for Irene who on various occasions plays the role of spiritual director to him, and secondly, by the horrible suspicion that Hervé sows in the mind of Marcel regarding Tota's extravagant affection for her brother Alain. The suspicion seems to be wholly unfounded, but it grows on Marcel and ruins any possibility of happiness with his wife. In the end the old father dies, Alain goes off to be a priest, and Tota returns to La Hume, whether for a time or permanently we do not know. Hervé's mother, a devout Catholic though somewhat annoying and ridiculous in her piety, influences her son to repentance and a possible change of heart. Although the novel contains some excellent scenes (for instance, Chapter XII, in which Irene pleads with Hervé not to leave her over the weekend, and Chapter XX, in which mother and son meet after Irene's funeral), still there is something unsatisfactory about it. Marcel's suspicions are too monstrous, Irene's suicide too disappointing, and Hervé's conversion too unexpected. Mauriac does better when he treats a single, unified theme, and, though his effort to introduce the supernatural element is laudable, it is done with awkwardness and constraint.

The novel that many consider Mauriac's masterpiece is *Le Noeud de vipères* ("The Vipers' Tangle"). It illustrates the epigraph from St. Theresa placed at the beginning: "O God, consider that we do not understand ourselves, and that we do not know what we wish, and that we deviate infinitely from what we desire." The main character is Louis (the family name is not mentioned), an enemy to his whole family on account of the passions of hatred and avarice that are devouring his heart. The story is cast in the form of a diary or a long letter, written by Louis to his wife Isa. She dies without ever reading it, and it falls to his uncomprehending son and daughter. Only a granddaughter Janine appreciates the change that came over this terrible man in his last days, when he seems to have caught a glimpse of the eternal. She realizes that the family are in a measure responsible for his sins, for they are all mediocre, superficial Catholics, who forget that the greatest of all virtues is charity. Instead of guiding him on to the light of faith, they have rather darkened his vision. In spite of the fact that Louis is a real monster, we cannot help feeling sorry for the lonely old man who passed his life in a nest of vipers. Benjamin Crémieux calls attention to the fact that in *Genitrix* Mauriac showed us the mother loving her son immoderately, and in *Le Noeud de vipères,* the father (genitor) passionately hating his children.[18]

In *Le Mystère Frontenac,* on the other hand, Mauriac emphasizes the mysterious bond that unites the family. Michel Frontenac possessed at Bordeaux a great commercial house. He dies and Blanche, his widow, devotes herself to the five children. Her brother-in-law, Xavier, does not want to leave Angoûlème (or his mistress), so, though he is generous with his advice and assistance, he leaves the real management of the fortune of his brother's family to Dussol, Michel's partner. Blanche reproaches him for this lack of active interest, but fails to persuade him to come to Bordeaux. We follow the fates of the children, of whom Yves, the youngest, and Jean-Louis, the eldest, are the most important. Yves is a poet, dreamy, ardent, and eccentric, evidently the author's favorite. The mother insists that before her death

"Jean-Louis should become the head of the business, the master of their fortune, the protector of his younger brothers and sisters."[19] So, though he wants to be a professor of philosophy, he sacrifices his ambition to follow in his father's footsteps and preserve the old homestead. Thus, "the Frontenac mystery would escape destruction, for it was a ray of eternal love refracted across a race."[20] The plot is slight and easy to follow. Mauriac seems to have turned aside for a while from his dramas of passion to sing a lyric hymn to the family.

The latest novel of Mauriac, *Les Anges noirs*, savors of the *roman policier*, and is somewhat different from his other works. Gabriel Gradère is as thoroughly wicked and perverse as any of Mauriac's heroes, corrupting those with whom he comes in contact and finally murdering his mistress. Still he retains some redeeming qualities — pity for the calumniated priest (Alain Forcas, Tota's brother in *Ce qui était perdu*) and love for his son Andrès. These two virtues finally save him, for he ends his days in the home of the priest, is converted by him, and promises him the soul of his son: " 'In exchange for what you have brought me, what can I give you on this earth? But I have the promise of my son. . . . You understand me? Have no more fears for him. Isn't that right, Andrès? Tell him yourself.' The boy, without turning, nodded assent. A profound silence reigned in the room."[21] It is a book of paradoxes, and Jean Baudry hardly exaggerates when he calls it "a mixture of mysticism and sensuality . . . sentimentality and sense, Freudianism and simplicity, purity and perversion, anguish and rapture, grace and fatality."[22]

Much has been written about Mauriac's Catholicity, which has been a source of worry to himself as well as to his critics. All his works are full of Catholic allusions, and he has definitely discussed his position in *Petits essais de psychologie religieuse* (1920), *La Vie et la mort d'un poète*

author, not always as the crown of his work, but as the key; thus he thinks of Maynard as a poet of color, although he likes other of his poems just as well as *A Song of Colors*. This expresses the attitude of many readers toward *Lazare*. It shows us Mercier primarily as a religious poet, but traces of *Poème de la maison* and *Voix de la terre* are very evident. The critics are particularly generous in their tributes to *Lazare*. Gohin says that it shows "with what surety and art Louis Mercier knows how to treat such a grandiose subject."[19] Jean Tenant asks permission to place it at the top of the list of Mercier's works.[20] Henri Bremond tells us that our English Browning recoiled before this subject, as one to which it was impossible to do justice, but he commends Mercier's treatment of it in the words: "No one, indeed, since the author of the *Dream of Gerontius,* has translated in a manner more human and poignant the emotions of a heart about to cease beating."[21] Henry Bordeaux considers it a "strange, moving poem, worthy to be a classic."[22] The only objection to it worthy of note is that it introduces the Person of Christ, and puts into His mouth words that are not sanctioned by Scripture. Still, since we do not forbid our painters and our sculptors to represent Christ according to their own interpretation, why should we deny the same privilege to our poets?

Lazare is a poetic commentary on the gospel narrative of the resurrection of Lazarus from the dead. This man was permitted a glimpse beyond the veil, down the arches of the eternal years, into the hidden mysteries of the future life. Back to earth, he burns to tell his secret. But when he opens his lips to speak, his mind is a blank. To the eager questions of his loving sisters he can only reply, "I cannot remember!" When the people crowd around him and beg him to tell them the wonders he has experienced, he gives them the same answer. A mother hastens up to him to ask news of her child taken from her by cruel death:[23]

dis-moi,

Ce que font les enfants que l'on a mis en terre!
Où vont-ils? Ont-ils faim? Ont-ils peur? Ont-ils froid?
Et que deviennent-ils sans leur mère dans l'ombre?
Le mien était si frêle! Il pleurait pour un rien.
Il avait peur, le soir, quand la chambre était sombre,
Alors, je réchauffais ses doigts entre les miens!
Oh! lorsqu'il vit la mort s'approcher pour le prendre
Comme il serrait mon cou avec ses petits bras,
Blottissant contre moi son corps farouche et tendre!
. . . .
Il ne supportait pas qu'aucune main le touche
Hors la mienne. Il m'aimait comme un lis le soleil.
. . . .
O Lazare, pitié! Dis-moi ce qu'il faut croire . . .
Les enfants qu'on nous prend nous seront-ils rendus?
Comment les retrouver en cette foule noire
Où, parmi tant de morts, ils errent confondus?*

There is a terrible silence, then Lazarus tries in vain to answer her. He moves his lips but utters no sound, and the secret of the grave remains unbroken. In this description Mercier shows himself a master of pathos. He does not jar upon the feelings, but with a few touching and powerful expressions he arouses in the reader intense emotions. The grief-stricken mother and the helpless babe look out from the page, and demand our pity and sympathy. Not even by André Chénier, in his famous ode, *La Jeune captive,* is the pathos of early death more fittingly treated.

---

* Tell me, what do the children do that they have put in the earth? Where do they go? Are they hungry? Are they afraid? Are they cold? And what becomes of them in the darkness without their mothers? Mine was so frail! He used to weep for a trifle. He was afraid, in the evening, when the room was dark, and then I warmed his fingers between mine! Oh! when he saw death coming to seize him, how he clung to my neck with his little arms, pressing against me his frightened and tender body! . . . He could not bear to have any hand touch him but mine. He loved me as a lily loves the sun. . . . O Lazarus, have pity on me! Tell me what I must believe. Will the children who are taken from us be returned to us? How shall we be able to find them in that dark crowd, where, among so many dead, they wander about?

There are many other passages in the poem which deserve special attention — the picturesque and lifelike scene of the feast at the house of Caiphas; the temptation of Lazarus, which comes to him in a terrible dream, a *vision dantesque,* as it has been called; the fury of the crowd ready to stone this *faux ressuscité* until abashed by the presence of Christ. All attest the richness of imagination and the force of expression which the writer possesses in an extraordinary degree.

Lazare proves that Mercier's genius is suited to long compositions as well as to "short swallow-flights of song," and *Ponce Pilate* is an evidence of the same thing. This graceful poem is a far-off twentieth-century echo of the mystery plays of the fifteenth. It is a little religious drama, written to be read rather than acted. There are striking scenes, interesting dialogues, and well-drawn characters. The courageous faith of the Christian Procula stands in bold relief to the pitiful cowardice of her pagan husband. In the last scene, when the disreputable Barabbas and his wretched companions ask to speak to Pilate, Procula entreats him not to admit the robber. She declares that to receive this man will dishonor the Roman toga, the Roman name, and, most of all, himself. But he, although convinced that she is right, is too weak to act according to his convictions, and as he goes out to meet Barabbas she cannot refrain from whispering "with more pity than scorn, 'Coward!'"

Mercier writes not only of man here on earth, but his pen follows the soul beyond the grave. We have seen that he presents Lazarus to us with his lips sealed, but in other poems he tells us some of the secrets of the future life, as his own imagination guided by faith has revealed them to him. *Purgatoire* is a piece of great beauty, alive with religious feeling. The unreal becomes so real that we find ourselves ready to converse with those souls which the poet sees in his dream. This dream takes place on Toussaint, the very eve of the day when the Church offers all her prayers for these poor souls. The poet finds his way down a stairs of which no man could count the steps, and there he sees souls bent under the heavy burden of sorrow, with no body but a "pale light," resembling somewhat the figure they had while on earth. They are mounting toward the *haute blancheur* afar off but ever visible, and their great joy comes from the fact that they are certain of attaining their goal. He speaks to one of these souls and it answers him, and in this short dialogue the whole doctrine of purgatory is explained. Then with a touch of tenderness the poet recognizes his mother, but she turns away from him, and he adds:[24]

> Il me semble
> *Que j'avais vu trembler un instant son image,*
> *Et je ne la vis plus. Puis, un long temps coula.**

In verses in which there is not the slightest deviation from the Church's teaching about purgatory, she tells him not to weep but to pray, for that is what will profit him.

Purgatoire is the only one of Mercier's poems the whole of which is about purgatory, but in several others he has references to this land of mourning. Part of the congregation assisting at the *Première Messe* are those who "do not cast a shadow behind them." In *Prière devant les tombes des nôtres,* he speaks of and to the dead. His *Ex Votos* are short and simple, but full of meaning as they exhibit not only poetic thought but also deep religious faith. In the first of these, *À la Memoire d'Arsène Vermenouze,*[25] he takes up a line that his friend himself had written, and applies it to him, now forever silent:

> "*L'âme mystérieuse et flottante des prés.*"
> *Quand tu rythmas ce large vers, ô Vermenouze,*

---

* It seems to me that I saw her tremble an instant, and after that I lost sight of her. Then a long time passed by.

La mort avait déjà mis son ombre jalouse
*Sur les derniers des jours qui t'étaient mesurés.**

This calls to the minds of us Americans Father Tabb's
lines, *At Keats' Grave,* which he begins by a quotation from
the dead poet:

> *"I feel the flowers growing over me."*
> *Prophetic thought! Behold no cypress gloom*
> *Portrays in dim memorial the doom*
> *That quenched the ray of starlike destiny!*

From purgatory we look up to paradise, which Mercier,
with his usual simplicity and vividness, presents to us in a
single verse, "And in heaven it is always Sunday." Most of
his poems relating to heaven are prayers to God or to His
saints, filled with touching humility and pathos. *Le Cantique d'action de grâces* is a rapturous burst of adoration in
honor of the Blessed Trinity, sung by the Church after its
consecration. In the *Procession des jours* which follows it,
each day sings the praise of some saint, as the procession
wends its way through the fields, vineyards, and meadows.

Among the saints, his favorite — or at least the most
favored — is St. Jeanne d'Arc. Five poems comprising
Vitraux pour Sainte Jeanne, portray her life, and twelve
others are contained in *Litanies de Sainte Jeanne d'Arc,*
which Giraud calls "the most poetic litanies that have ever
been put in verse."[26] Why does Mercier show this preference
for the Maid of Orleans? Because his three loves are God,
France, and country life, and St. Jeanne d'Arc was a saint
of God, a heroine of France, and a peasant girl. Giraud gives
us another reason why these litanies bring to an end the
Poèmes de la tranchée written of the World War: "It is

---

* "The soul mysterious and floating over the meadows." When you rhymed
that verse full of meaning, O Vermenouze, death had already cast its jealous
shadow over the last of the days which had been measured out to you.

because the author through the history and the soul of Jeanne allows us to see with infinite art, the history and the soul of our heroic and modest soldiers."[27]

Practically all of Mercier's war poems are prayers. Here he differs from other writers, who, from the author of the *Chanson de Roland* down to our own day, have expressed their enthusiastic admiration both in prose and in verse for brilliant deeds, glorious victories, and mighty heroes. We look in vain for such sentiments in Mercier. Perhaps he felt them, but with his wonted modesty, he writes not of the great and illustrious, but of the humble and unknown. A glance through the titles of the volume *Poèmes de la tranchée* will make this evident: *Prière pour les sentinelles, Prière pour ceux qui portent les rondins, Prière pour les soldats paysans,* etc. Not a word about the battle of the Marne, no mention of Foch! And yet, far from being disappointed, we are pleased and agree with Jean Tenant: "We rejoice to see him, by a miracle of good taste, avoid the dangers with which the enterprise was sown."[28] In the awful crisis he showed exactly what he was, the Catholic soldier-poet of France. The following, from *Prière à Notre-Dame de prompt-secours,*[29] is a beautiful and characteristic verse:

> *Je pense à vous, ce soir, dans la tranchée, à vous*
> *Madone aux pieds de qui, tel un beau livre, s'ouvre*
> *L'horizon d'un pays majestueux et doux.*
> *Je pense à vous, ce soir, Madone de Coutouvre.**

Les Cinq mystères joyeux, a tiny volume of eight poems, is, as the name indicates, a tribute to the Blessed Virgin Mary. It contains brief poetic meditations on the first five mysteries of the rosary, each being based on some text from Scripture. The deep spirituality and fine lyrical qualities of

---

* I am thinking of you this evening, in the trenches, of you, Madonna, at whose feet the horizon of a majestic and lovely country opens, as a beautiful book. I am thinking of you, this evening, O Madonna of Coutouvre.

these poems appear again in *Virginis corona,* published in 1929, which proves that age has not lessened Mercier's powers.

Such then are the religious poems of Louis Mercier. It is true that his life is limited, almost the whole of it having been spent at Forez. But perhaps the dazzling glare of the nooaday sun would blind that inward eye that sees so keenly in the shadow of retreat. His art is not an end but a means. Poetry is for him, not a substitute for religion, but an inspiration that makes religion more necessary. Therefore, in spite of the variety of subject matter, there is an essential unity in his poems, for between the lines of every one of them we read his faith. His muse is, indeed, grave and contemplative, but if what Jules Bois tells us is true, "Let us say without hesitation that France is a land of faith. We are a serious people, though on the surface gay and ironic,"[30] then France will never tire of such poems as *Pierres sacrées* and *Lazare.* The strain of sadness in Mercier's poetry is doubtless what won for him the appellation of "L'Alfred de Vigny du nouveau siècle."[31] But while Vigny's sadness and pessimism reveal a bitterness and even a revolt against nature, Mercier's is permeated with Christian hope. Contrast the famous *Mort du loup* of the former, with the *Cri de la femme* of the latter. Both present death in all its cruelty, but while Vigny preaches a pagan stoicism, Mercier would have us accept death as the just punishment of original sin.

Mercier's religious poems are many, and in this brief sketch we have not even touched on some of them. Gabriel Aubray wrote in 1903: "Louis Mercier is a great, a very great poet, the greatest that has appeared during the last fifty years."[32] He is now an old man of sixty-eight, but still we hope that his strains of melody have not ceased, but that his harmonious songs of heaven and earth will continue to attune this discordant world to God.

PRINCIPAL WORKS OF LOUIS MERCIER

1897 *L'Enchantée*
1903 *Voix de la terre et du temps*
1906 *Le Poème de la maison*
1907 *Les Contes de Jean-Pierre*
1910 *Lazare le ressuscité suivi de Ponce Pilate*
1911 *Hélène Sorbiers*
1916 *Poèmes de la tranchée*
1920 *Les Pierres sacrées*
1923 *Les Petites géorgiques*
1924 *Les Demoiselles Valéry*
1929 *Des Contes et des images*
1929 *Virginis corona*
1932 *Témoignages*

REFERENCES

Aguettant, Louis, "Un fils de Virgile, Louis Mercier," *Correspondant,* CCXCLX (1925), pp. 191-209.

Aubray, Gabriel, "L'Alfred de Vigny du nouveau siècle, M. Louis Mercier," *Mois littéraire et pittoresque,* June, 1903, pp. 741-751.

Beaunier, André, "Un Poète en province, M. Louis Mercier," *Revue des deux mondes,* XVII (1923), pp. 698-710.

Bernard, Paul, "Louis Mercier et la poésie des champs," *Études religieuses,* CXXXVII (1913), pp. 323-354.

Bordeaux, Henry, "*Les Pierres sacrées* de Louis Mercier," *Monde illustré,* CXXVII (1920), p. 66.

Bremond, Henri, "Poètes d'aujourd'hui," *Correspondant,* CCXXXIII (1908), pp. 895-925.

Giraud, Joseph, "Les Poèmes de la tranchée de L. Mercier," *Études religieuses,* CLI (1917), pp. 346-360.

Gohin, Ferdinand, *Le Poète Louis Mercier,* Paris, 1922.

Tenant, Jean, "L'Oeuvre de Louis Mercier," *Minerve française,* V (1920), pp. 51-61.

Théolier, Louis, "Les Pierres sacrées de Louis Mercier," *Études religieuses,* CLXX (1922), pp. 650-670.

CHAPTER XI

Charles Péguy

(1873-1914)

PÉGUY, AS A MAN AND AS A WRITER, IS SOME-
what of an enigma. He was a genius, a solitary, and more or
less of an outlaw all his life. Théodore Quoniam, his
nephew, complains that he has not been understood,[1] and
Daniel-Rops voices the general opinion when he says that
"Between him and those who write of him or study him,
there is a zone of essential incomprehension."[2] The cause of
this lack of understanding is perhaps the fact that many read
Péguy's works without knowing anything of his life or
character. He lived and worked and thought in a region
far above the plane of most men, especially in this materialistic age, and he consistently refused to lower his
standards. He reminds us of the prophet, who from up on
his wall replied to those beneath: "I am doing a great work,
and I cannot come down." It is impossible to interpret
Péguy's works apart from himself for, to quote Mounier,
"He thought his life and lived his thought."[3]

Péguy's grandparents came from a little village, Genne-
tines, in Bourbonnais in the heart of France, and settled in
Orléans, where the family remained and where the grandson Charles was born on January 7, 1873. His father died
before his birth and he grew up under the care of two
women, his grandmother, who did not even know how to
read but who was a good storyteller, and his mother, who
recaned chairs at the cathedral. At the age of seven he entered the primary school recently laicized (an annex to the
École Normale) and attended catechism class at the parish

church. He was a serious child, and performed conscientiously all the duties imposed on him. In 1884 M. Naudy obtained for Charles a *bourse municipale* which enabled him to continue his studies at the lycée of Orléans. At sixteen he went to Paris, first to the Lycée Lakanal and then to Louis-le-Grand. He was always an excellent student and speaks gratefully of his "kind and patient teachers."

All his life Péguy had a way of doing the unexpected. In 1891 he suddenly left school for a year, and engaged in military service in the 131st regiment of infantry. After this surprising interruption he resumed his studies at Sainte-Barbe, and began a lifelong friendship with Jérôme Tharaud, Louis Baillet, Joseph Lotte, François Porché, Charles de Peslouan, and Marcel Baudouin. He became a Socialist, and in his zeal for humanism lost his faith in Christianity. Many anecdotes are told about Péguy during these days at Sainte-Barbe. Perhaps the two best known are the one which relates how he, at the head of a group of companions, served soup to the poor on winter nights, and the other which states that, an unbeliever, he was elected, through the influence of his friend Lotte, to the presidency of the Society of St. Vincent de Paul, to meetings of which he came late — by agreement — so that he would not have to lead the prayers.

In August, 1894, Péguy was received at the École Normale. Here he was definitely influenced by two men, Lucien Herr, the eccentric and scholarly librarian, and Henri Bergson, the professor of philosophy, for whom he ever retained a faithful affection. After two years at this institution came another *coup de tête*. He returned to Orléans and his mother, and wrote his *Jeanne d'Arc*. Probably the monotonous life of a teacher in a provincial lyceum did not appeal to him, so he chose the uncertain joys of a literary career.

When the Dreyfus Affair was agitating all France, Péguy

threw himself into it heart and soul, considering it an opportunity to express his love of justice and truth, in conflict with the rights of the State. Marcel Baudouin, his college friend, died in 1896, and soon after Péguy married his sister. He went to Msgr. Battifol, his old chaplain at Sainte-Barbe, to tell him of his marriage, a civil one, but refused to listen to any suggestion about having it validated. With his wife's dowry he set up a socialist bookstore, named for a friend, Librairie Bellais. In 1900 he founded the *Cahiers de la Quinzaine* and, after several moves, established his shop at 8, Rue de la Sorbonne. The *Cahiers* came out every two weeks, and henceforth Péguy's life was bound up with their publication. The subscribers paid when and as much as they pleased, according to their means and generosity, so the editor often suffered poverty and even hunger.

When the World War broke out, Péguy departed as for a Crusade. He was commander of the 276th company of infantry. The story of the last month of his life (August 4–September 5, 1914) is told by one of his soldiers, Victor Boudon.[4] Recklessly brave and indifferent to fatigue, hunger, and other hardships, he was an example to his men, especially during the demoralizing retreat from the Somme. On September 5, 1914, he was one of the thousands killed by a bullet in the awful battle of the Marne.

The first great event in Péguy's life was the Dreyfus Affair. He gallantly espoused the cause of the Jewish captain, not for the sake of the man but because of the principle involved. He had already found in Socialism a form of altruism, and he was imbued with the idea of aiding the masses physically and morally. His ambition was to cure the *mal humain* which he found in the world. All his life the problem of evil haunted him, and he was unwearying in seeking its solution. His Socialism was idealistic, for he imagined that a society could be created where the first place would be ceded to the workers, where there would be no tyrannical laws, but where all would willingly obey the wise decrees of justice. He visioned a "harmonious city," which would take care of the corporal and spiritual wants of its citizens. It was to be established by persuasion, not by force, and absolute liberty of thought would be the privilege of all. As in the Dreyfus Affair, "a single injustice, a single act of cruelty exercised by the city against a man, plunges, so to speak, the whole country into the state of mortal sin."[5] As soon as he realized that Jaurès, the great Socialist leader, wanted to draw political profit from the Affair, he broke with him.

Péguy's concept of charity (love of the people) was noble and unselfish but entirely human, little more than a Utopian dream. Later, however, it caught the spark of the Divine and led him back to Catholicity. He was never *converted* in the usual sense of the word, but rather, he returned to himself. He had been baptized and brought up a Catholic, and as a child had learned his catechism well. He lost his faith during his years at the lyceums, under the influence of atheistic professors and their false philosophy. He always believed in the spiritual, however, and writes in *Le Porche du deuxième mystère:* "Soul and body are two hands clasped."[6]

By Bergson, who gives first place to intuition, Péguy was led to a mystic aestheticism. He never relinquished his respect for Christianity, in spite of the anticlerical jests scattered through his works, and he regained his faith fourteen years after he had lost it. He who had always loved the truth and had spoken it,[7] even brutally at times, was bound to find it in the end, if he continued faithful in his search. Moreover, he discovered in Catholicism the solution to the problem of evil and suffering. Of course, the real cause of his conversion was the grace of God, granted, we may venture to suggest, in answer to the prayers of Dom

Baillet, his college friend, who had become a Benedictine monk, and who never ceased interceding for Péguy. We have the story from another friend, Joseph Lotte. In 1908 he visited Péguy, who was ill. The patient talked about his poverty, his lassitude, and his longing for repose. Then suddenly, raising himself on his elbow, his eyes filled with tears, he exclaimed: "I have not told you all . . . I have regained the faith. I am a Catholic."[8]

Although there is no question about the honesty of Péguy's conversion, he did not become a *practicing* Catholic. As far as we know, he never attended Mass on Sunday nor received the sacraments. On the eve of the great battle which brought his death, he gathered flowers and put them on the Blessed Virgin's altar in an old convent, but he did not go to confession nor receive Holy Communion with his fellow officers and soldiers. Only God can see the heart, and man must observe the *Nolite judicare,* but several attempts have been made to explain this seeming inconsistency. Msgr. Battifol says that in order that their civil marriage be validated, Péguy's wife would have to consent to have the children baptized and brought up as Catholics.[9] This Péguy would not ask her to do, so he remained a sincere but *incomplete* Catholic the rest of his life. Daniel-Rops suggests another rather ingenious explanation. He says that Péguy, with mistaken generosity, did not want to be saved alone. If his wife and family, and, in fact, all mankind could not enjoy with him the benefits of salvation, he refused to accept them for himself.[10] Nevertheless he prayed earnestly and was devoted to the Blessed Virgin. When one of his little boys, Pierre, was ill with diphtheria, he made a pilgrimage to Chartres, and with humble confidence recommended his three children to our Lady. He wrote to Lotte: "I cannot look after everything. My life is not an ordinary one. No one is a prophet in his own country. My little ones are not baptized.

The Blessed Virgin must take care of them."[11] She did take care of them. The boy was cured, and later on, after their father's death, all three sons became Catholics.

Most of Péguy's works were first published in the *Cahiers de la Quinzaine*. Unlike most writers, he began with prose and wrote all his poetry during the last few years of his life. When he started this journal, his friends prophesied that it would not last six months, but it appeared regularly every two weeks until 1914. The bulk varied according to the importance of the matter published. In its pages Péguy poured out without restraint his ideas about men, the country, the government, his joys and sorrows, dreams and fears. He wrote in a rambling, loquacious style, repeating himself and digressing from the main topic constantly.

Among his best prose works we may cite *Notre Patrie, Notre Jeunesse, Victor Hugo,* and *L'Argent. Notre Patrie* recounts a week in the life of a bourgeois in Paris. The king of Spain is visiting the city, and the air is full of joy and happiness. Suddenly an anarchist shoots at the royal carriages, but fortunately no harm is done and the affair is passed over. This seems a presage of the bad news to follow, however, which comes in the menace of a German invasion. There is a long digression on Paris and its people, and another on Victor Hugo, the glory of Paris. Péguy takes this opportunity to express his patriotism, especially in his meditation on the French nation, according to him the *peuple élu*. He was nearly forty when he wrote *Notre Jeunesse,* which Tharaud calls his *chef d'oeuvre*.[12] In this, as in most of his works, he converses with himself, and the subject of the conversation is, in this case, the bygone glories of the Republic.

In *Victor-Marie, comte Hugo* the author discusses the rhymes of Hugo, then the rhymes of Corneille and Racine, and ends with a comparison of Classicism and Romanticism. His ideas are more those of a moralist than of a literary critic.

The long preface and conclusion devoted to his friend Daniel Halévy, with whom he had just had a rupture, are excellent. *L'Argent* contains reminiscences of his childhood when he was taught by both lay and clerical teachers. The title seems to come from his contention that most authors are willing to write whatever the public asks, and thus to barter their principles for money.

We find terrible inequalities in Péguy's prose, excellent passages in the midst of much that is mediocre. When he treats a concrete subject (himself, his friends, his enemies, his projects, ambitions, difficulties, etc.), he hammers home his meaning with a sincerity and irresistible force which compel attention, even though his opinions may be debatable. When he gets into the abstract, he is apt to become verbose and obscure, to stammer and prattle, and to repeat incessantly. Suarès says that his books are always beginning and never end.[13]

Péguy's great work is in his drama, *Jeanne d'Arc,* which is a reminiscence of the medieval mystery plays. He came from Orléans, and the inspiration of his life was the Maid who had saved the city in 1429. He grew up in the shadow of the old cathedral, and from babyhood listened to stories of *la Pucelle.* She was everything to him, his model, his heroine, his saint. Daniel-Rops says that Jeanne d'Arc is for Péguy the symbol of the union of the spiritual and temporal. In the temporal, she represents what he loved most: the people, the country, military life. In the spiritual, she incarnates his pet virtues: heroism, faith, hope, love of men, and a desire to save all.[14] For several years after the completion of his enormous manuscript (800 pages), he kept it locked up in his trunk, having found no publisher. There are three acts, relating the life of Jeanne at Domrémy, during her battles, and at Rouen. We are admitted into the secrets of her heart, her sufferings, distresses, temptations,

and sanctity. The dedication, which Sénéchal says contains
in germ the whole work of Péguy,[15] is:

> À toutes celles et à tous ceux qui auront vécu
> À toutes celles et à tous ceux qui seront morts
> Pour tâcher de porter remède au mal universel.*

The drama is too long and cumbersome to be played,
though the characters act and speak very naturally. There
is a charm of youth about it which is wanting in the *Mystère de la charité de Jeanne d'Arc,* written in poetry ten
years later. This latter is really a meditation on the Passion
of Christ and on the problem of evil. André Gide tells how
he fled from Paris for a few days' rest, and took with him
among other books this *Mystère* of Péguy. "I opened it," he
says, "and almost immediately I had no more attention for
anything else. What an astonishing book! What a beautiful
book! Nothing, since *L'Arbre* of Claudel, had taken such a
hold of me."[16]

The keynote is Jeanne's question to Madame Gervaise:
Qui donc faut-il sauver? Comment faut-il sauver?, a question
which Péguy spent his life trying to answer. The book is
really made up of the prayer of Jeanne d'Arc, two dialogues
of Jeanne with Hauviette, her little peasant friend, and a
very long dialogue between Jeanne and Madame Gervaise,
a nun.

In *Le Porche de la deuxième vertu,* Madame Gervaise,
without a pause through two hundred pages of verse, unfolds the mystery of Hope, *la fille chérie du Père.* Péguy
meditates on the three theological virtues, but he gives the
palm to Hope. *Le Mystère des Saints Innocents* is really a
continuation of *Le Porche.* Madame Gervaise is again supposed to be the speaker, but Péguy seems to forget her completely and God speaks directly in this as in *Le Porche.*

---

* To all those men and women who will have lived, To all those men and
women who will have died, In an effort to remedy the universal evil.

There is a long introduction of a couple of hundred pages before we actually come to the story of the baby martyrs. Among the *Tapisseries* of Péguy — collections of poems written, one group to honor St. Genevieve, one to Notre Dame — we find the exquisite *Présentation de la Beauce à Notre Dame de Chartres:*[17]

Étoile du matin, inaccessible reine,
Voici que nous marchons vers votre illustre cour,
Et voici le plateau de notre pauvre amour,
Et voici l'océan de notre immense peine. . . .

Vous nous voyez marcher sur cette route droite,
Tout poudreux, tout crottés, la pluie entre les dents.
Sur ce large éventail ouvert à tous les vents
La route nationale est notre porte étroite . . .

Quand on nous aura mis dans une étroite fosse,
Quand on aura sur nous dit l'absoute et la messe,
Veuillez vous rappeler, reine de la promesse,
Le long cheminement que nous faisons en Beauce.

Quand nous aurons quitté ce sac et cette corde,
Quand nous aurons tremblé nos derniers tremblements,
Quand nous aurons râlé nos derniers râclements,
Veuillez vous rappeler votre miséricorde.

Nous ne demandons rien, refuge du pécheur,
Que la dernière place en votre Purgatoire
Pour pleurer longuement notre tragique histoire,
*Et contempler de loin votre jeune splendeur.**

---

* Star of the morning, inaccessible queen, Behold us advancing toward your illustrious court, And behold our poor love like a bare plateau, And our grief like an immense ocean.

You see us traveling along this straight road, Covered with dust and mud, facing the rain, On this wide expanse open to the wind, The great highway is our narrow gate.

When they will have laid us in a narrow grave, When they will have said over us Mass and absolution, Deign to recall, queen of the promise, The long pilgrimage we made to Beauce.

When we will have put aside this sack and this cord, When our last trembling will be stilled, And the last death rattle will be silenced, Deign to recall your mercy.

We ask nothing, O refuge of sinners, But the last place in your purgatory, To weep without ceasing our tragic history, And to contemplate from afar your never changing splendor.

This recalls Péguy's tender devotion to Mary, and his yearly pilgrimage to Chartres. In one of the last notes he wrote before his death, he says to Mme Garnier-Maritain: "I shall tell you perhaps some day in what church I heard Mass on the Assumption. If I do not return, you will go to Chartres once a year for me."[18]

Ève is an immense poem recounting the story of our first parents in the earthly Paradise, their temptation, fall, and banishment. It celebrates the mother of the human race, of which the Redeemer was born, true man as well as true God. An invective against the modern world with its false pastors follows. We can hardly agree with Joseph Lotte, who wrote: "*Polyeucte* excepted, which Péguy has taught us to put above all, everything points to the conclusion that this *Ève* is the most considerable work which has been produced among Catholics since the fourteenth century."[19] Most readers find these 8,000 verses very monotonous, though there are fine passages, such as the oft-quoted and prophetic lines:[20]

> *Heureux ceux qui sont morts pour la terre charnelle,*
> *Mais pourvu que ce fût dans une juste guerre.*
> *Heureux ceux qui sont morts pour quatre coins de terre,*
> *Heureux ceux qui sont morts d'une mort solennelle.* *

Péguy's personality is apparent in all he wrote. He himself says that he does not need to sign his name, as it is indelibly written on every line of his poetry and prose.[21] Tharaud remarks: "That which is beautiful and great in Péguy is the character of the man, and the temperament of the writer."[22] Suarès agrees: "Péguy was not the greatest writer of France, nor the best poet of his time. But he was Péguy, great by his force, great by his conscience and character."[23] He always exercised an ascendancy over those

---

* Happy are those who have died for the carnal earth, But provided it was in a just war, Happy are those who have died for their own four corners of earth, Happy are those who have died a solemn death.

around him, from his days at school when he was incontestably the leader in the yard, to his later years, when the new generation (Psichari, Massis, Alain Fournier) looked up to him as to a sage and prophet. He wrote a book every time he took an important step, and his *Cahiers* are a faithful reflection of his exterior and interior life. Perhaps the most striking characteristic is his perfect sincerity as he practiced in an eminent degree the injunction "To thine own self be true." He hated anything that savored of artificiality or hypocrisy, and was absolutely lacking in human respect when there was question of plain speech. He wrote: "I say what I write, and I write what I say."[24] His friends recognized this honesty and respected him for it. Barrès begins an article on Péguy with the words: "I loved Péguy . . ."[25] and he goes on to enumerate a long list of other friends who were equally devoted to him.

Many of Péguy's critics speak of his "immense pride." There was undeniably a semblance of tranquil egoism in him which emanated from his self-respect and nobility of purpose. He had "hitched his wagon to a star" and he was determined to drive straight ahead in quest of his ideal. He was likewise stern in his judgments of others, terrible in his anger, and intolerant of cowardice and injustice. Though not a pessimist, his outlook on life was rather misanthropic, for he realized profoundly that the modern world is terribly out of joint. There was in him a touch of naïve vanity, exhibited in such statements as the following: "A Catholic renaissance is being accomplished by me."[26] Of his *Ève,* he wrote: "It will be an *Iliad.* It will be more powerful than the *Paradiso* of Dante."[27] He proclaimed his intention of covering in the Christian field the same ground that Goethe covered in the pagan. But at heart, Péguy was truly humble in the real Christian sense of the word. He realized his own shortcomings and did not excuse them. He wrote to Lotte: *"Je suis un pécheur, un bon pécheur."*[28] His love for truth saved him from the blindness and rebellion resultant from real pride, and a genuine sense of humor made him as ready to smile at himself on occasion as at others.

Turquet-Milnes remarks that many "share Péguy's ideas, but detest his style,"[29] while others (and among them critics whose judgment is not to be despised) admire it. Some see in it only a confused mass of thoughts, reiterations, long sentences, faulty syntax, strange vocabulary and hyperbole. All these faults can be found in Péguy's works in abundance. To give only one illustration:[30]

C'est une des plus grandes sources de sophismes et d'erreurs, ou, pour demeurer dans notre comparaison, je dirai: c'est un des plus grands magasins de sophismes et d'erreurs, que cette négligence de considérer, cette faute de considérer, ce défaut de considérer, je veux dire que cette négligence qui consiste à ne pas considérer, à négliger de considérer que du tout neuf n'est pas forcément du tout nouveau.*

On the other hand, Daniel-Rops reminds us that an author, who elsewhere has given so many proofs of his qualities of order and method, must have left in his work this irregularity and excess knowingly and willingly.[31] Péguy believed that the flow of thought should be unrestrained, that it should not be spoiled by exterior discipline. He consciously disregarded elegance and polish as a detriment to freedom of expression, and considered poetry, not a matter of technique, but an ability to grasp and convey the reality of things. His repetitions and digressions are often due to a scrupulous anxiety to make his meaning clear. Though he could say in ten sentences what he says in five hundred any attempt to summarize would spoil the effect. After all, we rather like his artless prolixity, which is far removed from the

---

* One of the greatest sources of sophisms and errors, or, to keep our comparison I will say, one of the greatest storehouses of sophisms and errors, is this negligence of considering, this fault of considering, this lack of considering, I mean this negligence which consists in not considering, in neglecting to consider that everything new is not necessarily original.

artificiality of style and thought of so many of his contemporaries.

André Gide writes of Péguy's style: "The style of Péguy is like that of the very ancient litanies. . . . It is like the Arab songs, the monotonous songs of the moor; it is comparable to the desert, desert of alfa, of sand, of stones. . . . The style of Péguy is like the pebbles of the desert which follow each other and resemble each other, where one is like the other, but a very little different. . . ."[32] Péguy's style is indeed somewhat more tumultuous than a desert, the reflection of his troubled and heroic soul. It is essentially an oral style, better when read aloud than silently. Mounier says that Péguy is more of a musician than an architect.[33] Porché aptly compares Jammes' poetry to an altar of the Blessed Virgin covered with roses in May, Claudel's to High Mass in St. Peter's with all its pomp and ceremony, and Péguy's to the plain chant of the liturgy with its solemn monotonous cadence.[34]

Péguy was perhaps one of the four or five writers of his age who really had a message for the world and who fearlessly delivered it. Whether future generations will be interested in that message or not, only time can tell; but that he was desperately earnest in uttering it, no one will ever doubt. It is a message of truth, of Christian charity, and of unswerving devotion to an ideal, colored with poetry, it is true, but emphasized by civil as well as military heroism, and crowned by a glorious death.

PRINCIPAL WORKS OF CHARLES PÉGUY

1897 *Jeanne d'Arc*
1905 *Notre Patrie*
1906 *Le Mystère de la charité de Jeanne d'Arc*
19:0 *Notre Jeunesse*
1911 *Un Nouveau théologien, M. Fernand Laudet*
1911 *Le Porche du mystère de la deuxième vertu*

1911 *Victor-Marie, comte Hugo*
1912 *Le Mystère des Saints Innocents*
1913 *L'Argent*
1913 *La Tapisserie de Sainte Geneviève et de Jeanne d'Arc*
1913 *La Tapisserie de Notre Dame*
1914 *Ève*
1914 *Note sur Bergson et la philosophie bergsonienne*
1917 *Oeuvres complètes* (15 volumes)

REFERENCES

Boudon, Victor, *Avec Charles Péguy de la Lorraine à la Marne, août-septembre, 1914,* Paris, 1916.

Daniel-Rops, Henry, *Péguy,* Paris, 1933.

Halévy, Daniel, *Charles Péguy et les Cahiers de la Quinzaine,* Paris, 1918.

Johannet, René, *Charles Péguy et ses Cahiers,* Paris, 1914.

Maxence, Jean, et N. Gorodetzkaya, *Charles Péguy,* Paris, 1931.

Mounier, Emmanuel, *La Pensée de Charles Péguy,* Paris, 1931.

Pacary, Pierre, *Un Compagnon de Charles Péguy, Joseph Lotte,* Paris, 1919.

Porché, François, *Charles Péguy et ses Cahiers,* Paris, 1914.

Quoniam, Théodore, *De la Sainteté de Péguy,* Paris, 1929.

Suarès, André, *Péguy,* Paris, 1915.

Tharaud, Jérôme et Jean, *Notre cher Péguy,* Paris, 1926.

CHAPTER XII

Ernest Psichari

(1883-1914)

PERHAPS NO CONVERSION TO THE CATHOLIC faith in modern times caused such a stir in literary circles as did that of Ernest Psichari, grandson of the rationalistic philosopher, Ernest Renan. More than one critic has undertaken to show how the law of compensation has worked out in him, who, an unbeliever in early life, later became a Dominican Tertiary, thus repairing in some measure the perversion of his epicurean grandfather, who began a cleric and ended an agnostic. This motive of reparation, read into his life by so many of his biographers,[1] was probably much less apparent to Psichari himself. His sister, who knew him intimately, writes: "The conversion of Ernest, following so closely his grandfather's renunciation of the faith, the hope that he would be a great Catholic writer, that he would destroy by his writings and by his deeds the influence of his grandfather, arose forcefully not only in the minds of earnest and zealous priests, but also among the greater part of the writers and thinkers of the party. This idea of revenge, Ernest himself must scarcely have foreseen, hardly suspected. He never knew, for the peace of his soul, the avenging articles which appeared on the morrow of his death."[2] His literary fame rests on four works, which were written before he was thirty years old, and which form an integral part of his short but heroic life.

Ernest Psichari was born at Paris on September 27, 1883, the son of Jean Psichari and Noémie Renan. According to the wishes of the paternal grandmother, he received baptism of immersion in the Greek Orthodox church. His father, director of the École des Hautes Études, was a noble, intelligent man, who took a personal interest in the education of his children. To him Ernest owed his love of Greek and Latin, while from his mother, his lifelong confidante, he derived his moral loftiness and his tenderness. He was the eldest of four children in a family where, as Henriette writes, "the love of letters and, in general, the appreciation of beauty held first place."[3] Renan tells a charming story about Ernest, who used to visit him at his home in Brittany: "My little five-year-old grandson," he writes, "has such a good time in the country that he has only one dread, that of going to bed. 'Mama,' he asks his mother, 'will the night be long today?' "[4] As he grew older, he liked music and played the violin. He learned by heart several stanzas of some favorite poet each morning while he was dressing, and he wrote verses himself, though not very good ones. He was a rather delicate boy, much more nervous and high strung than his brother Michael, whom friends styled Sancho Panza, while he was Don Quixote.

He studied at the Lycée Henri IV and at Condorcet, passed a brilliant licentiate of philosophy in 1902, and then enlisted for his year of military service. Great was the surprise of his family and friends when, this year being completed, he voluntarily signed a re-engagement in the army in 1904, and in 1906, as sergeant-major, departed with Colonel Lenfant for central Africa. This decision seems to have been principally due to the fact that Ernest had just passed through a grave malady followed by a severe mental crisis. His sister tells us that at twenty he had a love affair with a girl seven years his senior, and that when she married another, his despair was so complete that he attempted suicide.[5] In order to get hold of himself he turned to the army, hoping that its discipline and action would quiet his interior tumults. He was admirably adapted to the life, and almost joyfully abandoned the capital, the Sorbonne, a position of ease and happiness in the midst of his family, to follow for eighteen months untold hardships in a barbarous country under a scorching sun.

His impressions of this first expedition to Africa are recorded in *Terres de soleil et de sommeil,* the most poetic perhaps of his four works, though it shows signs of an amateur whose talent is not fully developed. The influence of Barrès is evident in the tendency to moralize, and that of Loti in the languorous descriptions and in the harmony of words which seem to exhale some of the charm of the primitive beauty he is portraying. *Terres de soleil et de sommeil* is not a novel, neither is it a travelogue. It simply recounts his first glimpses of the country and of the people, the episode about Sama, his stay with the Foulbés, and his return to Paris, emphasizing throughout his personal reaction to these exterior events. There is no religion in the book, in fact, the tone is decidedly pagan, as the following incident exemplifies: Among the porters in his caravan is a young Baya, for whom Psichari takes a liking. He makes him his "boy," and tries to study him, to know him intimately, but does not succeed, for the blacks are a silent people, who jealously guard their secrets. Sama grows thin and weak, fails visibly, and finally dies, and Psichari reflects: "What a strange death! How queer that one can die thus! What has happened? I touch the body of Sama; it is already cold. It is over. . . . And it is such a trifling thing, this black, who died one evening at Zalé. . . . He has departed into nothingness, the strange friend of far-off roads, the ephemeral companion whom I would have liked to know."[6] . . . That is all the death meant to him. It aroused no supernatural sentiments whatsoever, nor did it lift his mind beyond the grave.

Nevertheless the army did much to strengthen him physically and morally. He says in the dedication to *Terres de soleil et de sommeil:* "You [Lenfant] have initiated me into a new life, the rude and primitive life of Africa. You have taught me to love this land of heroes which you have traversed without truce for nearly fifteen years. I owe a debt to you for having given to my life its motive and its end." He was freed from the dangerous dilettantism of his youth, for the silence and austerity of the desert taught him patience, renunciation, and endurance. He had passed the first stage on the road that was leading him directly to Catholicism.

In 1908 Psichari returned to France, to his home, his books, his family and friends. Goichon tells us that three editors offered to publish *Terres de soleil et de sommeil* for him, and that it won a prize from the Academy.[7] He took a trip into Brittany and saw again "the pine forest which ascends from the harmonious shore, the path where, very small, I followed with my eyes the old Renan, heavy with thoughts and with genius."[8] But his mind and heart were still in Africa, "the land of sleep, lying down there under the sun."[9] At Paris he renewed his acquaintance with Péguy and Maritain, both of whom he had known in school, and who had since been converted to Catholicism. Dietz says that the superiority of Psichari over the group of patriots whom he found in the capital lay in the fact that "he lived his theories before proclaiming them, acted instead of discoursing upon action, and went to the desert to risk his life for France while others glorified sacrifice in their private offices."[10] Péguy himself seems to have had the same conviction, for he concludes his *Épître votive,* which he addresses to him at the end of his *Victor-Marie, comte Hugo,* thus: "You who know what it is to blaze a trail and to pitch a tent, to construct a road and to build a camp; you who know what the desert means, and a journey on camel's back; you who alone of us all have heard silence — in the

solitudes of three and four months — and who have thus
kept the purity of your soul."[11]

Psichari entered the military school at Versailles, principally to satisfy his mother, and after a year was sent to
Cherbourg as second lieutenant. In 1909 with Colonel Paté
he departed again on a three-year expedition to organize
and pacify Mauritania, recently conquered by the French.
In 1912 he returned to France with the manuscript of
L'Appel des armes, and also a notebook full of impressions
and personal reflections, which were published after his
death under the name of *Les Voix qui crient dans le désert.*
L'Appel des armes, dedicated to Péguy, is very different
from *Terres de soleil et de sommeil,* though they are both
patriotic and idealistic. This book "begun in the ardor of the
twenty-sixth year and finished under the Saharian tent during the long hours of a magnificent exile,"[12] describes the
birth and development of Psichari's military vocation. It is a
mixture of fiction and autobiography, in which there are
few events but living characters. A young man, Maurice
Vincent, son of an anticlerical pacifist, becomes acquainted
with an officer, Captain Timothy Nangès, who is proud of
his profession and contented in it. Vincent greatly admires
Nangès, engages in his regiment of colonial artillery, and
goes with him to Mauritania. He loves the life, but unfortunately is wounded, and returns to France, regretting
the happiness he has to relinquish. The dominant theme of
the book is, as Psichari himself expresses it, *"militarisme in-
tégrale."* His thesis is explained in the following oft-quoted
passage: "I esteem it necessary . . . that there be in the
world a certain number of men who are called soldiers,
whose ideal is to fight, who have the taste for battle, not for
the victory but for the struggle, as hunters have a taste for
the chase not for the game. Our role (or we lose our reason
for existence and our life has no more meaning) is to main-

tain a military ideal, not, note it well, nationally military, but, if I may so express it, militarily military."[13] Psichari was influenced by *Servitude et grandeur militaires,* but his attitude toward the army is quite the opposite of Vigny's. While the latter deplores the life of the garrison, its necessary hardships and humiliations, and calls it *"un vice des temps,"* Psichari is enthusiastic in his praise of army life, for to him the soldier is the incarnation of heroism. He had begun to grasp, moreover, the mysterious relationship existing between the army and the Church; he saw in both a power and a tradition. His conception of military training led him to realize that true discipline must command both body and soul. Hence *L'Appel des armes* completes a second stage on Psichari's road to conversion, though as yet he is without the faith. There are great beauties in the book. The style still reflects Barrès at times, but is more original and sincere than in *Terres de soleil et de sommeil.* The description of the battle of Tichitt, the return of Maurice to his home and his rejection by his father are especially good. Occasional prayers full of touching confidence are interspersed, while on the other hand, we are rather surprised at the nonchalance with which the author relates the immoralities of Nangès without in any way condemning them.

Les Voix qui crient dans le désert, which first appeared in *Le Correspondant* from November 25, 1919, to January 25, 1920, is a history of the different stages of his conversion. It is a confession rather than a novel, a drama in which his own soul is the chief actor. It relates the exterior and interior events of his life in Africa from February 17, 1910, to November 16, 1912. He sums up the spiritual progress he has made in the last chapter. "A heavy twilight was closing over my years of misery. But then a dawn was also breaking, a dawn of youth and purity, and a celestial brightness lighted up the horizon in front of me. This time I knew where I was going. I was going toward the holy Church, Catholic, apostolic, and Roman. I was going toward the dwelling of peace and of benediction. I was going toward joy, toward health, I was going, alas! toward my cure."[14] He defines his belief in the chief doctrines of the Catholic Church, the Trinity, Incarnation, Redemption, grace, the communion of saints, the last judgment, the Holy Eucharist, etc. The solitude of the Sahara, the simplicity of nomadic life, military training, the reading of Pascal and Bossuet, and above all, the grace of God did their work in his soul, and by degrees he was changed, and inspired with the desire of perfection. It is interesting to follow him from his first determination to travel through Africa, not as a tourist, but as one seeking from her "the true, the good, the beautiful, and nothing less."[15] He began with a good will, an open mind, and a humble spirit, and thus prepared the way for grace which is never denied. Prayer followed naturally and faith came in its wake. One day Sidia, his faithful Mussulman guide, said to him: "I know that Issa [Jesus] is a great prophet, but what do you say, you Nazarenes, on the subject?" Psichari did not hesitate a moment for his answer. "Issa, my friend, is not a prophet, but, in all truth, He is the Son of God," and he went on to explain clearly the mysteries of the birth, death, and resurrection of Christ. "Then," he adds, "I stopped, my throat tight, my eyes full of tears. For was this adorable story really mine? Had I the right to grasp it, to preach Jesus Christ without believing in Him? I was then in the strangest state of mind, for I did not believe that Jesus Christ was the Son of God, and I did not know how to pray. And yet, I was speaking from the depth of my conscience, and it seemed to me that I did not lack frankness. . . . At this moment I knew I was lying, but I also knew that I would have lied more if I had not confessed the truth of my God."[16] Thus, almost without knowing it, he believed. A short time after this, just as spontaneously he fell on his knees and realized that soon he would be a professing

Catholic. Henceforth all his plans are made with the sub-conscious provision, "When I am a Catholic."[17]

Le Voyage du centurion ("A Soldier's Pilgrimage") is also the story of his conversion, this time told in the form of a novel. It is an apologetic work to the glory of the Church, a loyal testimony to Christ who had led him into the way of perfection. Maxence, the hero and a French officer, travels through Mauritania, fighting, exploring, organizing villages, and establishing peace in the colony. He also travels through a spiritual realm in quest of faith and perfection. The two voyages are woven into each other and so intimately united that they form one perfect whole which shows no confusion nor artificiality. The closing lines, in which Maxence addresses his soul and finally bows down to recite the Our Father, are exquisite. "What, Lord," he asks, "is it then so natural to love You?"[18] The novel was not finished until the winter of 1914. Psichari remarked to Paul Bourget on its conclusion: "It is a tremulous thing to write in the presence of the Most Holy Trinity!"[19] Dietz says that it is one of the most pathetic and sincere works of contemporary mystic literature.[20]

Psichari returned to France on December 3, 1912. Jacques Maritain introduced him to a Dominican priest, Father Clérissac, who became his spiritual adviser and friend. On January 26, 1913, Maritain led him to Mass, on February 8 he was confirmed, and on February 9 he received Holy Communion and made a pilgrimage to Chartres. In October, 1913, he went to Rijckholt in Holland to make a retreat, at the end of which he was admitted to the Third Order of St. Dominic, taking the name, "Frère Paul." He spent the months from June, 1913, until August, 1914, at Cherbourg, leading a saintly life in his little house, Rue Asseli. His time was given to prayer, reading, writing, and his military duties. Goichon tells us that he recited the rosary and Little Office of the Blessed Virgin and visited the Blessed Sacrament daily.[21] He was thinking seriously of joining the Dominicans, as the following letter to Father Clérissac shows: "I need not tell you that my only thought is the great affair with regard to which you have so kindly said a word of hope. With all my heart . . . I feel myself called by our Holy Father, to whose service I am burning to consecrate my life, in the full measure of my infirmity. But I also realize all that still remains in me of the old man to be overcome. I know all the progress that remains to be made, and so I have decided to wait as long as you advise, in study and interior effort, the day when I shall be worthy to possess the only happiness which remains for me to desire upon earth. . . ."[22]

In the meantime the World War broke out, and he departed among the first with the second regiment of colonial artillery. He was killed at Rossignol in Belgium on August 22, 1914. Around his neck were a medal and a cross, and under his coat was the scapular he had received at Rijckholt. A rosary entwined his fingers, and the calm expression on his face betokened the peace of his soul.

The important event in his life, from which all else radiates, is his conversion. This conversion, Loisy contends, was not "according to formula,"[23] but he forgets that very often God's ways are beyond our ken. Faith is a grace given freely to those on whom He sees fit to bestow it. Nevertheless, even humanly speaking, few adults have prepared the way for conversion so thoroughly, and arrived at it by such definite, logical steps, as did Psichari. It was not at all sudden, but the inevitable evolution of an upright conscience. His ascetic life in Africa, his honesty and sincerity, his eagerness to know the truth and follow it, were so many magnets attracting the grace of God to him. He wrote in Les Voix qui crient dans le désert: "Nothing causes us to advance in the spiritual life so much as to live daily on a handful of rice and a little salty water."[24]

Psichari's literary fame is probably in part a light reflected from his grandfather. He realized that himself. When his friend, John Dietz, congratulated him on the favorable reception of his book, *L'Appel des armes,* he turned to him rather brusquely and asked: "Come, old man, between us, do you think that all this success would be mine if I were not the grandson of my grandfather?"[25] Still he has claims all his own that cannot be overlooked. He has a rare gift of expression, a power of psychological analysis, an easy, animated, interesting style. His descriptions are rapid and picturesque, and his reflections sincere and convincing, those of a poet rather than of a philosopher.

He was only thirty when he died, leaving two novels which had been published and two others unfinished. It is vain to try to predict what he might have done had he lived another decade. Paul Bourget, in his preface to *L'Appel des armes,* speaks of him as a *"noble promesse brisée."* On the monument erected by the youth of Belgium on November 9, 1924, to mark the spot where he fell, are inscribed the words which he himself wrote, and of which his life is a proof: "The blood of martyrs is worth more than the ink of savants."

PRINCIPAL WORKS OF ERNEST PSICHARI

1908   *Terres de soleil et de sommeil*
1913   *L'Appel des armes*
1916   *Le Voyage du centurion*
1920   *Les Voix qui crient dans le désert*

REFERENCES

Aguettant, Louis, *Ernest Psichari,* Paris, 1920.
Barrès, Maurice, *Le Tombeau d'Ernest Psichari,* Paris, 1921.
Dietz, John, "Ernest Psichari," *Revue de Paris,* VI (1924), pp. 90–114.

Goichon, Amélie, *Ernest Psichari d'après des documents inédits*, Paris, 1921.

Grandmaison, Léonce de, "L'Aïeul et le petit-fils," *Études religieuses*, CXLVI (1916), pp. 451–471.

Massis, Henri, *La Vie d'Ernest Psichari*, Paris, 1916.

Psichari, Henriette, *Ernest Psichari, mon frère*, Paris, 1933.

Psichari, Jean, *Ernest Psichari, jugements et souvenirs*, Paris, 1925.

CHAPTER XIII

Louis Le Cardonnel

(1862–1936)

ON JUNE 27, 1936, THERE PASSED AWAY AT Avignon, France, Louis Le Cardonnel, a poet really great, but too little known and appreciated by his contemporaries. His lack of celebrity is due in great part to his own modesty, for besides being a poet, he was a priest, every inch a priest in fact, and far from seeking applause and fame, he constantly hid himself from the public eye. According to Louise Delpit, the great charm of his work is the intimate mingling of the sacred and profane, the perfect equilibrium between ancient aesthetics and his Christian faith.[1] With a profoundly human note he continually echoes songs that seem to have been born in eternity. Biographical details are meager, but his poems live after him to attest the sincerity of his quest for true beauty, found as nowhere else, in the stupendous mysteries of Christ.

He was born in 1862 at Valence in Drôme, and the exquisite loveliness of this French valley with its poetic ruins and southern skies left its imprint on his susceptible mind and heart. Later on he wrote:[2]

> Je suis né dans Valence, aux mémoires romaines,
> Qui voit les monts bleuir dans ses horizons clairs.
>
> L'écho des chants venus de la belle Provence,
> Aux aèdes brunis par l'éternel été,
> A bercé ma jeunesse, et j'ai dès mon enfance
> Connu l'enchantement de l'antique Beauté.*

---

* I was born in Valence, with its Roman memories, gazing at the blue moun-

His home was built on the site of an old Visitation convent founded by St. Jane Frances, and tradition handed down stories of personal visits there from St. Francis de Sales, St. Vincent de Paul, and Richelieu. From his Irish ancestors, "a melodious race and a race of warriors,"[3] he inherited "the soul of a constructor of mystic churches, the desire to roam, and the attraction for exile."[4] Both his Norman father and his Lorraine mother were devout Catholics and took care to sow the good seeds of piety in the heart of their son. Henri Clouard tells that one day Louis left home "to live the life of nature in the plains. They brought back this young John the Baptist, occupied in gathering locusts which he did not have time to eat."[5]

He studied at the Collège and at the Petit Séminaire of his native city, and his two vocations, to seek beauty and to enter the priesthood, developed hand in hand. In his mind they were one, for beauty appeared to him not in its sensuous, languid aspect which enticed too many Latin poets, but as a reflection of Divine Beauty "in a chapel with mystic, stained-glass windows, and no other than the religious rite seemed sufficient to adore it."[6] At twenty he went to Paris and joined the group of young poets who were advocating Symbolism as a reaction against the crude coarseness of the Naturalists, and the cold analytic perfection of the Parnassians. He became acquainted with Verlaine, Samain, Moréas, and Mallarmé, and frequented the numerous salons of the day. He even recited verses at the *Chat Noir,* and felt the enchantment of gay young companions and the questionable joy of late hours. But he never lost sight of his one great end, and entered the seminary of Issy in 1886. After various doubts and difficulties he was ordained priest ten years later,

---

tains on the clear horizon. The echo of songs from beautiful Provence, of bards tanned by an eternal summer, has rocked my youth, and from childhood I have known the enchantment of antique beauty.

and in 1900 went to Ligugé, where he found Huysmans, a Benedictine oblate. He himself became a monk there under the name of Frère Anselme, but, owing to his delicate health, was obliged to leave the order after two years. His poems entitled *À Saint Benoît, Les Exilés, À une Benedictine, La Lampe, Sous un tableau de Saint Benoît*, etc., all prove his love for the cloister and his deep disappointment at being unable to embrace the monastic life.

The next years were spent in Italy, at Florence, Assisi, and Rome. His poems are filled with expressions of love and admiration for his adopted land. Assisi especially attracted him and he remained there for years in a Benedictine monastery guarded by one monk. He returned for a time to his native city, but his last years were spent at Avignon, in an old palace restored and rebuilt by some generous benefactor. There he had a room, "the cell of a humanist and ascetic, radiating a spiritual light,"[7] and there he died.

All Le Cardonnel's poems are contained in two small volumes. They include *Carmina sacra* (1912), *De l'une à l'autre aurore* (1924), and numerous other poems (about sixty), most of which were written between his twentieth and fortieth year, and published in periodicals. They all testify to his high ideal of poetry, his passion for beauty, and his classic taste. Although in his early poems there is evidence that the author had not yet attained the heights of mysticism and the perfection of art that he reached later, still we find some exquisite verses. They are fashioned from "webs of light sounds, woven by the feeble wind, noises of stray brooks, and the voluptuous laughter of the elfs."[8] In them he dreams of "cold castles on the side of a lonely hill," of "distant queens, all white, who, once loved by princes, now lie buried there."[9] He hears the vesper bell in the silent city, "where a clucking idiot and a coughing old lady are the only living creatures visible."[10] He regrets his

youth, "abandoned to singing dreams which will all too
soon be consumed."[11] One of the best of these early poems is
entitled *Le Piano*.[12] In a gloomy house on the deserted quay,
an unknown woman is playing a piano:

> *Phrase lente, elle conte une longue misère;*
> *C'est un De Profundis qui ne croit pas en Dieu,*
> *Et supplie, en sachant le néant de son voeu.*
>
> *Et l'on sent, reflétée en sa monotonie,*
> *La monotone horreur de ce vide infini.* *

And the succeeding verses go on to tell how the melody
betrays her empty heart and the hidden tragedy of her life.

The volume, *Carmina sacra*, reflects a happy serenity in
the author. Many of his early doubts and dreads have evidently left him and he sings a gladder song. It contains
Chants d'Ombrie et de Toscane, Épigrammes, Orphica,
Élégies chrétiennes, and *Méditations et cantiques.* Most of the
Chants d'Ombrie et de Toscane are, as their name implies,
hymns in praise of his beloved Italy. The two dominant
notes are his delight in Italian spring, and his affection for
St. Francis (*Au printemps d'Assise, Saint François à la*
cigale, Assisium, Primavera, etc.). He loves April with its
lilies, daffodils, and anemones:[13]

> *Ce mois, les cheveux lourds de ses roses nouvelles,*
> *Ce mois qui chante, il a sur la bouche un rayon;*
> *Il est ceint de feuillage; à son front bat des ailes,*
> *Comme au front de Psyché le jeune papillon.* **

In his more solemn moments, autumn appeals to him with
its melancholy tones and its somber colors:[14]

---

* A slow phrase, it recounts a long period of suffering; it is a *De Profundis*
without any belief in God, and it prays, knowing the nothingness of its prayer.
And one feels, reflected in its monotony, the monotonous horror of this infinite
void.

** This month, its hair thick with new roses, this singing month which has on
its mouth a beam of light; it is wreathed with leaves; on its brow flutter wings,
as the young butterfly on the brow of Psyche.

Un bel automne, encor, dans l'abîme se couche:
La vendange est finie, et l'arrière-saison,
À travers les champs nus, que bat le vent farouche,
Nous ramène attristés vers la triste maison. *

Many of these poems express sublime transports, and seem almost to be snatches from Verlaine's *Sagesse.* They were written at Assisi with its sacred memories of the gentle saint who 'abode there, "his soul on fire, heedless of all but of praising God,"[15] and they voice the author's search after "ecstatic love won through suffering."[16] Occasionally we find dashes of realism, as, for example, in *Jeunes ombres,* he describes his visit to a cemetery where he reads the names of so many *young* people on the tombstones:[17]

Que reste-t-il de vous dans la nuit sépulcrale?
Ces cheveux qui paraient vos têtes de vingt ans,
Que jamais une main n'effleure, nuptiale:
Et la blancheur, hélas sans bouche, de vos dents. **

Orphica, written in much the same strain but more Mallarmian, contains his theory on poetry, and is addressed to his disciples. He speaks to them as a father to his sons, and warns them of the storms they will have to weather if they will be faithful to their ideal. His advice can really be summed up in one line:

Sois noble, sois divin, afin de l'inspirer.[18]

Méditations et cantiques include poems to the Blessed Mother, St. Michael, and St. Benedict, meditations on the Holy Scriptures, Easter, and Ascension, and sighs for the cloister, "where the fall of day is infinitely sweet."[19]

---

* A lovely autumn once more has gone to sleep in the abyss: The vintage is finished and the late fall days, through bare fields beaten by the fierce wind, send us sadly back to the dreary house.

** What remains of you in the sepulchral darkness? This hair which adorned your heads at twenty years, that a bride's hand will never stroke: And the whiteness of your teeth, without mouth, alas!

We find new accents in *De l'une à l'autre aurore*, though Le Cardonnel still sings of Italy and spring. He is forty years old now, and in his *Maturité* he looks back at his youth as a dream of yesterday. He thinks of all his friends who have already fallen along the way, and realizing that he is in the summer of life, advancing with heavy step under an arid sun, he begs God to sustain him for he is alone and overburdened with the weight of work and days. This fearful accent, characteristic of those who are growing old, is heard again and again in this volume, but it is always blended with a hopeful cry to God and His Blessed Mother. Several poems echo the War, and one of the finest things Louis Le Cardonnel ever wrote is his *Trains qui passent*. He is tossing about during a sleepless night, gazing through the cold windowpanes "at the infinite harvest of stars in the sky." They remind him of other fires, where France and Italy are fighting the *Barbares,* when he hears passing a train full of wounded and dying:[20]

> *Trains, passez, emportez vers des hôpitaux calmes*
> *Ces enfants; que, là-bas, des mains de nobles soeurs,*
> *S'ils doivent s'en aller, jonchent leurs corps de palmes.*
>   *Et maintenant, en haut les coeurs!*
>
> *Nous avons tant souffert déjà; tant de ruines,*
> *Tant de mères sans fils, d'épouses sans époux:*
> *Trains, une horrible angoisse a serré nos poitrines,*
>   *Comme si vous passiez sur nous.*
>
> *Mais rien ne peut tuer l'Italie; et toi, France,*
> *Ton astre, sans déclin, pour les Nations luit,*
> *— Vous n'écraserez pas dans nos coeurs l'espérance,*
>   *O trains qui roulez dans la nuit.**

---

* Trains, pass on, carry to the calm hospitals these children; so that, down yonder, if they must die, the hands of noble sisters may strew their bodies with palms. And now, lift up your hearts! We have suffered so much already: so many ruins, so many mothers without sons, wives without husbands: Trains, a horrible anguish wrings our hearts, as if you were passing over us. But nothing can kill Italy; and you, France, your star, never declining, shines for the nations. You will not crush hope out of our hearts, O trains that roll on in the night.

Édouard Schuré remarks that what distinguishes the poems of Louis Le Cardonnel from "hundreds of other contemporary volumes of vapid piety and feigned religiosity, is the vivacity of their sentiment and the originality of their artistic form, at the same time hieratic and modern. Here the dogmas, rites, and symbols are revived by individual sentiment."[21] On the other hand, Georges Duhamel read the *Carmina sacra* and was disappointed. He concedes that the verses are scrupulously correct, but at the same time banal and monotonous. He complains that in the poem *À l'enfant Simplicius,* the cares are *poignant,* the virgins *pure,* the angels *charming;* that sleep is *sweet,* and poetry *wingèd.* He also dislikes the metaphysical vocabulary with its capitalized *Essence, Cause, Word, Rule, Beyond, Peace,* etc.[22] There is ground for this adverse criticism, as we do find among Le Cardonnel's poems some that are rather commonplace and others that are too abstract. But few, even of our greatest poets, are always at their best. Wordsworth, for instance, has written both the finest and the worst verses ever printed. To offset these trite connotations pointed out by Duhamel, we may quote dozens of others that are fresh and original, as, for example: Long veils of night, proud gardens, distant midnights, cold castles, reeling skeletons, starry silences, pale space, discolored azure, harmonious and sober gold, the nostalgic flight of the swans, etc. Even in the above condemned poem (*À l'enfant Simplicius*),[23] the last verse contains a charming figure:

> Et, dans le doux sommeil, quand notre corps repose,
> Parfume-nous un peu des aromes du ciel.
> Âme de saint enfant, nouvellement éclose,
> Comme une fleur vivante, au Jardin eternel.*

---

* And, when our bodies repose in sweet sleep, perfume them sweetly with the aromas of heaven. Soul of an innocent child, newly budded, as a living flower, in the eternal garden.

The beauty of Le Cardonnel's poetry is not, however, derived from striking epithets, but rather from its mystic aspirations and the intensity of the emotion. In his early work he follows Mallarmé (though he is never as obscure as his master),[24] singing to the lyre, and praising those whose ideal of poetry is sublime and inaccessible. He lived above the vulgar realities of daily life, and was beyond the reach of many of his readers. His *Chant Platonicien*[25] sums up his early manner:

> *Auprès de vous, j'entends l'infini qui m'appelle;*
> *La Vérité me parle, ineffablement belle.*
>
> *Et je lui chanterai, l'adorant dans ses voiles,*
> *Des hymnes pleins du feu glorieux des étoiles.*
>
> *Inspirez-moi, sereine, en robe blanche et droite,*
> *O vous que nul désir vulgaire ne convoite.**

But the Latin and Celtic in him soon brought him back to the classic standards of traditional French poetry. He told a friend, "I feel something within me that aspires to clarity, severity, and strength. I feel that I shall not be a Baudelaire, that I shall be the very opposite, that my work will not have the confusion of darkness. . . . Something tells me that I shall be a poet of light."[26] And so he was — a poet of light pointing out in simple but vivid language, the luminous way that leads to the vision of eternal brightness which he himself sought so faithfully. The idea which dominates all his work, according to Praviel, is "the union of a form always beautiful, always voluntarily harmonious, with the *élan* toward the ideal."[27] His inspiration came from his deep spirituality and burning love of God, which at times burst out in tumultuous songs of joy, but more often found ex-

---

* Near you, I hear the infinite calling me; truth speaks to me, ineffably beautiful. And I will sing to it, adoring it under its veils, hymns full of the glorious fire of the stars. Inspire me, serene beauty, in your robe simple and white, O you who inspire no unworthy desires.

pression in calm and peaceful prayers. Charles Terrin sums up his genius when he says: "He allies to the vigor of Bossuet, the evangelical simplicity of St. Francis, and the serene adoration of Racine."[28]

PRINCIPAL WORKS OF LOUIS LE CARDONNEL

1912 *Carmina sacra*
1920 *Du Rhone à l'Arno*
1923 *A Sainte Thérèse de Jésus*
1924 *De l'une à l'autre aurore*
1928 *Poèmes. Chants d'Ombrie et de Toscane*
1929 *Oeuvres*, 2 vol.

REFERENCES

Aykroyd, Phyllis, *Louis Le Cardonnel*, London, 1928.

Bersaucourt, Albert de, *Louis Le Cardonnel*, Paris, 1909.

Hugues, P. d', *Louis Le Cardonnel, Poète mystique*, Paris, 1927.

Langevin, Eugène, *Louis Le Cardonnel*, Paris, 1927.

Richard, Paul, *Le Poète Louis Le Cardonnel*, Paris, 1925.

Ryan, Mary, "Louis Le Cardonnel," *Dublin Review*, CLXX (1922), pp. 256–273.

Terrin, Charles, "Louis Le Cardonnel, poète Catholique," *Revue des deux mondes*, June 1, 1936, pp. 649–665.

CHAPTER XIV

Paul Claudel

(1868–   )

PAUL CLAUDEL HAS BEEN CALLED THE "UN-usual ambassador."[1] It seems to be an unwritten axiom of the human race that a poet should be more or less of a dreamer, so we scarcely expect him to exhibit in a marked degree the practical turn of mind required in a good diplomat. On the other hand, we cannot name many foreign ambassadors who write mystical poetry flavored with medievalism. But Claudel is recognized by critics, not at all given to exaggeration, as the greatest living French poet,[2] while there is no question in the United States about his ability and success as an ambassador of the first rank. Perhaps no other literary man has ever combined in so admirable a manner the contradictory qualities of the intuitive lyrist and the practical man of action. His dramas and poems do not, indeed, afford matter for light reading, but anyone who seriously devotes himself to study the mystery of his genius will be amply repaid.

Better to understand his work, we shall cast a hasty glance at his life, to find out whence he came and what were the influences that helped to mold his genius. Paul-Louis-Charles-Marie Claudel was born, on the sixth of October, 1868, at Ville-Neuve-sur-Fère in Tardenois, the same district where the scene of his *L'Annonce faite à Marie* ("Tidings Brought to Mary") is laid. His family moved to Paris in 1882, in order that his sister Camille might study sculpture with Rodin. He attended the famous Lycée of Louis le Grand, where his companions were Léon Daudet, Fortunat Strowski, and Joseph Bédier. Strowski tells us that "little Claudel had a round face with a frank expression, a rather harsh accent, lively manners, and a robust build."[3] At the distribution of prizes in 1883 at the close of his college career, he was crowned by Renan himself, whom at the time he idolized, but of whom he wrote later: "Do not destroy me with the Voltaires, and the Renans, and the Michelets, and the Hugos, and all those other villains."[4]

Shortly after this, his grandfather, whose lingering sufferings the boy had been watching for years, died of cancer. The thought of his death, and the works of Arthur Rimbaud which he began to read about this time, made a profound impression on Claudel. Though he had been baptized a Catholic, he was quite indifferent, even hostile to religion, until his eighteenth year. He himself relates the story of his conversion.[5] It took place on Christmas day in 1886, when he and some companions went to Notre Dame in Paris, not out of reverence for the feast which was being celebrated, but hoping to gain inspiration from the poetry of the ceremonies. Like his great patron, St. Paul, he was struck down by grace that very day, though he acknowledges that it was four years later that he gave a wholehearted submission, wrestling meantime with grace. Since 1890 he has been an undoubting and militant Catholic.

He attended the École des Sciences Politiques for a short time, and then entered consular service. His first appointment was in 1893 as vice-consul in New York. Since then he has successfully held diplomatic positions in China, Austria, Germany, Italy, South America, Denmark, and Japan. In 1926 he became ambassador to the United States, which position he held until 1933, when he returned to France with his wife (nee Mlle Reine Sainte-Marie-Perrin) and five children. Later he was appointed French ambassador to Belgium.[6]

Claudel is the author of some twelve dramas, of numerous

lyric poems, and of several volumes in prose, most of which are collections of critical or philosophical essays.[7] He is probably best known to Americans for his *L'Annonce faite à Marie,* which was played in translation by the New York Theater Guild in 1923–24. His first dramatic effort[8] was *Tête d'Or,** written before his conversion in 1889. It is a violent drama, showing the earmarks of youth and resembling the extravagant performances of the Romanticists more than the artistic plays of the Symbolists. It tells the story of Simon Agnel, the "man of desires," who later becomes Tête d'Or, the reckless hero who kills the king, conquers the country, and makes himself a demigod. But after having reached the heights of human power and glory, he meets defeat and death in a solitary spot in Asia. The meaning of the play is obscure, but the author evidently intended to present the emptiness of egoism and the helplessness of man without God; for if there is no eternity, life is full of bitterness and despair.

The first version of *La Ville* ("The City"), a social drama, followed in 1893 without the name of the author. On the whole, it is perhaps less intelligible even than *Tête d'Or,* though in the second version (published in 1901) the characters are not so abstract as in the first. The hero is the City itself, whose downfall is caused by the strife and rebellion of restless men. Then it is for the poet-priest Couvre and his son Ivors to build a new city, whose laws shall be based on the divine law and whose inhabitants shall be wiser and more God-fearing.

Le Repos du septième jour is an oriental play which shows that death and hell are the punishment of sin. It contains beautiful passages, dantesque in their grandeur. The emperor of China descends to the lower regions to find out from the Prince of Darkness the cause of the evils that have

---

* Translated into English under the same title.

come upon his country. The Angel of the Empire is sent
to him and explains that the people are being chastised for
their wickedness and forgetfulness of God. He says:

> Six days, then, let him do his work, nourish his body and his mind,
>   And on the seventh, as a servant who, having adorned his house,
> introduces his master into it,
> Let him raise his hands toward heaven.
> Such is the law which you have transgressed, and that is why the
> Earth,
>   Seeing that you use badly the fruits which are given to you,
> wishes to take back from you that which belongs to her.[9]

L'Échange is simpler and more direct than the three preceding dramas. The scene is laid in America and there are
only four characters. Louis Laine, led on by avarice and
cupidity, proposes to give his wife, the honest Marthe, to
Thomas Polluck Nageoire, in exchange for money and for
Polluck's mistress, the wicked Lechy Elbernon. Tragedy
results from this flagrant violation of the sacredness of the
marriage bond, and the reader is convinced that there are
many precious things in life which have no monetary value.

The four preceding plays, together with *La Jeune Fille
Violaine,* appeared in one volume entitled *L'Arbre* in 1901.
A revision of this last play was published in 1912 under the
title *L'Annonce faite à Marie.* It is much more dramatic
than the earlier work and is, in many ways, Claudel's most
perfect production. Both versions tell of the lovable Violaine, who is to marry Jacques Hury, but who, on account of
the jealousy and calumny of her sister Mara, is driven from
home and leads a solitary life of penance and suffering.
Later, when this same Mara is in trouble and grief, she
comes to Violaine for help; for, though she is wicked herself, she recognizes the power of sanctity in her elder sister.
Neither is she disappointed, for Violaine's prayer obtains a
miracle. There are many minor changes in the later play.
For example, in it Violaine is struck with leprosy as a result

of an innocent kiss of sympathy given to the church builder, Pierre de Craon, while in *La Jeune Fille Violaine* she becomes blind on account of the ashes thrown in her eyes by her cruel sister. Again, in this earlier play, Violaine's prayers cure Mara's baby boy, Aubin, of blindness, while in the later one it is Mara's baby girl, Aubaine, who is restored to life. Perhaps the greatest improvement is that *L'Annonce* is put back in the Middle Ages, while *La Jeune Fille Violaine* has a modern setting.

Le Partage de Midi, like *L'Échange* a drama of passion, appeared in 1906. Ysé, the woman with a too human outlook on life, is redeemed by Mesa, the man in whom the spirit triumphs over the flesh. It is a work of transition, leading up to the next group of plays, and presents a peculiar combination of simplicity and sublimity.

The idea of the beauty of Christian sacrifice is again stressed in *L'Otage* ("The Hostage") published in 1911. It was followed by *Le Pain dur* in 1918[10] and by *Le Père humilié* in 1919.[11] These three plays form a trilogy, in which the same characters or their descendants appear. They all have a historic background and give a rather vague picture of France after the Revolution. In *L'Otage,* Sygne de Coufontaine, to save the Pope who was hidden in her home, offers herself as a hostage to the brutal Toussaint Turelure. She becomes his wife and lives a martyr. *Le Pain dur* recounts the life of their son Louis, Count de Coufontaine, who seems to have inherited all the bad qualities of his father and none of the virtues of his mother. His greatest ambition is to destroy Christ in himself and to rid his home of the family crucifix venerated by Sygne. *Le Père humilié* is the story of the unfortunate Pensée, Louis de Coufontaine's blind daughter, who is loved by the two nephews of the Pope. She has a child by one of them, who is killed in battle, and the other marries her to save his brother's honor and to protect mother and child. The first of these plays is probably the best on account of its genuinely human appeal, its dramatic action, and the exquisitely drawn character of Sygne de Coufontaine.

The most remarkable of Claudel's dramas, the colossal one that seems to sum up his genius, is *Le Soulier de Satin* ("The Satin Slipper"), (1929). Its message, like that of *L'Annonce*, is that "all things minister to a Divine Purpose and so to one another, be it events or personalities. Even the falterings of circumstance and the patternings of personality, sin and falsehood, are made to serve truth and justice, and above all, salvation in the long run."[12] The plot is complex with many scenes and characters, but the main theme is the tale of the noble lady Prouhèze and her lover Rodrigo, who play an important part in the history of sixteenth-century Spain. Duty and honor prevent the union their passion would desire, so Rodrigo plunges into the feverish life of the New World, while Prouhèze marries the hateful Camillo to save his soul for God, and Africa for Spain. Rodrigo, after years of glory in America, again seeks Prouhèze, encouraged by a letter which had been written long before but which had not been delivered. She rejects his love, having found happiness in sacrifice to duty, and in the end Rodrigo follows her example of renunciation and allows himself to be sold as a slave to the nuns of St. Teresa. The play takes its title from Act I, Scene 5, in which Dona Prouhèze, standing in her saddle, takes off her little satin slipper and puts it in the hands of the statue of the Blessed Mother, begging the Virgin to prevent her from being to her house a cause of corruption, from doing any dishonorable act. She prays thus:

See, while there is yet time, holding my heart in one hand and my shoe in the other,

I give myself over to you, Virgin Mother; I give you my shoe, Virgin Mother, keep in your hand my luckless little foot!

I warn you that presently I shall see you no longer and that I am about to set everything going against you!

But when I try to rush on evil, let it be with limping foot! The barrier that you have set up,
    When I want to cross it, be it with a crippled wing!
    I have done so much as I could; keep you my poor little shoe,
    Keep it against your heart, tremendous Mother of mine![13]

Claudel's *Book of Christopher Columbus* stands somewhat apart among his works. It is a lyrical drama in two parts,[14] interpreting the life of the great discoverer and showing once more the futility of human endeavor against divine appointment. The story is rather fragmentary and the whole impression somewhat confused. This impression is increased rather than lessened by the illustrations, powerful but grotesque, of Jean Charlot.

Claudel's dramas form the major part of his work. Spiritual and idealistic in tone, they are often abstruse and lack popular appeal. They belong to that class of books which Bacon says must be "chewed and digested." Several critics have called attention to the fact that, to appreciate them fully, we must be in a state of receptivity. The longer we study them, the more they grow upon us and the more we grasp the unity in them; for each one expresses an idea, and this idea is an integral part of a great harmonious whole. As Jacques Rivière says: "Each drama is a verse of the immense poem of life."[15] God is the explanation of the world, and all the events that take place in it are directed by Him. Claudel does not attempt to explain further these events, but simply relates them as an absorbed onlooker. He believes that "all things minister to a Divine Purpose." Still he makes it evident that, in this drama of life, God does not interfere with human liberty. Man can choose to be saved or lost, his soul can progress toward God or retrograde. Claudel's main interest is not, however, in the moral struggle of his characters, but rather in their destinies, often influenced in the plays (as in life) by external events even more than by personal choice. Here he differs widely from Corneille and

Racine, whose plots represent the inner strife between the will and the passions.

Claudel has been called a *"peintre d'ensembles."*[16] His very setting and stage directions emphasize this. Often no date nor country is mentioned. The names of his characters are usually strange and give no hint as to nationality. We know neither the race nor century to which Tête d'Or belongs. *La Ville* might be situated anywhere in the world. *L'Annonce* takes place "at the end of a conventional Middle Ages."[17] The note at the beginning of *Le Soulier de Satin* is typical: "The scene of this play is the world, and more especially Spain, at the close of the sixteenth, unless it be the opening of the seventeenth century. The author has taken the liberty of compendiating countries and periods, just as at a given distance several separate mountain chains make but one horizon."[18] We realize then that dates and geography are secondary in the author's mind. As a dramatist he is interested in neither history nor politics, but in individuals. Yet he is noticeably specific about time and atmosphere, since these have an effect on the soul. The first scene of *Le Père humilié* takes place on "a beautiful night, when the glow of twilight is still afloat." *Le Pain dur* is set in the gloom of November, and *L'Otage* opens in a violent storm.

Man must seek God, and according to Claudel the way to find Him is renunciation and sacrifice. If we refuse this, life will be a failure. Thus Tête d'Or dies in despair, the City perishes miserably, Louis Laine is punished for grasping forbidden goods, while on the other hand Marthe, Violaine, Mesa, the emperor of China, Sygne, and Prouhèze find salvation and redemption through suffering and self-immolation. Nearly all Claudel's dramas are tragedies, and realistic ones at that. He does not convert his characters and crown them with halos in the last act (as some might expect from a mystic). They are natural and very human, even the best of them. Sygne, in spite of her heroic act of submission, comes near breaking under the awful strain, and we are left in doubt about her final repentance. Her death is almost a suicide, and the dispositions of her last hour remain a secret in the drama as they would have in life. Violaine, in spite of her sanctity, retains her love for Jacques Hury — purified, it is true, but nevertheless unlawful. Most dramatists would have seen to it that Mara turned to a life of penance and reparation after her child's resurrection, but human nature is not changed so easily even in the presence of a miracle, so Mara remains the malicious, jealous sister. Again, Orian, notwithstanding his noble ambitions, is not careful to avoid the occasion of sin and so falls pitiably.

In the earlier plays the characters are somewhat vague and abstract. We hardly get acquainted with Besme, Lala, Avare, Couvre, and Ivors in *La Ville*. The emperor of China and his followers have little individuality. In *L'Échange*, however, and the later dramas the characters become more clearly defined. We feel that we know Sygne, Violaine, Marthe, Ysé, Prouhèze, and Rodrigo personally, while even the secondary characters such as Anne Vercors, Pierre de Craon, Orso, Sichel, and Musica are less shadowy and more natural. Some of these are types, while others have a symbolic meaning — for example, Tête d'Or represents egoism; Violaine, renunciation; Orian, weakness; Camillo, selfishness; Polluck, greed, etc. Katherine Brégy says that "Claudel's women, when they are decent at all, have a unique, unearthly quality not unlike the fragrance of incense, and Violaine is the essence of this pitiful and mysterious charm."[19] Of course, some of them are not "decent at all," but others, such as the Princess (in Tête d'Or), Sygne, Pensée, and Prouhèze, are simply unforgettable.

The lyric element often predominates over the dramatic, especially in the early plays. Thus *Tête d'Or, La Ville,* and

Le Repos du septième jour are full of platonic dialogues and poetic monologues which often have very little to do with the plot. The author allows the characters to express their individual ideas, and sometimes he even forgets all about his characters and speaks himself. Take, for instance, Couvre's dissertations on poetry in *La Ville*[20] and the demon's dogmatic explanation of the three degrees of sin in *Le Repos.*[21] This lyricism is much less noticeable in the later plays, where we find some examples of the most direct and perfect dialogue in modern French literature. Anne Vercor's conversation with his wife concerning the future of their two daughters,[22] and Mara's talk with her mother in which she persuades her to forward her plans for marriage with Jacques Hury in *L'Annonce*,[23] are masterpieces of simplicity and naturalness. Sometimes the tone becomes vulgar and almost brutal, as the remarks of the soldiers in *La Ville*[24] and the sallies of the workers in *L'Annonce.*[25] In *Le Soulier de Satin* such a passage (the conversation of the Chinaman with the Negress)[26] is wedged in between two of the most poetic and beautiful scenes in the book. This combination of gross realism with sublime idealism is one of the surprising qualities of Claudel's work. It is what Cunliffe calls "a poetic materialism."[27]

Few of Claudel's plays have ever reached the stage,[28] and the difficulty of presenting them is evident. Nevertheless there are some excellent dramatic scenes in nearly every one of them. To mention only a few: the miracle scene in *L'Annonce*,[29] Sygne's struggle with her spiritual director in *L'Otage*,[30] Pensée's confession of blindness to her lover in *Le Père humilié*,[31] Louis Laine's acknowledgment to his wife that he is exchanging her for money in *L'Échange*,[32] Rodrigo's encounter with Camillo in the fortress of Mogador,[33] Prouhèze's conversation with her Guardian Angel[34] and her final choice between love and duty[35] in *Le Soulier de Satin*. Probably the author never intended some of his dramas to be played. This does not necessarily detract from their merit or his reputation. André Gide says: "At present there are two kinds of plays: the one kind is not played, but it is important; the other kind is played, but is without any importance. Claudel's plays are more important than all the products of Donnay and Capus."[36]

As a dramatist Claudel has often been compared to Aeschylus, three of whose plays he translated into French.[37] As a poet, too, he shows Greek influence, especially that of Pindar. His master in France was, according to his own testimony, Arthur Rimbaud,[38] who "tried to express the inexpressible." We are not surprised, then, that his lyric poems, even more than his dramas, must be read and re-read, literally ruminated upon. His principal volumes of verse are: *Cinq grandes odes* (1910), *Corona Benignitatis Anni Dei* (1914), *Cette heure qui est entre le printemps et l'été* (1913), *La Messe là-bas* (1919), and *Feuilles de Saints* (1925).

Jacques Rivière calls the odes "an immense act of thanksgiving."[39] The first, *Les Muses,* is in praise of the figures of the nine Muses sculptured on a sarcophagus in the Louvre. The second, *L'Esprit et l'Eau,* is an abstruse philosophical treatise showing that water (tears), vivified by the spirit of penance, cleanses the soul. The third, *Magnificat,* is a canticle of love and gratitude to God for His gifts to the poet. The fourth, *La Muse qui est la Grâce,* is a dialogue between the poet and the Muse, who little by little is transformed into Grace. The fifth, *La Maison fermée,* is an answer to those who reproached the poet for the "closed" character of his art. In these odes, Claudel gives us many interesting hints about his theories as a lyric poet. He tells us that "the poem is not made up of these letters which I plant as nails, but of the white spaces which remain on the paper."[40] When accused of obscurity in his verse, he answers with supreme disdain: "I do not care whether you laugh or cry, nor whether or not you like my language, and no praise nor blame from you will change its modesty. I have nothing to do with you, it is for you to find your account with me."[41]

The *Processional* (which follows *Cinq grandes odes*), *Corona Benignitatis Anni Dei,* and *La Messe là-bas* are all liturgical poems much easier to follow than the odes. The *Processional* deals with the Mass, the sacraments, the litany of the saints, and the Blessed Trinity, while *La Messe là-bas* follows the Holy Sacrifice from the Introit to the last Gospel, with appropriate reflections on each part, varying from sublime outbursts of praise in the Gloria to the touching, homely picture in the Pater Noster, where the husband and father is departing for the War thinking of his wife: "And all the long years which are beginning during which she will never cease to be a widow."[42] The *Corona Benignitatis Anni Dei* has been appropriately styled "an ornamental breviary of poetry, an illuminated missal, a liturgical year in colours."[43] It proves that the author is deeply familiar with the Bible and the Divine Office, for almost unconsciously he uses their phraseology. He begins with the Epiphany and leads us with triumphant note through the glorious chain of feasts that adorn the Church's calendar. Each poem is full of elevating thoughts, expressed in simple but lofty style.[44] For example, in the hymn to St. Benedict, he assures us: "Rather than to return to God, it is simpler never to leave Him."[45] In *Le Jour des cadeaux,* he tells God that if He wants heroes, virgins, Christians who will follow Him bravely and gladly, there is Dominic, Francis, Lawrence, and Cecilia; but if He has need of a sluggard and an imbecile, a proud man and a coward, ungrateful and sinful and hard-hearted — then "You will always have me!"[46]

Most of these poems are written in what is called "Claudelian verse." It is a form of expression which should hardly be called verse at all, though it is more rhythmic than ordinary prose, and reminds one of the cadence of the Psalms.

Usually there is no rhyme nor assonance, but occasionally
we find both. The length of the verse varies from one
syllable to five lines. Claudel's poetic instinct and sense of
harmony enables him to use this verse-form with marked
success and to obtain admirable effects from it at times. Yet
we must confess that there are many lines and passages that
differ not at all from pure prose, and that, on the whole, it
is not as musical and effective as the Alexandrine. Claudel
uses this classic verse in a few instances, as, for example, in
Vers d'exil.[47] But this meter is rare, and by far the greater
part of his lyric poetry and practically all his dramas are
written in his own *vers libre.*[48]

Besides his poetry, Claudel has published several volumes
of prose, of which the most important are: *La Connaissance
de l'Est, L'Art poétique,* and *Ways and Crossways.* The first
of these is considered by many the author's most readable
book. Peyre calls it "Claudel's masterpiece in the Mallarmé
manner."[49] It is a collection of short sketches written in racy,
picturesque prose, and dealing with a variety of widely
different subjects with which Claudel became acquainted
during his years in China and Japan. We read of cocoa
trees, cemeteries, tombs, rice, feasts, Chinese writing, cities,
gardens, pigs, pagodas, etc. Sometimes we find the crudest
realism; for instance, in describing the leper in *La Pagode,*
he notes the single eye full of blood and water, the mouth
despoiled of its lips by leprosy and discovering even to the
roots the teeth, yellow as bones and long as the incisors of
the rabbit; "and the rest of the face is gone."[50] Other
sketches are real little prose poems, idyllic and charming:
"O God, what novelty this blue has for me! how tender is
this green, and how fresh! And looking at the far-off sky,
what peace to see it still so dark that the stars are blinking
in it."[51]

L'Art poétique, the most abstract of his works is a metaphysical treatise which only a philosopher can understand.

It deals with the meaning of time, our knowledge of the exterior world, vegetal and animal life, man with his intellect, and finally the development of the Church. *Ways and Crossways,* published only in English translation,[52] is also philosophical, but not so abstruse as the former work. It is a collection of essays on such subjects as art, religion and poetry, the physics of the Eucharist, an underground church, etc., between which there is no relation excepting that they all disclose the author's sound Catholic philosophy.

The universal complaint against Claudel is that he is difficult to understand, and this criticism is often justified, especially (as we have pointed out) in the case of his lyric poetry. Whence this obscurity? First of all, Claudel is synthetic, while the French genius is, as a rule, analytic. He rarely explains a subject or mentions details, but rather gives a mere suggestion and leaves the reader to follow it out. This is true in his dramas as well as in his poems. For example, who is the woman that Simon Agnel buries in the first scene of *Tête d'Or?* The author hints that she is the daughter of the old Peasant and that Cebes had loved her, but that is all. Again, in *Le Soulier de Satin* the tortures to which Camillo puts Don Sebastian makes the reader feel that Prouhèze's life must be one of horror, but we know nothing more. In his poems this tendency to compactness is even more marked. His odes are crammed with original but undeveloped thoughts. The author seemed to realize this, for he wrote an "argument" at the beginning of each. Even with the aid of this argument, most readers find it difficult to follow the theme.

Claudel was a Symbolist in his early years, and learned from Mallarmé and Rimbaud to express by symbols the inner relations that exist between our souls and the exterior world. His own prodigious imagination saw resemblances which sometimes seem strained to his less gifted readers. He looks down from an eminence on a village and sees "in the midst of the trees . . . the poem of roofs."[53] In the *Présen-tation* he finds only Simeon and Anna in the temple to welcome Christ, all the other Jews are "reading the newspaper or playing at politics against the Romans."[54] *In Feuilles de Saints* he describes the outbreak of war thus: "The monstrous torso of War appears at the end of the embankment, and with a turn of her shoulder she uproots the gate of the city."[55] Every page of his works contains breathtaking similes and metaphors, and this power of imagination plus a desire to express his whole thought rapidly, results often in peculiar syntax, ellipses, omission of verbs, inversions, etc. We like writers whose sentences can be analyzed and whose paragraphs can be outlined, and Claudel deliberately rejects this order. He says in Ode I: "O my soul, we must not draw up any plan." He has a rich, colorful vocabulary, containing unusual French words and words with foreign flavor. Jacques Rivière says: "His words have not only light and sound, but also a consistency, an odor and a taste."[56]

We must confess that, on account of his tendency to synthesize, his vivid imagination, his unusual expressions and unfamiliar vocabulary, his peculiarities of syntax and versification, Claudel is frequently obscure and almost never easy reading. But on the other hand, we insist that he is well worth study and effort. He opens to us a new world, a world full of mysterious beauty and charm, vibrating with vigorous Catholicity, which at first seems unreal and strange, but after we become accustomed to the energizing atmosphere, it fills us with delight. Of course, as Mme Sainte-Marie-Perrin says, some never appreciate lyrists and mystics,[57] so there will always be a coterie who consider Claudel half mad. So precise and clear in his diplomatic writings, he seems to prefer that poetry be shrouded in mystery.

We Catholics find a further reason for this strange, primitive, unearthly note in Claudel's works, which to many is wholly inexplicable. When we ponder that in 1900 he made a retreat with the Benedictines at Ligugé and received the habit of an Oblate of St. Benedict;[58] that through his influence many others have been brought into the Church (notably Francis Jammes and Gabriel Frizeau); that for years he has been a daily attendant at Mass; that while a busy ambassador at Washington, he found time to spend an hour every day in front of the Blessed Sacrament; then we begin to grasp the source of his power. He rises before us as one of the inspired prophets with a message all his own, pleading eloquently by his life and by his writings for Christ, whose standard he chose once and forever in 1890. And the world never will understand this language, for its ears are not attuned to the melodies of heaven.

PRINCIPAL WORKS OF PAUL CLAUDEL

1890   *Tête d'Or*
1892   *La Ville*
1900   *Connaissance de l'Est*
1901   *L'Arbre (Tête d'Or, L'Échange, Le Repos du septième jour, La Ville, La Jeune Fille Violaine)*
1906   *Partage de Midi*
1907   *Art poétique*
1910   *Cinq grandes odes*
1911   *L'Otage*
1911   *Le Chemin de la croix*
1912   *Théâtre (4 vol.)*
1912   *L'Annonce faite à Marie*
1914   *Corona Benignitatis Anni Dei*
1915   *La Nuit de Noël*
1918   *Le Pain dur*
1919   *La Messe là-bas*
1919   *Le Père humilié*
1925   *Feuilles de Saints*
1926   *Correspondance avec J. Rivière*
1927   *Protée*
1927   *L'Ours et la lune*

1928   *Positions et propositions*
1929   *Le Soulier de Satin*
1931   *La Cantate à trois voix*
1933   *Ways and Crossways*
1935   *Le Livre de Christophe Colomb*
1936   *Figures et paraboles*

REFERENCES

Benoist-Méchin, Jacques, *Bibliographie des oeuvres de Paul Claudel*, Paris, 1931.

Cattaui, Georges, "Paul Claudel and the *Satin Slipper*," *Dublin Review*, CXC (1932), pp. 268–279.

Chaigne, Louis, *Le Chemin de Paul Claudel*, Paris, 1931.

Dimnet, Ernest, "Paul Claudel as a Diplomatist," *Outlook*, CXLV (1927), pp. 337–339.

Duhamel, Georges, *Paul Claudel. Le Philosophe, le poète, l'écrivain, le dramaturge*. Paris, 1919.

Goldbeck, Edward, "Paul Claudel," *Bookman*, LXVII (1908), pp. 501–506.

Madaule, Jacques, *Le Génie de Paul Claudel*, Paris, 1933.

—— *Le Drame de Paul Claudel*, Paris, 1936.

Peyre, Henri, "The Work of Paul Claudel," *Living Age*, CCCXLIII (1932), pp. 225–231.

Rivière, Jacques, *Études*, Paris, 1911.

Sainte-Marie-Perrin, E., "M. Paul Claudel," *Revue des deux mondes*, Feb. 15, 1914, pp. 871–903.

Tonquédec, Joseph de, *L'Oeuvre de Paul Claudel*, Paris, 1917.

Truc, Gonzague, *Paul Claudel*, Paris, 1928.

CHAPTER XV

Henri Ghéon

(1875–   )

HENRI GHÉON IS KNOWN TO THE MODERN literary world as a poet,[1] a novelist,[2] a critic,[3] a hagiographer, and a dramatist. As a poet he is mediocre,[4] but in the other fields, especially the drama, he has accomplished important and original work. His real name is Dr. Henri Vangeon, and he writes and practices medicine in Orsay, an ancient town in the shadow of Versailles. He is one of *les grands convertis,* for, though he was born a Catholic and made his First Communion on what he terms "the most beautiful day of my life,"[5] he fell away soon after. In *L'Homme né de la guerre* (1919), the book he wrote about his conversion, he describes the pathetic scene.[6] It was Easter Sunday morning, and he was sitting in one of the downstairs rooms reading, while his mother was above getting ready for Mass. She calls down, "Hurry up, Henry, or we shall be late!" He rises, puts down the book, and goes up to his mother's room. She is drawing on her gloves, and repeats, all unsuspecting his reply, "Hurry, or you will miss Mass." "I am not going," he answers, shamefaced but resolute. "What do you expect, Mother? I do not believe any more!" And he leaves her, a knife in her heart.

He himself analyzes the situation thus: "Between the good, pious mother, and the godless father . . . the young man hesitates, wavers. He had two examples, and one single way to choose. My father had not said a word to tear me from the maternal faith, and, God knows . . . what secret preference attracted me to my mother; it was my father,

however, that I followed."[7] He persevered in this unbelief
until 1915. Even at his loved mother's death (she was killed
in an accident) he did not repent, but was filled with bitter
rebellion against God. At the consecration during the
Requiem Mass, he uttered blasphemous reproaches: "You
are not . . . No, You cannot be . . . You would not have
taken from me her whom I loved, after having thus
mangled her."[8]

Then came the World War. He was exempt from service
on account of poor health, but went as a doctor of the Red
Cross.[9] Through his friend, André Gide, he was introduced
to a man who changed his whole outlook on life, Dom-
inique-Pierre Dupouey, lieutenant-commander of a bat-
talion of Marines. Ghéon met him only three times, for
Dupouey was killed on the Yser on Holy Saturday, 1915,
but he was vitally affected by the unostentatious sanctity of
the officer. He writes in *Foi en la France*:[10]

> *Ami, vous êtes le reflet*
> *De Dieu dans mon âme terrestre:*
> *Je vous garde, comme un secret*
> *Comme un talisman,*
> *Comme une promesse.*
> *Ce que de vous j'attends*
> *Le sais-je?*
> *Attendrais-je*
> *Si je le savais?*
>
> *Ami, vous êtes mon attente,*
> *Mon recours et ma dernière heure:*
> *Je l'ai trop peu mérité, ce bonheur*
> *Qui m'inquiète et qui me tente;*
> *La pensée du vôtre est douce et mon coeur,*
> *Ami, s'en contente.*
>
> *Ami, le peu que j'ai de foi*
> *Je vous l'offre; priez pour moi.**

---

* Friend, you are the reflection of God in my terrestrial soul: I keep you as a
secret, as a talisman, as a promise. What do I expect from you? Do I know

It is interesting to note that it was this same Gide, himself so far from the truth, who thus urged Ghéon to the final step: "At the point where you are, your hesitation seems unpardonable to me."[11] So the wanderer came back to the fold, and on Christmas, 1915, received Holy Communion once more. Since then, like Claudel, he has been fulfilling a lay apostolate, earnestly defending the faith with dauntless zeal. Unlike his illustrious contemporary, however, who deliberately addresses himself to the élite and delights in abstruse diction difficult to interpret, Ghéon chooses as his audience the people, the Catholic people, whom he wishes to instruct and entertain.

Perhaps it was the fact that he owed his own conversion to the example of a holy man, that determined Ghéon to write attractive and comprehensible lives of the saints, both in the form of biography and of drama. He has given us *Le Saint Curé d'Ars* (1928), *Sainte Thérèse de Lisieux* (1934), and *Saint Jean Bosco* (1935),* all brilliant and appealing studies.[12] The saints in his books are real, living, breathing people, free from the meaningless halo of awesome and even repellent sanctity so commonly found in our hagiographies. He undertook the task with some trepidation: "I was not too sure myself that I would not find the saints rather boring company. . . . They gave me the same sense of wonder and surprise as one of those medleys of people that you get whenever many races mingle."[13] His success has been so marked that Mr. Sheed considers him the greatest living portrait painter of the saints. His intelligent and sympathetic presentation clears away all the misunder-

---

myself? Would I expect it if I knew? Friend, you are my hope, my recourse in my last hour: I have merited it too little, this happiness which disturbs and tempts me. The thought of your happiness is sweet, and my heart, friend, rejoices at it. Friend, the little faith that I have, I offer to you; pray for me.

* These three books have been translated into English under the titles, *The Secret of the Curé of Ars*, *The Secret of the Little Flower*, and *The Secret of St. John Bosco*, respectively.

standing that has blinded us to the fascinating reality of the saints, and makes us see them as their contemporaries saw them, as they actually were.

Ghéon's real field is the drama. First he undertook the *tragédie populaire* in blank verse, in which, without preaching directly, he teaches a lesson through the characters themselves. In *Le Pain* (1912), for example, the hero is a baker who, in spite of the opposition of his miserly wife and her father, gives generously of his bread in time of famine. But he receives only ingratitude from those he tries to benefit. The play is rather too long and overcrowded with lyricism, although it shows definite dramatic ability in the author. Another play of this type is *L'Eau de vie* (unpublished) which portrays a family of peasants to whom drink has brought ruin. One son, the youngest, tries to remedy the evil, but becomes the enemy of his own household and suffers the bitter consequences. In both these early plays there is life and color, deepened by a shade of pessimistic realism.[14]

His next venture was to introduce the saints to the modern world through the drama. He declares that we do not know the saints any more, though a movement for renewal of acquaintance does seem to be on foot. His intention is to "reaccustom the century to the *merveilleux chrétien* as to a reality; to work to render faith more concrete, more familiar, and more intimately blended with our everyday life; finally, to bring back to society these men of yesterday and yore, today saints, who, sharing our condition, our temptations, our weakness, won heaven while on earth and fought the good fight before triumphing."[15] He has exploited Catholic history and legends, and put on the stage SS. Cecilia, Alexis, Francis, Benedict, Scholastica, Martin, Nicholas, Genesius, Thomas, and a host of others.[16] As we said, he wishes to appeal to the people, so his settings are simple, and his favorite actors amateurs, modern *Confrères de la*

Passion. He mingles comedy and tragedy, realism and ideal-ism, backyards and fairyland. His dream is that each parish celebrate the feast of its patron by *un beau miracle* to be given after the liturgical service, in the hall or yard of the church. Thus *La Triomphe de Notre Dame de Chartres* (1927) was played in the open air at Chartres on the sixth of June, our Lady's feast, by the *Compagnons de Notre Dame*. His Eminence, Cardinal Dubois, presided, and the actors opened the performance by the recitation of a *Pater* and an *Ave,* to ask the Blessed Virgin to bless their efforts. *La Rencontre de Saint Benoît et de Sainte Scholastique* (1927) was played by the pupils in the abbey school of Maredsous to honor their patron saint and his twin sister.

Four of the best known of Ghéon's dramas are *La Farce du pendu dépendu* (1921), *Le Comédien et la grâce* (1925), *Aventures de Gilles, ou le Saint malgré lui* (1922), and *La Bergère au pays des loups* (1922). *La Farce du pendu dépendu* is a miracle play in three acts, which was presented for the first time on May 25, 1920, at the Théâtre Balzac in Paris. It is based on a dateless anecdote related in *La Légende dorée,* translated by Wyzewa, and modified somewhat to suit Ghéon's purpose. A father and his son (evidently a moron) are making a pilgrimage to the tomb of St. James at Compostela. They stop at an inn where their host and his wife, moved by cupidity, make them drunk, and during their sleep put into their sack a silver marriage cup. The next morning they are formally accused of theft, and de-clared guilty by the judge, who conveniently happens to be lodging at the same inn. They must turn over all their goods to the innkeeper, and one of them is to be hanged. In spite of the father's protests, the son claims the privilege, so the old man continues on his way to Compostela. On his return a month later, he stops to mourn at the foot of the gibbet where his son is hanging, and, to his amazement, finds him still alive, thanks to St. James, and, moreover, grown wondrous wise. They take down the boy and are about to hang the perfidious innkeeper in his place, but the father and son plead for his life.

Le Comédien et la grâce ("The Comedian") is a more serious drama,[17] which has the same subject as Rotrou's famous *Saint Genest*. It tells how the actor, Genest, at the command of the emperor Diocletian, takes the part of a Christian in a play. He throws himself into his role so completely that he is actually converted and dies a martyr. Ghéon's play is superior to Rotrou's in one point especially. It reveals more perfectly and analyzes more thoroughly the interior sentiments of the hero. We follow Genest step by step from his initial repugnance to play the part of a Christian, counteracted only by a direct command from the emperor, through his professional endeavor to learn more about the Christians and his stubborn resistance to the advice and prayers of his brother Felix, to his final complete and heroic surrender to grace. We must recognize, however, that while this character analysis adds to the psychological interest, it somewhat lessens the dramatic action of the play.

Saint Gilles, the saint in spite of himself, has infinitely more difficulty in persuading the world of his lack of sanctity than Molière's Sganerelle ever had in proving that he was not a doctor. The play contains four main episodes: in the first, Gilles heals a paralytic child bitten by a serpent and frees a woman possessed by a devil; in the second, he assists Bishop Césaire, and works extraordinary cures among his parishioners; in the fourth, he enjoys the solitude of the desert, having for companion only a young doe, "the most adorable of all M. Ghéon's parabolic beasts,"[18] according to Katherine Brégy; but in the end he must return to apostolic labors. The main action of the play revolves around the earnest but hopeless endeavor of Gilles to escape the praise and admiration aroused by his holiness and miracles.

Perhaps the loveliest of Ghéon's miracle plays is *La*

Bergère au pays des loups ("St. Germaine of the Wolf Country"). It is a sacred pastoral, consisting of a prologue, three tableaux, and an epilogue. It relates the story of a poor little shepherdess, Germaine de Pibrac, whose own mother died when she was a baby, and who is left to the mercy of a cruel stepmother and a spineless father, who really loves his daughter, but is afraid to display his affection. There are four first-class miracles in the play, as the *meneur du jeu* announces at the beginning: "Each morning ·she [Germaine] left her flock to go to hear Mass, and yet never did the wolf carry off a lamb during her absence. In order to get to the church, she had to cross a stream, torrential during the time of the great rains: she was seen walking on the waters like the Master whom she loved. Gentle to children and charitable to the poor, she was protected, as was St. Elizabeth of Hungary before her, by the charming miracle of the roses. And when she died, having passed scarcely twenty years on this earth, our Lord sent His angels to conduct her soul to Him."[19] To those who insist that this is entirely too much supernatural intervention in one play, Ghéon points to the miracles which are daily occurrences at Lourdes and like places of pilgrimage. Moreover, says he, the dramatist often chooses as subject exceptional events rather than the banalities of life.

Besides these four, Ghéon has numerous other miracle plays[20] of the same type, though each has its individual charm. There is the delightful *Débat de Nicolazic entre Sainte Anne et le recteur* (1923) which relates the difficulties Nicolazic had in carrying out the orders given him by St. Anne to build a church in her honor. *Les Trois miracles de Sainte Cécile* (1922) shows in scenes of poetic loveliness the virgin martyr's noble life and death, with very little departure from tradition. *Le Miracle de l'enfant bavard* (1925) recounts how a gossipy boy (strange it was not a woman!) had his tongue cut out until he learned to use it only in praise of the Blessed Virgin. *Le Bon voyage, ou le Mort à cheval* (1923) is another story of a pilgrimage to St. James at Compostela in which five men vow to make the journey, but only one is faithful and is rewarded by the Saint accordingly. *Le Dit de l'homme qui aurait vu Saint Nicolas* (1922) is the tale of a man to whom a false and a true St. Nicholas appear, and the false is converted by the true. In *Le Pauvre sous l'escalier* (1920), we learn how St. Alexis, the night before his marriage, abandons his wife to roam the world, a beggar. Years later he returns, and, unknown to his family, lives on charity under the stairs of his own father's house, the constant witness of his poor wife's grief. *Les Trois sagesses du vieux Wang* (1927) is a Chinese drama whose central figure is the heroic Lao Wang, who for love of God pardons his cruel enemy. *La Vie profonde de Saint François d'Assise* ("The Marriage of St. Francis"), *La Triomphe de Saint Thomas d'Aquin, Saint Maurice ou l'obéissance,* and *La Merveilleuse histoire du jeune Bernard de Menthon* ("The Marvelous History of St. Bernard"), all narrate episodes from the lives of the respective saints, in dramas which mingle the most sublime mysticism with astounding but genuine naïveté.

Most of these plays, modeled on the mystery and miracle plays of the twelfth century, are at the same time farces, for Ghéon succeeds admirably in joining mirth to malice, and laughter to tears. He keeps the direct and popular accent of the Middle Ages and of Molière. His aim is to convey to this supremely modern world an echo of those mystic tones of trustful faith that haunted the people of long ago, and that resound so clearly in his ears above the din of the centuries. His plays are best interpreted by the *Compagnons de Notre Dame,* who serve gratuitously, and were founded "for the praise of God and the exaltation of His saints," for they present these moral heroes to us in all their simple grandeur and artless wisdom, encouraged by angels and tempted by devils who appear in the guise of human beings. We all believe that spirits exist and that they take a prominent part in the battle for souls. Why not show them on the stage as actually fulfilling the role that faith ascribes to them? Ghéon laments that so many Catholics relegate them to the sphere of mythology with the fairies, nymphs, satyrs, elfs, and dwarfs of pagan worship.[21]

What shall we say of his style? At times it is delicate, light, and poetic, with a tenuous, elusive charm, as, for instance, in *Les Trois miracles de Sainte Cécile,* that touching tragedy told in strains of lyric beauty. After Cecilia has sent her brother Tiburtius and her husband Valerian to martyrdom, she battles thus in prayer:[22]

> *Mon père, votre nom se fige entre mes lèvres;*
> *Votre règle est de fer, j'en ai le corps brisé.*
> *Ah! que de ma froideur et de ma fermeté*
> *Votre compassion pour un temps me relève.*
>
> *Mes frères sont à vous: que voulez-vous de plus?*
> *Je vous les ai remis et ma besogne est faite:*
> *Permettez-moi, Seigneur, de détourner la tête*
> *Afin de mesurer les biens que j'ai perdus.*
>
> *Seule en face de vous, me faut-il feindre encore?*
> *N'ai-je pas bien celé à vos deux serviteurs*
> *La vérité sur la misère de mon coeur? . . .*
> *Ils sont partis . . . Seigneur, mes larmes me dévorent.*
>
> *Oh! de grâce, daignez desserrer votre main!*
> *Mon coeur contraint pèse à mon flanc comme une pierre*
> *Il veut battre aujourd'hui d'un battement humain,*
> *Il veut faiblir . . . et sa vertu le désespère.*
>
> *Ce n'est pas que j'oublie en quel lieu doit finir*
> *Mon veuvage d'un temps, ni dans quelle allégresse*
> *Mais qu'il est malaisé d'épouser l'avenir*
> *Quand l'horreur du présent de toutes parts vous presse!*
>
> *Seigneur, je reviendrai vous demander secours*
> *Quand le délaissement excédera mon âme . . .*

Écartez-vous de moi, je ne suis qu'une femme
*Qui rappelle à grands cris tout un passé d'amour.**

In *La Triomphe de Notre Dame de Chartres,* the three young girls address to the little wooden statue of Mary, still unknown to them, the following plaintive prayer:

Kind black goddess, O you who have no name, behold us here at your feet without father or mother.

For the wind will not blow any more, the god, brother of the wind, is dead.

For the flowers will not bloom any more, the goddess of the flowers is dead.

For our voices will not sing any more, even the god of song is dead.

The world will not be any more: the god who sustained the world Has followed into the tomb the other gods.

But if you remain, you will take the place of the others.

Black goddess, protect us![23]

At times, Ghéon shows a delightful wit and humor, in which there is often a streak of the *esprit gaulois,* that satirical, mocking, jovial spirit which characterizes French literature from *Le Roman de Renard* to the present day. For example, in *L'Impromptu du charcutier,* after St. Nicholas has

---

* My Father, your name freezes on my lips: Your rule is iron, and I have only a broken body. Ah, from my coldness and hardness, may your compassion lift me for a time.

My brothers belong to you: what more do you wish? I have returned them to you and my work is done; permit me, Lord, one last look, that I may measure the treasures that I have given up.

Alone in front of you must I still dissemble? Have I not carefully concealed from your two servants the truth about the misery of my heart? They have departed . . . Lord, my tears consume me.

O Lord, have mercy, deign to relax your hand! My heavy heart is like a stone within me. It wishes to beat today with a human beat, it wishes to weaken, and its strength torments it.

Not that I have forgotten in what place must end my widowhood of a time, nor in what joy, but it is hard to espouse the future when the horror of the present oppresses you on all sides.

Lord, I will return to ask your succor, when the abandonment is more than I can bear . . . Depart from me, Lord, I am only a woman, who recalls vehemently a whole past of love.

restored to life the three boys ground up in the sausage mill
of Créon, he points to the devil and rebukes Créon:

> Imprudent butcher, for your penance you are going to seize that
> fellow firmly; you are going to throw him into the very jaws of your
> machine, with all your sins, and start the mechanism. I warn you
> that nothing edible will come out of it, and that your instrument
> will become worthless. But so much the better. I forbid you to buy
> another. This is the price of your pardon.[24]

In *La Vie profonde de Saint François,* when the wood-
pecker declares that birds cannot talk to men, an old crow
replies:

> I beg your pardon. The uncle of the great-grandfather of my
> parents' great-great-grandfather used to tell (it's my parents who told
> me) that in the days of the great-great-uncle of the great-great-grand-
> father of his parents' great-great-grandfather (it was they who told
> him) all the birds used to talk with men, even birds of prey. And
> when I say with "men" I mean with the man, for there was only one
> then, who lived with his wife and was king on land and sea.[25]

In *Le Grand combat entre l'ermite et le dragon,* the holy
hermit Armel comes to chide the dragon, who has eaten a
number of people.

> St. Armel: Sir Dragon, I am sorry to disturb you, but all my
> time is taken; I must settle this affair on my way.
> Dragon: What affair? What affair?
> St. Armel: You are not behaving yourself well.
> Dragon: That is my business. I have a right to all the spoiled
> meat. I devour sinners. The good God has no reason to complain.
> St. Armel: Yes, He has. He wants to save them.
> Dragon: So much the worse for them! I will not give them up.
> You have finished your sermon, holy man?
> St. Armel: It has done no good, I see?
> Dragon: None.
> St. Armel: Then it will be necessary to settle our affair other-
> wise. Sir Dragon, I challenge you.
> Dragon: The deuce! An affair of honor! I do not know what
> you are talking about. I have no honor.

St. Armel: Then I will be forced to kill you in your lair. I would have preferred a loyal combat.

Dragon: You cannot kill me.

St. Armel: You know nothing about it.

Dragon: Since St. George and St. Michael, no one has been found with strength! Keep away, Your Reverence. With all your abbey, esteem yourself fortunate that I allow you to depart. Mou . . . Mou . . .[26]

Thus his style is always suited to the subject. It may even seem loose and careless at times, but that is exactly what we should expect when humble folks are talking. If little Brother Genièvre cuts off the leg of a poor peasant's pig to satisfy the hunger of his sick brother Lucide,[27] who would ask him to explain in polished phrases? Ghéon is also condemned for lack of psychology, but when we remember that he wrote about saints who glory in being fools for Christ, and who often defy all psychological analysis, we are inclined to grant that the difficulty lies more in the subject matter than in the writer. Again, critics reproach him for his verbosity and lengthy discourses. In *Saint Maurice ou l'obéissance*, Maurice makes an address of twelve hundred words to his soldiers to persuade them to die as Christians without resistance to the unjust order of the Emperor Maximian. A long speech for a drama, no doubt, but necessary to show the power of the saintly leader over his six thousand men, who, rebellious at first, accept with resignation and finally with joy the prospect of martyrdom which awaits them. Sometimes there is humor in this prolixity. For example, in *La Farce du pendu dépendu*, the judgment scene could be condensed to a few lines, but the laughter aroused by the pretended sagacity of the pompous judge and garrulous gendarme (alias lawyer) would have to be sacrificed.

The popularity of his plays and the unexpected welcome they received in theaters, colleges, and open-air performances are the greatest proof of their success. Jacques Maritain shows how they combine the elements of the early

Greek tragedy with the liturgical Christian drama and the medieval allegory.[28] The secret of Ghéon's genius lies in his familiarity with the supernatural, and his ability to present it to us in a pleasing manner. This gift, combined with his ingenuous simplicity, superb imagination, freedom from rhetoric, and vividness of characterization, makes him stand out, original and alone. Father Martindale's remark about *La Vie profonde de Saint François* applies in a manner to all Ghéon's religious dramas: "Provided that the play be acted without the remotest suspicion of sentimentality, of pomposity, of pseudo-mysticism, of pose (ecclesiastical, or of the stage), it must admit us to some at least of the profundity of the fathomless life of St. Francis."[29] And Praviel sums up his influence thus: "This primitive has returned to us our primitive mentality of the time before the epoch of false elegances, borrowed graces and literary ruses."[30]

PRINCIPAL WORKS OF HENRI GHÉON

1897   *Chansons d'aube*
1906   *Algérie*
1911   *Nos Directions*
1912   *Le Pain*
1916   *Foi en la France*
1919   *L'Homme né de la guerre*
1920   *Le Miroir de Jésus*
1920   *Le Pauvre sous l'escalier*
1921   *La Farce du pendu dépendu*
1922   *Le Dit de l'homme qui aurait vu Saint Nicolas*
1922   *La Bergère au pays des loups*
1922   *Les Trois miracles de Sainte Cécile*
1922   *Aventures de Gilles, ou le Saint malgré lui*
1923   *Le Bon voyage, ou le Mort à cheval*
1923   *Le Débat de Nicolazic entre Sainte Anne et le recteur*
1923   *Saint Maurice ou l'obéissance*
1924   *Jeux et miracles pour le peuple fidèle*
1924   *Partis pris*
1925   *Le Comédien et la grâce*

1925 *Le Miracle de l'enfant bavard*
1925 *Triomphe de Saint Thomas d'Aquin*
1926 *L'Impromptu du charcutier*
1926 *La Joyeuse farce des "Encore"*
1926 *La Merveilleuse histoire du jeune Bernard de Menthon*
1926 *La Vie profonde de Saint François d'Assise*
1926 *Les Propos interrompus*
1927 *Les Contes de Perrault en action*
1927 *Triomphe de Notre Dame de Chartres*
1927 *Les Trois sagesses du vieux Wang*
1927 *La Rencontre de Saint Benoît et de Sainte Scholastique*
1928 *Le Saint Curé d'Ars*
1929 *Les Jeux de l'enfer et du ciel*
1930 *La Vieille dame des rues*
1931 *Sainte Anne d'Auray*
1931 *Sainte Marguerite-Marie*
1932 *Promenades avec Mozart, l'homme, l'oeuvre, le pays*
1934 *Sainte Thérèse de Lisieux*
1935 *Féeries*
1935 *Saint Jean Bosco*
1936 *Chants de la vie et de la foi*

REFERENCES

Bateman, May, "Henri Ghéon," *Fortnightly Review*, CXXV (1929), pp. 234–248.

—— "Henri Ghéon," *Dublin Review*, CLXXX (1927), pp. 73–86.

Brégy, Katherine, "Concerning Henri Ghéon," *Catholic World*, CXXX (1929), pp. 1–13.

Gide, André, "Le Lieutenant de vaisseau, P. Dupouey, avec des lettres de H. Ghéon," *Correspondant*, CCLXXV (1919), pp. 820–834.

Parvillez, Alphonse de, "La Diligence qui porte des âmes," *Études religieuses*, CCI (1929), pp. 718–733.

Praviel, Armand, "Un Primitif de France, M. Henri Ghéon," *Correspondant*, CCXCVII (1924), pp. 181–195.

CHAPTER XVI

Women Writers

THE HISTORY OF FRENCH LITERATURE HAS
presented during every century some noted women writers,
from Marie de France and Christine de Pisan of the Middle
Ages down to the Comtesse de Noailles and Colette of our
own day. Their particular fields seem to have always been
poetry and the novel. Braunschvig explains this fact by
showing that these two forms lend themselves best to the
expression of personal sentiments, and, as women are inclined to be subjective and like to recount themselves, they
are not attracted to the drama, which requires a certain
objectivity and effacement of the author behind his characters, nor to history, criticism, or philosophy, which call
for abstract thinking and detachment from self.[1]

There are a number of Catholic women who deserve
mention in the literary history of the present day. We shall
give a brief account of the work of five who have attracted
special attention among littérateurs: Henriette Charasson,
Marie Noël, Jean Balde, Colette Yver, and Geneviève
Duhamelet.

HENRIETTE CHARASSON (*1890–   *)

Henriette Charasson (Mme René Johannet) is probably
best known in the literary world as a poet though she has
written several works of criticism (*Jules Tellier*, 1922, *La
Littérature féminine*, 1923, *M. de Porto-Riche ou le "Racine
Juif,"* 1925), two books on feminism (*Faut-il supprimer le
gynécée?*, 1924, and *La Mère*, 1931), a few comedies, of which
the best known is *Le Saut du diable*, 1931, a biography,
Soeur Claire de Jésus, religieuse Bénédictine, 1930, the story

of a little boy, *Grigri,* 1923, and numerous articles in periodicals.

She tells us that her main purpose in writing is "to show foreigners that all French women are not hoydens, Thérèse Desqueyroux's, or Albertines dear to Proust. I believe that I express with my soul the soul of the greater part of the French bourgeoise, who are the true French women."² She leaves no doubt in the mind of her reader about her opinion with regard to the education of girls and the duties of a wife and mother: "Lead the married woman to recognize that she is made above all to have children and to raise them, so as to render agreeable to her husband this home where maternity and her role of educator confine her."³ She insists on this: "I have already said it and I repeat it, one fact dominates and orients the whole problem of féminism, *maternity.*"⁴ She dreads to see the day when "all the women would wish to play the man, taking as ideal the existence of man,"⁵ for she knows that then they will lose their own characteristic charm and barter their subtle civilizing influence. She warns the young bride that married life is not a continuous honeymoon, and that with the joys and compensations, she should be willing to expect the burdens and trials: "Little lady, you will disembark as others, and then you will no longer find at your arm a prince of dreams and legends, but *a man,* made like you, of matter. . . ."⁶ Her ideas may seem old fashioned to many of the younger generation, but she is simply expressing sound Catholic traditions with regard to woman's rights and duties.

Her poems voice the same sentiments as her prose, though in a less direct and definite manner. She has published four volumes: *Attente* (1919), *Les Heures du foyer* (1926), *Deux petits hommes et leur mère* (1928), and *Mon Seigneur et mon Dieu* (1934). *Attente* is a collection of poems dedicated to her brother Cam, who fought in the World War, and on September 28, 1915, was reported missing. They are some of the most beautiful poems that the War inspired, though they are not, strictly speaking, *war poems* as they do not sing battles or victories but simply depict the author's grief over the absence of one she loves. They reflect the doubt and despair that ravaged her mind and have been aptly called "a little collection of sobs mingled with hope."[7] She had lost her faith when she was about eighteen years old and did not regain it until some fourteen years later. She prays in the opening poem:[8]

> *O mon Dieu, si vous existez au fond de votre ciel,*
> *Au fond de votre ciel si noir où descend seulement ce soir un*
> *croissant de lune pâle,*
> *Est-ce que vous n'entendez pas la triste clameur qui monte de*
> *votre terre ravagée?**

Les Heures du foyer which was awarded the Prix de littérature spiritualiste and the Médaille de l'union féminine et sociale is dedicated to her husband and to her three little boys, and celebrates her conjugal happiness. Her first-born child, Claude, had died and she wrote a touching *Dialogue de la mère et du petit enfant mort:*[9]

> *Est-ce que tu joues, mon enfant, toi qui n'as pas joué sur terre?*
> *Est-ce que tu ris, toi dont je ne connais pas la douce petite*
> *cascade?*
> *Te berce-t-on parfois? as-tu grandi? es-tu toujours cette blanch-*
> *eur sans voix et sans pensée qu'on m'a ravie?*
> *Joues-tu parfois avec l'Enfant Jésus de Prague, et vous relancez-*
> *vous gaiement sa boule qui est un Monde?*
> *M'entends-tu, comprends-tu que je m'adresse à toi?***

---

* O my God, if You exist in the depths of Your sky, in the depths of Your sky so dark, where this evening only the crescent of the pale moon goes down, do You not hear the sad clamor which arises from Your ravaged earth?

** Do you play, my child, you who did not play while on earth? Do you laugh, you whose sweet little ripple I do not know? Do they rock you sometimes? Have you grown? Are you still that pale silent form that they took away from me? Do you play sometimes with the Infant Jesus of Prague, and do you gaily throw back to Him His ball which is a world? Do you hear me, do you understand that I am speaking to you?

In some of the poems of this volume, the author introduces rhyme, as, for instance, in the following:[10]

> *Mon Dieu m'a dit, mon Dieu m'a dit:*
> *— Tu ne sais que faire de ta peine?*
> *Offre-la-moi.*
> *J'étais seule, j'étais triste, je marchais*
> *lentement dans le jardin autour*
> *de la fontaine,*
> *Portant ma croix.**

The whole tone of *Les Heures du foyer* is different from *Attente,* for in it we have the devout Catholic, expressing her trust in God, resignation to His will and joy in His service. It seems to be a diary of a happy wife and mother, who makes note of her daily emotions and sentiments and later converts them into prayers. Paul Fierens, in his review, concludes with the words: "Pity the man who will read this book without being filled with a greater love for his mother, his wife, his children, his very life."[11]

Deux petits hommes et leur mère is dedicated to her boys, to gentle Antoine and ardent José, and most of the poems are about them, although in some she writes of her husband, and in many of God. She tells us about her babies' eyes, their hands, their sandals, their kisses, their play, and their sleep. Antoine, whom she calls *ma douceur,* is chubby and sweet, a dreamer with poetic instincts; José is more fragile, but active and impulsive, inclined to *boss* his elder brother, and she calls him *ma colère.* She loves them both passionately and she expresses her love with an art, which according to Jean Charpentier, excels in revealing the secrets of the heart without sacrificing spontaneity.[12] In the first poem of the volume entitled *J'écris afin que vous sachiez,* she says that others leave their heirs beautiful castles, old gardens, val-

---

* My God said to me, my God said to me: You do not know what to do with your pain? Offer it to Me. I was alone, I was sad, I was walking slowly in the garden around the fountain, carrying My cross.

uable papers, precious jewels, shining gold, a boasted name, a proud title; she cannot leave such things to her children, but she writes in order that, if she should die before they grow up, they may know how much she loved them. The second part of the book, *Images de piété,* contains poems to the Blessed Virgin, the Stations of the Cross, reflections on Lent and on death. André Fontainas remarks, in speaking of the volume, that "her sincerity, her delicacy of feeling, and the suppleness of her talent, are beyond question."[13]

Her latest volume, *Mon Seigneur et mon Dieu,* which André Thérive hailed in *Le Temps* as an original and beautiful book, is, as the title indicates, a collection of prayers. Six thousand five hundred copies of it were sold within two months of its publication. Quite a record for a volume of religious poetry! Sometimes the author expresses herself in a few, brief, well-chosen words, as:[14]

> *Deux morceaux de bois cloués en haut d'une colline,*
> *   C'est tout et c'est la Croix.*
> *Regarde quelle ombre gigantesque font sur le monde qu'elle*
> *   domine*
> *   Ses deux bras où pend le Roi.**

Again she is more effusive, and we have the long poem entitled *Vacances de Pâques,*[15] which begins:

> *La nuit est tombée, les visiteurs sont partis, la campagne noire*
> *   regarde à la fenêtre.*
> *Seul dans la cuisine, près du fourneau je veille le dîner, la soupe*
> *   bout à petit bruit.*
> *Et tout à coup, dans mon travail de ménagère, une grande paix*
> *   m'envahit.*
> *Et c'est une telle détente que ma pensée naturellement jaillit vers*
> *   vous et vous rejoint, mon Maître!***

---

* Two pieces of wood nailed together at the top of a hill, that is all and that is the Cross. See what a gigantic shadow is made on the world that it dominates by its two arms where hangs the King.

** Night has fallen, the visitors have departed, the dark country is looking in

Henriette Charasson's poetry is characterized by its sincerity, simplicity, and spontaneity. She relates the happenings of daily life, tells her experiences as a mother and prays to God for the things for which all women pray, but she clothes these commonplace acts with poetic sentiments and sings them in lyric notes. Still there is no pose nor affectation. As Jean Larnac says: "Often she approaches banal naïveté, but she never falls into it: the delicacy of her smile charms us; the aristocratic finesse of her sentiments moves us."[16] Charles Le Goffic calls her a *racinienne née.*[17]

In her verse form she follows Paul Claudel, writing in *versets,* in some using neither rhythm, assonance, nor rhyme, and in others, rhyme but no regular meter. The rhythm seems to follow her mood, feeling, and emotion, and, as she possesses real poetic instinct, she has attained success. At the end of the poem she often returns to the same motif with which she opened it. Her language and syntax are more simple than those of her great master, and there is in them a feminine grace. Vallery-Radot says: "These poems have the silence of the countryside and the odor of stone and holy water of country churches; they seem to come from a little swallow's nest, hidden with love in the great belfry of the Claudelian cathedral."[18]

MARIE NOËL (*1883–*   )

Marie Noël (Mlle Rouget) has given us only three small volumes of poetry, *Les Chansons et les heures* (1920), *Chants de la merci* (1930), and *Le Rosaire des joies* (1930), but in them she displays real talent. André Billy remarks that "she does not imitate anyone, which is, you will agree, a rare merit."[19]

---

through the window. Alone in the kitchen near the stove I am watching the dinner, the soup boils with a little noise. And suddenly, in the midst of my household duties, a great peace fills me. It is such a great calm that my thoughts naturally turn toward You and are united to You, my Master!

The opposing influences of her gentle pious mother and her stern Jansenistic father are seen in her work, which is marked by sweetness and simplicity but also by virile strength. She has lived a very quiet, retired life at her home in Auxerre on the Yonne, teaching catechism to the children, rarely going to Paris, shunning publicity, and even refusing to allow Lucien Descaves to have her photograph for the paper.[20] But, hidden away in the quaint old home behind the great cathedral, she has dreamed her dreams and sung her songs more for God's ear than for man's. Unlike so many other poets, she tells us little about herself in her verses, and we find few personal confessions in them. She has never married, though she has written some exquisite love songs. In one of them she sighs:[21]

> Mon bien-aimé passe voilé de rêverie,
> L'âme ailleurs
> Sans me rien dire, hélas; sans me voir
> Et j'en meure.*

Again, in a gayer mood, she writes the round:[22]

> Mon père veut me marier,
> Sauvons-nous, sauvons-nous par les bois et la plaine,
> Mon père veut me marier,
> Petit oiseau, tout vif te laisseras-tu lier?**

Les Chansons et les heures (1920) is a book of poems, most of which were written before the World War, and which express her own sentiments and those of her fellow-sufferers of that heroic generation. Victor Giraud says of it: "She makes herself the echo of their intimate aspirations, of their disappointed dreams, of their secret lamentations, of their silent resignation, of their manly and religious ac-

---

* My beloved passes wrapped in reverie, his mind elsewhere, without saying anything to me, alas! without seeing me, and it is killing me.

** My father wishes to marry me, let us run away, let us run away through the woods and the plain, My father wishes to marry me, little bird, full of life, will you let yourself be caught?

ceptation. And she does it in such a manner, with so much sincerity, depth and art, that no one, it seems to me, will open her collection without feeling himself in the presence of a true poet."[23] The book went through three editions (1920, 1928, and 1930). Raymond Escholier called it an *enchantment,* and its author a *genius.*[24] The French Academy awarded her part of the Archon Despérouses prize (1923), and through the influence of Mme Gerard d'Houville and Henri de Régnier, she received the José Maria de Hérédia prize in 1929.

Her next volume, *Les Chants de la merci,* appeared in 1930. In the foreword Mlle Noël says: "To the friends of my first book, I give this second, and I apologize for it. It is not of much value for them or for me. They will find in it less of poetry than of eloquence, of dreams than of reality; more of virtue than of charm, nothing or little of what they desire." She goes on to explain that these poems are written for the poor, for whom she is filled with compassion and love, as many of the titles indicate: *Prière pour toutes sortes de nécessités, Souci, Bataille, Chant de la compassion, Pleurs sur la foule,* etc. She makes herself one with the sufferers, for she says:[25]

> *Je suis*
> *Celle blessée entre toutes qui pleure.*
> *Et je serai les pauvres tout à l'heure.**

Le Rosaire des joies is a collection of poems on the joyful mysteries of the rosary, as the title indicates. One of the most beautiful is the long poem *Annonciation,*[26] which begins:

> *La Vierge Marie est dans sa maison.*
> *Son petit jardin par la porte ouverte*
> *Respire. Une abeille entre. La saison*
> *Qui vient de très loin n'est pas encor verte.*

---

*I am the wounded one weeping among all others who weep. And I will be one with the poor by and by.

L'air joue au soleil avec un fétu.
Je me suis assise à ton seuil, Marie,
Sur la marche tiède. . . . O ma soeur, sais-tu
Si la fleur de Pâque est tantôt fleurie?

Marie Noël's poetry is impregnated with the supernatural, and it has an other-worldliness about it that reminds one of the Spouse in the Canticle of Canticles. Robert Honnert says: "As one feels Mme Delarue-Mardrus, in spite of the aspirations of her soul, solidly anchored in the world of appearances, so Mme Marie Noël moves with ease in the world of faith and in mysteries."[27] She is essentially religious, even in her poems on profane subjects, but in her hymns and canticles she often reaches the sublime. Her gift of picturesque and original expression lends a charm to verses that might otherwise be trite and commonplace, as, for instance, the one[28] in which she reminds God that He created

*Le bleu de Votre ciel, cette inutile chose.***

She writes in regular verse that seems to reflect her thoughts, and the rhythm and rhyme flow on without effort, quite spontaneously. Lucien Descaves says that her poetry is that which Barbey d'Aurevilly has defined as *la poésie du cri.*[29] She herself tells how she writes:[30]

Les chansons que je fais, qu'est-ce qui les a faites?
Souvent il m'en arrive une au plus noir du moi . . .
Je ne sais pas comment, je ne sais pas pourquoi,
C'est cette folle au lieu de cent que je souhaite.

Dites-moi . . . Mes chansons de toutes les couleurs,
Où mon esprit qui muse au vent les a-t-il prises?

---

* The Virgin Mary is in her house. Her little garden breathes its fragrance through the open door. A bee enters. The season which comes from far away is not yet green. The wind plays in the sun with a straw. I am seated on your door sill, Mary, on the warm step. . . . O my sister, do you know whether the Easter flower will be blooming soon?

**The blue of Your sky, that useless thing.

Le chant leur vient — d'où donc? — comme le rose aux fleurs,
Comme le vert à l'herbe et le rouge aux cerises.

. . . .

Et quand je ne sais plus, j'attends que Dieu me souffle.*

JEAN BALDE (*1885–*   )

Mlle Jeanne Alleman, poet and novelist, was born at Bordeaux of an old Girondin family. It was from her great-uncle, Jean François Bladé, who collected the *Contes et poésies populaires de la Gascogne,* that she took her pen name.[31] Her first publication was a volume of poetry, *Âmes d'artistes* (1908), and it, as well as a later one, *Mausolées* (1916), was awarded the Prix Arachon. She has also written a few biographies (*Madame Elizabeth,* 1935, *Les Dames de la miséricorde,* 1932, etc.), but it is her novels that have brought her fame.

Her first attempt, *Les Ébauches* (1910), is the story of a young Catholic of Bordeaux, who comes to Paris with high hopes in 1840, but is quickly disappointed and disillusioned. He returns to the province a few years later, and there in *la terre* finds the real meaning of life. *Les Liens* (1920) portrays the unselfish motherly devotion of an elder sister to her younger brother, who shows scant gratitude. *La Vigne et la maison* (1921) is an interesting study of provincial life in the Gironde. *La Survivante* (1923) relates how a young widow, Elizabeth Borderie, consecrates her life to the glory of her dead husband, an artist, and refuses the love of Lucien Portets, who would persuade her to rebuild her happiness with him.

---

* The songs that I write, who has written them? Often they come when I least expect them . . . I do not know how, I do not know why, it is this foolish fancy instead of the hundred others that I am wishing for. Tell me . . . my songs of all colors, where my mind musing in the wind, has caught them? Melody comes to them — whence then — as the pink to the flowers, as the green to the grass and the red to the cherries . . . and when I no longer know what to write, I wait until I hear God's whisper.

Le Goëland (1926) is considered by many to be Jean Balde's masterpiece. The theme is the loneliness of an adolescent, over whom hangs the cloud of a secret that no one will explain. He lives at Arès with the fisherman Picquey and his wife, and his most sympathetic companion is Estelle, their little daughter. A beautiful, nameless woman comes to see him occasionally, but, though she shows him great affection, she refuses to answer his questions. His uneasiness and anguish increase until she takes him to Bordeaux to live apart from her in a little room by himself. The climax is reached when she meets him one day in the city, and turns away without any sign of recognition. Then he realizes his solitude, that he is an outcast from society, a bastard. His grief turns into anger and hatred, and he flees from this woman who has not the courage to acknowledge him in spite of her evident love. He goes back to Arès, marries Estelle, and finds in humble labor an emancipation. Later on he has one more fleeting glimpse of his mother in a street car, and from the sorrow written on her face he realizes that she is paying the penalty of her sin.

None of Jean Balde's more recent works surpass *Le Goëland* in psychological analysis, delineation of character, or power of description, though *Reine d'Arbieux* (1928) is an excellent study of an ardent, sensitive young girl, and it brought its author the Prix du Roman of the French Academy. Reine is an orphan who lives with a selfish aunt. She loves Régis Lavazan, but he is poor and goes off to Senegal to seek his fortune. Encouraged by her relatives, she marries the rich Germain Sourbets, who loves her with an impetuous, passionate, jealous love. She meets Adrian Bernos, whose father had been ruined by Germain's father, and who determines to avenge himself on Germain through his wife. He succeeds in winning Reine's confidence and almost persuades her to embark with him for Casablanca. But she suddenly realizes what type of man he is, and in what a dangerous and unworthy position she has placed herself. She bravely retraces her steps, physically and morally, and in the end regains her husband's love and her own happiness.

La Maison Marbuzet (1934) gives us a vivid picture of Berthe Marbuzet, the antique dealer, of Line Vairon, her wily clerk, and of Gilbert, her gullible secretary. The author tells us: "La Maison Marbuzet completes the cycle of my Girondin studies. In La Vigne et la maison I have written of the anguish of the earth and the courage of the vine-dresser; Le Goéland is the novel of the sea; La Touffe de gui, that of feminine solitude. La Maison Marbuzet opposes in the incomparable scenery of a palace erected at Bordeaux by Gabriel, the world of the brocante with its traditional bourgeois salons. Two epochs, that of bric-a-brac and that of sports."[32]

Jean Larnac calls Jean Balde a "Catholic George Sand,"[33] because she is a regional novelist who has upheld the love of moral traditions and of her native country, and because of the moderation, delicacy, and clearness of her style. She likes to use bourgeois settings, and she has given us some delightfully true pictures of the Gascon peasants. We are told that before writing Le Goéland, she spent a year living in Arès with the fishermen and the oyster catchers in the basin of Arachon.

Her books remind us somewhat of those of Henry Bordeaux, as they glorify the family without slighting the rights of the individual. Henri Pourrat says: "It seems indeed that the dominant feature of her talent as a novelist is the double faculty that she has of conceiving all things under the angle of the family and yet of going profoundly into the analysis of the individual soul, fatally condemned to a more or less great solitude."[34] Again, her novels are honnête, like Bordeaux's, and usually contain a certain amount of moralizing. In the best ones, the thesis, though ever present, is concealed

in the folds of the story, and is absorbed almost unconsciously by the reader. In others, however, it is thrust upon
him directly, and impairs the novel from the artistic point
of view. For example, *La Pylône et la maison* (1936), her
most recent work, is an indignant protest against the modern
vandals, who, with no eye for beauty and no regard for sentiment, do not hesitate to ruin beautiful private estates, by
erecting upon them ugly structures that serve for modern
convenience. This is supposed to be a long short story, but
so eager is the author to convince her readers, that she practically forgets plot and characters, and appeals directly to
them to prevent such absurd and unjust depredation, done
in the name of public utility.

Sometimes Mlle Balde's characters are rather colorless,
tiresome people, but more often they are the results of her
penetrating observation and keen analysis, and are painted
with a strong and sure hand. Women usually hold the important place and are the guiding force of the story (Elizabeth in *La Survivante*, Cécile in *Les Liens*, Reine in *Reine
d'Arbieux*, etc.). Her style is pleasing and harmonious, com-
bining masculine vigor with womanly grace. François
Mauriac says that "her prose is that of a poet."[35]

COLETTE YVER (*1874-*   )

Colette Yver (Mme Huzzard, née Antoinette Bergevin)
is a native of Segré (Maine-et-Loire). She began by writing
stories for children and then turned to social novels, which
are an exposition of the rights and duties of women. Her
first great success, *Princesses de science* ("The Doctor's
Wife") of 1907, is typical. Thérèse Herlinge, an attractive
young *doctoresse,* is loved by Dr. Fernand Guémené. He
asks her to marry him, at the same time sacrificing her professional studies for his sake. She refuses at first, but later
accepts his proposal, made this time without conditions. For

a while all goes well and they seem happy, she preparing
for her thesis, and he studying cancer and tending to his
patients. But soon they realize how far apart they really are,
and how little their house resembles a true home. Then
their first child dies, owing to the fact that the mother will
not nurse it herself, but leaves it in the hands of a careless
maid. Fernand seeks sympathy from a widow, Mme Jourdeaux, and by degrees falls in love with her. Thérèse finally
sees that their happiness is all but lost, and gives up her
profession to win it back. Mme Yver is persuaded that
woman is made for the home: "It is just that woman
abandons herself entirely to her sovereign function, which
is to live for her husband, for her children."[36] She believes
in the equality of husband and wife, but not in their simili-
tude, as man and woman are essentially different. Fernand
says to Thérèse: "The intellectual equality which will be
between us seems to me to constitute the best element of our
happiness. I like your luminous thought and I am proud of
it, but I claim to enjoy it alone."[37]

Les Dames du palais ("Love vs. Law"), published in
1910, is an analogous story, but the heroine this time is an
avocate. Henriette Marcadieu attains greater success in her
profession than her husband, André Vélines, who is also a
lawyer. She, too, is only able to save their happiness by sacrificing her ambition and accepting the role of secretary to her
husband, demonstrating once more that a married woman's
first duty is in the home. Mme Colette Yver has never re-
tracted these opinions expressed in her early works. She
reiterated them distinctly in 1920 in a book entitled *Dans
le jardin de féminisme,* a study of the duties of wives, and
again in 1929 in *Femmes d'aujourd'hui,* which contains
chapters on women as doctors, lawyers, dentists, chemists,
etc. She writes: "Even if, when she marries, a woman gives
up her position — and God knows how jealous the man is to
obtain this sacrifice — she is often, nevertheless, to her hus-

band a companion more informed and erudite than he is, and one who will judge him without ceasing, instead of admiring him. More than once, he will be lonesome for feminine ignorance."[38] It requires no little courage and independence in this progressive age to express so boldly ideas which undoubtedly seem exaggerated and antiquated to many readers.

Not all of Colette Yver's novels develop this theme, though most of them give the important place to women. In *Les Sables mouvants* (1913), Jeanne de Cléden is an exquisite young girl who struggles, suffers, and prays to retain the love of her adored artist-husband, though she realizes that he is not worthy of her and is even betraying her. *Le Mystère des béatitudes* (1916) also presents the picture of a saint, Abbé Naïm, the converted Jew who becomes a second Curé d'Ars. Both of these novels, however, lose some of their force because of the dualism and lack of unity in the plot. Each would make two separate stories and gain by the division. *Mammon* (1933) shows the evil effects of greed for money, a vice which taints practically everyone in the novel excepting the pure, innocent Marie du Cloiseau. In *Vincent ou la solitude* (1931) the main character is a man, but he draws his inspiration for his courage and heroism from Denise, the charming intern, whom he can never marry because he is tubercular.

In some of her recent books, we find a rather different attitude. *Le Vote des femmes* (1932), which is a romance in spite of its title, shows us Odile loved by three men: Bernard, a Catholic with high ideals, Hubert, an atheist but upright and generous, and Ignace, a voluptuary with a shady past. Against her reason and better judgment, she allows herself to be dominated by her passion for Ignace, which is stronger than her admiration and respect for the other two. *Les Deux cahiers de Pauline* (1935) is the story of the divorced Beatrice and Jacques told by their daughter. The first notebook presents Jacques as his wife and her family saw him, a tyrant full of faults. The second shows him as he really was, good-hearted but misunderstood. The book is well written, and, as the reader sees Pauline sit in judgment on her parents, and condemn first her father and then her mother, he is convinced of the evil of divorce. *Mirabelle de Pampelune* ("Mirabelle of Pampeluna") and *Cher coeur humain* (1932) are two volumes of short stories written by Colette Yver, but they have added little to her reputation.

In most of her books, Mme Yver presents two types of women, the modern intellectual type who emulate men and in so doing forget their duties as wives and mothers, and the other class, who are intelligent, educated, and well prepared for life, but at the same time full of devotion to home and family, and unwilling to sacrifice one iota of their feminine grace. There are many examples of these ideal women in her novels, and they are withal eminently human and lovable (Denise, Jeanne Cléden, Marie du Cloiseau, Olive de Charlemart, Dina Skaroff, etc.). Her psychology is true if not very deep, and her characters living and well-defined. Mme Yver is full of good sense, and one of her striking characteristics is her tact in smoothing out difficult situations. There are dramatic scenes in every one of her novels, as, for example, the tragic death of Jean Solème at Monte Carlo in *Le Mystère des béatitudes,* the return of the mutilated lover in *Mirabelle de Pampelune,* the meeting of Thérèse and Mme Jourdeaux in *Princesses de science.* Her style is clear and strong with an occasional touch of irony. Jean Charpentier, in speaking of *Mammon,* says that the shades are delicate and the scenes developed to perfection.[39] Her principal faults seem to be a fondness for long sentences and a lack of unity in construction.

She has evident talent which she is using to create ideals for the women of the present generation in a pleasing, attractive manner. Nevertheless, many of her novels, supposedly Catholic, lack the supernatural element which one would expect to find in them. In 1913 Louis de Mandadon reproached her for this: "There is a void in her work. The religious element is absent. . . . From the homes that Mme Colette has placed before our eyes . . . God has departed. We await pictures more real where He will be."[40] Some of these pictures she has since given us, so that this criticism is not as true now as it was when it was written. In *Le Mystère des béatitudes, Mammon, Vincent ou la solitude* Mme Yver has introduced a more genuinely Catholic atmosphere. The void that Mandadon found in 1913 has been partially filled also by her recent biographies of saintly French women (*L'Humble Sainte Bernadette*, 1934, *La Vie secrète de Cathérine Labouré*, 1935, *Histoire de Jeanne d'Arc*, 1936) and by a book entitled *La Femme et l'église* (1935), an orderly, convincing, well-written synthesis of what the Catholic Church has done for women down through the centuries.

GENEVIÈVE DUHAMELET (*1890–*   )

Another Catholic woman writer worthy of mention, though younger and less well known than Jean Balde and Colette Yver, is Geneviève Duhamelet. She has won her reputation by her novels, though she has published a volume of poems (*Pour l'amour de l'amour*, 1923, awarded the Jacques Normand prize), several biographies, and many short stories and plays for children.

She drew the material for her novels from her own experience, and most of them are either war stories (she served as a Red Cross nurse) or stories for children (she is a teacher). *Ces Dames de l'Hôpital 336* (1917) gives an account of the organization of a hospital unit during the World War, and *Les Inépousées* (1919) relates the lives of some young girls whose chances for marriage were ruined in

1914, when all the handsome French lads turned soldiers. Perhaps her best known book is *Rue du chien qui pêche* (1924), which was crowned by the French Academy and by the Academy de l'Humeur Français. It and its sequel, *Rue du chien qui pêche prolongée* (1931), are a collection of incidents, sad and joyful, that make up the life of a teacher in a French school in a district where most of the children live on the street. In *L'Espace d'un matin* (1929), the hero is a little nine-year-old boy, and *Tout feu, toute flamme* (1930) treats of the summer vacation of a little girl.

Mlle Duhamelet's style is simple and unadorned, her stories are interesting and uplifting, full of kindly sympathy and gentle humor. Without seeming didactic she teaches many a lesson in her own charming, pleasant way. It is evident that she is a great lover of children, for most of her books are either about them or for them. Alphonse de Parvillez, in his review of her volume of short stories entitled *La Dépossédée,* says: "Her stories have the tender grace of the best pages of Alphonse Daudet, while they avoid his sentimentality and affected style."[41]

PRINCIPAL WORKS OF AUTHORS

HENRIETTE CHARASSON

1919   *Attente*
1922   *Jules Tellier*
1923   *La Littérature féminine*
1923   *Grigri*
1924   *Faut-il supprimer le gynécée?*
1925   *M. de Porto-Riche ou le "Racine Juif"*
1926   *Les Heures du foyer*
1928   *Deux petits hommes et leur mère*
1930   *Soeur Claire de Jésus, religieuse Bénédictine*
1931   *La Mère*
1931   *Le Saut du diable*
1934   *Mon Seigneur et mon Dieu*

MARIE NÖEL

1920 *Les Chansons et les heures*
1930 *Les Chants de la merci*
1930 *Le Rosaire des joies*

JEAN BALDE

1908 *Âmes d'artistes*
1910 *Les Ébauches*
1916 *Mausolées*
1920 *Les Liens*
1921 *La Vigne et la maison*
1923 *La Survivante*
1926 *Le Goëland*
1928 *Reine d'Arbieux*
1930 *Un d'Artagnan de plume*
1932 *Les Dames de la miséricorde*
1934 *La Maison Marbuzet*
1935 *Madame Elizabeth*
1936 *La Pylône et la maison*

COLETTE YVER

1903 *Les Cervelines*
1907 *Les Princesses de science*
1910 *Les Dames du palais*
1913 *Les Sables mouvants*
1916 *Le Mystère des béatitudes*
1917 *Mirabelle de Pampelune*
1920 *Dans le jardin de féminisme*
1922 *Vous serez comme les dieux*
1925 *Le Festin des autres*
1929 *Femmes d'aujourd'hui*
1931 *Vincent ou la solitude*
1932 *Le Vote des femmes*
1932 *Cher coeur humain*
1934 *L'Humble Sainte Bernadette*
1935 *Les Deux cahiers de Pauline*
1935 *La Vie secrète de Cathérine Labouré*
1936 *Histoire de Jeanne d'Arc*

GENEVIÈVE DUHAMELET

1917 *Ces Dames de l'Hôpital 336*
1919 *Les Inépousées*
1923 *Pour l'amour de l'amour*
1924 *Rue du chien qui pêche*
1929 *L'Espace d'un matin*
1930 *Tout feu, toute flamme*
1931 *La Dépossédée*
1931 *Rue du chien qui pêche prolongée*

REFERENCES

Charasson, Henriette, "Marie Noël," *Études religieuses,* CXCV (1928), pp. 317–331.

Descaves, Lucien, "Marie Noël et les siens," *Nouvelles littéraires,* Sept. 29, 1928.

Faguet, Émile, Review of C. Yver's *Princesses de science, Revue Latine,* VI (1907), pp. 606–614.

Honnert, Robert, "La Poésie," *Correspondant,* CCCXXI (1930), pp. 133–137.

Le Goffic, Charles, "Nos poètes," *Revue hebdomadaire,* Aug. 7, 1920, pp. 77–95.

Mandadon, Louis de, "Madame Colette Yver," *Études religieuses,* CXXXV (1913), pp. 807–822.

——— "Mademoiselle Marie Noël," *Études religieuses,* CCIX (1931), pp. 200–216.

Parvillez, Alphonse de, Review of J. Balde's *Reine d'Arbieux, Études religieuses,* CXCVI (1928), pp. 207–214.

——— Review of G. Duhamelet's *La Dépossédée, Études religieuses,* CCIX (1931), p. 251.

Pourrat, Henri, Review of J. Balde's *Le Goéland, Revue hebdomadaire,* April, 1926, pp. 501–508.

Vallery-Radot, Robert, Review of *Les Heures du foyer, Correspondant,* CCCIV (1926), pp. 787–790.

Postscript

AS WAS STATED IN THE INTRODUCTION, THIS book is not intended to give a complete picture of Catholic literary France. It is merely an attempt to choose from among the numerous contemporary writers a few of the Catholic novelists, dramatists, and poets who seem to be leaders in the world of letters, and whose works will probably be read and esteemed through the coming ages. As a final word, it seems advisable to point out some of the marks of contemporary French literature, and to show how far they characterize the writings of the Catholic authors treated in the preceding chapters. In glancing back over the field there is risk, of course, of repeating much that has already been said, as there is also danger of prophesying rashly when we look into the future.

The first characteristic to be noted, is a reaction against the pessimism which was so noticeable during the last years of the nineteenth century and which was partly the result, no doubt, of the War of 1870. The nihilists, skeptics, naturalists, materialists, and positivists abounded to such an extent that even Renan exclaimed: "France is dying. Do not disturb her agony." This disenchantment can be found in the *Durtal* of Huysmans, and in the heroes of some of the earlier novels of Bourget and Mauriac. But most of the contemporary novelists (Catholic and non-Catholic) react against it. This is the era of great individualists, who surmount pessimism and eagerly seek reasons for living and for loving to live. Romain Rolland makes his Jean Christophe a powerful personality, Maurice Barrès calls his trilogy *Le Roman de l'énergie nationale,* Psichari extols military heroism, Péguy's whole doctrine is one of action, and Claudel continually preaches energy. The present generation has again found faith in itself and in God, after an era of melancholy and despair.

Closely allied to this renewal of vitality is an appreciation of the spirit of sacrifice and of the joy that comes from renunciation. Claudel, in his heroines Violaine, Sygne, and Dona Prouhèze, best illustrates this tendency, but many of the other writers, especially Bourget and Baumann, exemplify the same teaching. Even André Gide, who usually rejects discipline and glorifies the liberated man, idealizes the unselfish immolation of Alissa in *La Porte étroite*, although the last paragraph of the story does seem to imply that her offering was in vain.

Most of the present-day novels can be correctly classed as psychological. In fact, our generation is distinguished by its fondness for self-analysis. There is a growing propensity to study minutely the soul, to lay bare the inmost thoughts and sentiments, to trace with exactitude the rise and fall of temptation, and this with a pitiless frankness and sincerity. As Mauriac points out in his essay on the novel, one of the outstanding virtues of the people of this age is candor. His own books are full of private diaries, letters, journals, and confessions. For Gide, absolute sincerity is the supreme law, as it also seems to be for Proust, Rolland, and Duhamel among the unbelievers, and for Huysmans, Péguy, Baumann, and Bourget among the believers.

Partly as a result of this effort at sincerity, and partly owing to the French temperament, sins, especially sins of the flesh, are painted with utter frankness in contemporary novels. The principal difference between the attitude of non-Catholic and Catholic writers is that the former often show sin in attractive colors, make it inviting, and justify its commission by stressing the weakness of human nature and the impossibility of virtue. For them voluptuousness is the logical result of man's instincts, the marriage bond is unreasonable and cruel, sinners are not responsible to God or man and should be considered pathological cases. Moral obligations are no more serious than social conventions, and the just man and the chaste woman are objects of ridicule. Catholic novelists often describe sin and vice just as vividly as do unbelievers, but with this essential difference: they show that it is evil, and that it brings in its train untold miseries, temporal as well as eternal. They teach that man's duty and happiness lie in struggling against his fallen nature, and that, aided by the grace which flows from prayer and the sacraments, he can rise to heights of heroism undreamed of by those who have no faith in the supernatural. It is true that even these novels may be dangerous for certain classes of persons (adolescents, for instance), not because the philosophy in them is false, but because they are overgraphic in their portrayal of sensuous scenes and sexual irregularities. Some of the novels of Huysmans, Baumann, Bourget, and Mauriac fall into this class, as has been pointed out in the chapters which treat of their works.

A growing interest in social problems also characterizes contemporary French literature. Such topics as woman's station, the child, the family, education, the right to property, the use of leisure, etc., are becoming more and more common. The dramatists, following the example of François de Curel, Eugène Brieux, and Paul Hervieu, have given us numerous plays which are built around social theses. Bourget's *Le Tribun* and *La Barricade,* and some of his dramatized novels fall into this class. Among the Catholic novelists, there are many who try directly or indirectly to remedy social evils by their works. Bourget, Bazin, Bordeaux, Mauriac, Colette Yver, Jean Balde, and Henriette Charasson all belong to this group. Although their characters seem to be clearly conscious that they are not only individuals but members of a collective group which has definite rights and duties, these writers are conservative in their opinions, and bravely defend the family and tradition against innovators and radicals who advocate communistic principles.

Another feature of contemporary French literature is its tendency to become more-universal in spirit. It expresses the soul of the French people, but more than that, the soul of humanity. It is written not just for France, nor yet for Europe, but for the whole world. The word *Catholic* assumes its literal meaning, for the writers lose their narrow sense of nationality, and become "cosmic-conscious." Claudel, in the preface to *Le Soulier de Satin,* tells us that "the scene is the world," and Bourget chooses as one of his heroes the cosmopolite. The exotic and regional novel are both offshoots of this trend toward universality. Le Cardonnel sings of Italy, Frances Jammes of the Basque country, Psichari describes Mauritania, Bazin writes of La Vendée and Alsace, Barrès of Lorraine, and Bordeaux of Savoy. Exoticism and regionalism are not, however, new in French literature. Bernardin de Saint-Pierre in the eighteenth century and Chateaubriand at the beginning of the nineteenth, are really the fathers of exoticism, and George Sand was the pioneer in regionalism.

In contemporary French poetry there is much diversity. There are the Neo-classicists, including Louis Mercier and Le Cardonnel, who are attached to tradition and cling to classic standards. They believe that "what is not clear is not French," and faithfully follow the principles laid down in Boileau's *Art poétique.* Mercier's themes are usually very humble ones, while Le Cardonnel chooses more elevated subjects. There are the Neo-symbolists led by Claudel and Valéry, who have broken away from the traditional forms and incline to *vers libre* or rhythmic prose. Like their master, Paul Verlaine, they seek "Music before all else." Charles Péguy might be included among these, though he often employs the Alexandrine. These poets are apt to be obscure, owing to condensation of thought, exceptional subject matter, or unusual form. There is also a group who go to the other extreme and strive for absolute simplicity. Francis Jammes, for instance, is so naïve at times, that he appears to be affected. It is noteworthy that all these poets, no matter to which group they belong, have found their highest inspiration and done their best work when they chose as subjects the sublime truths of religion.

Claudel, Péguy, and Ghéon have all three done much to create an interest in the religious drama. Their work is similar in that they drew their themes from the Middle Ages, and endowed their plays with an atmosphere of faith and spirituality. Claudel's dramatic work, like his poetry, is impregnated with such lofty sentiments and cast in such a strange form, that often it is difficult to understand and almost impossible to represent on the stage, although the beauty and grandeur of the thought is beyond question. Péguy's *mystères* form an important part of his literary work, and they contain all the sincerity and ardor so characteristic of the author. They are really sublime hymns of faith, hope, and charity, written rather to be read than acted. Ghéon's miracle plays are much simpler and make a more direct appeal to the people. They are a serious attempt to present to the modern world the lives of the saints in dramatic form and in a medieval setting. They have been played in France and abroad, in theaters and in the open air, by professionals and by amateurs, and always with surprising success.

Finally, there are a few other influences which have affected contemporary French literature, which may be briefly mentioned. First, this is the age of literary schools — Humanisme, Synthétisme, Unanisme, Futurisme, École Romane, École Française, etc. — all of which have flourished since 1900. Let it be noted, however, that many of the greatest writers are outside of all the schools. Second, it is also the age of literary prizes: Prix de l'Académie Française,

Prix Goncourt, Grand Prix Balzac, Prix Femina-vie Heureuse, Grand Prix de Littérature, Prix du Roman, etc. These awards serve to stimulate writers in the different fields, and although public opinion does not always agree with that of the judges, the works that are crowned are usually of distinctive merit. Third, this is the age of journals and reviews, which have increased and multiplied astoundingly during the past fifty years. They have their disadvantages as well as their advantages, according to some thinkers, as they are apt to encourage hurried hack work to the neglect of greater things.

What may we hope for the future? We may hope and believe that France, in spite of all passing fads and fancies, will remain true to her glorious literary past, and will continue to exhibit in her literature the qualities that have always characterized French writing — clearness, brevity, simplicity, and grace. Every age has its geniuses, even though they are not recognized by their contemporaries. Perhaps the verdict of the next century will reverse many of our decisions, but it seems safe to wager that the Catholic Revival in France has produced a number of works that will always be shelved with the world's classics. We may envision the future without foreboding, trusting that the need of religious faith, which ever makes itself felt when men heed the call to higher things, will grow and increase until it thoroughly permeates the life and literature of the inscrutable tomorrow.

Notes of Chapters

CHAPTER I

[1] Cf. C. Alexander, *The Catholic Literary Revival*.

[2] Cunliffe and De Bacourt, *French Literature during the Last Half Century*, p. 9.

[3] J. Calvet, *Le Renouveau catholique*, p. 14.

[4] *En Route*, p. IX.

[5] Quoted by L. Chaigne, *Le Chemin de Paul Claudel*, p. 62.

CHAPTER II

[1] A. Symons, *The Symbolist Movement in Literature*, p. 94.

[2] E. Lepelletier, *Paul Verlaine, sa vie, son oeuvre*, p. 24.

[3] *Oeuvres complètes*, V, 6.

[4] *Ibid.*, IV, p. 212.

[5] *Ibid.*, I, p. 122.

[6] *Ibid.*, II, p. 35.

[7] Cf. *Ibid.*, V, p. 126.

[8] D. Mornet, *Histoire de la littérature et de la pensée françaises contemporaines, 1870–1927*, p. 48.

[9] *Oeuvres complètes*, V, p. 58.

[10] Quoted by E. Lepelletier, *op. cit.*, p. 381.

[11] J. Lemaître, *Les Contemporains. Études et portraits*, IV, pp. 90, 95.

[12] *Oeuvres complètes de Paul Verlaine*, Introduction, I, p. X. Cf. also *De Dante à Verlaine*, a study of Verlaine's religious poetry by J. Pacheu.

[13] C. Donos, *Verlaine intime*, p. 144.

[14] Cf. H. Nicolson, *Paul Verlaine*, p. 125.

[15] His wife married again in 1879.

[16] Those especially which were written after 1890.

[17] Cf. E. Lepelletier, *op. cit.*, pp. 544 ff.

[18] F. Gregh, *La Maison de Verlaine*, p. 224 (published in his *Étude sur Victor Hugo*).

[19] *Oeuvres complètes*, I, p. 78.

[20] A. Symons, *op. cit.*, p. 87.

[21] A. France, *Oeuvres complètes*, VII, p. 304.

[22] A. Séché, *Paul Verlaine*, p. 102.

[23] A. Bénéteau, *Étude sur l'inspiration et l'influence de Paul Verlaine*, pp. 18 ff.

[24] A. Symons, *op. cit.*, p. 81.

[25] G. Deschamps, *La Vie et les livres*, III, p. 40.

CHAPTER III

[1] Barbey d'Aurevilly, *Le Roman contemporain*, p. 381.

[2] *En Ménage*, p. 44.

[3] J. Besse, *Joris-Karl Huysmans*, p. 35.

[4] A. Symons, *Figures of Several Centuries*, p. 270.

[5] H. Ellis, *Affirmations*, p. 161.

[6] A. Symons, *op. cit.*, p. 274.

[7] *En Ménage*, p. 321.

[8] J. Huneker, *Egoists*, p. 197.

[9] *À Rebours*, Introduction, p. VI.

[10] *Ibid.*, p. 294.

[11] J. Huneker, *op. cit.*, p. 202.

[12] J. Besse, *op. cit.*, p. 11.

[13] *À Rebours*, Introduction, p. XII.

[14] *En Route*, p. 26.

[15] *Ibid.*, pp. 28, 29.

[16] *Ibid.*, p. 242.

[17] H. Peck, *The Personal Equation*, p. 152.

[18] V. Crawford, *Studies in Foreign Literature*, p. 79.

[19] *En Route*, p. 51.

[20] *Ibid.*, p. 18.

[21] *Ibid.*, p. 55.

[22] *Ibid.*, p. 57.

[23] *Ibid.*, p. 400.

[24] *À Rebours*, Introduction, p. XX.

[25] *Revue des Flandres*, June, 1907, pp. 177–180.

[26] Quoted in *Commonweal*, XIII (1931), p. 545.

[27] H. Ellis, *op. cit.*, p. 199.

[28] *En Route*, pp. 213, 214.

[29] *L'Oblat*, p. 171.

[30] *Ste. Lydwine de Schiedam*, p. 72.

[31] *Les Foules de Lourdes*, p. 148.

[32] *En Route*, pp. 119, 120.

[33] *En Route* (Introduction to English translation), p. IX.

[34] *En Route*, pp. 283 ff.

[35] A. Symons, *Symbolist Movement in Literature*, p. 273.

[36] For example, *concubiner, aumôner, cloportisme, inintime, ecclésiale.*

[37] *La Cathédrale,* p. 16.

[38] *Ibid.,* p. 250.

[39] *En Route,* p. 6.

[40] *L'Oblat,* p. 55.

[41] *En Route,* p. 36.

[42] *Ibid.,* p. 90.

[43] *Ibid.,* p. 9.

[44] J. Besse, *op. cit.,* p. 6.

CHAPTER IV

[1] J. Lemaître, *Les Contemporains,* III, p. 364.

[2] *Le Diamant de la reine,* p. 12.

[3] E. Dimnet, *Paul Bourget,* p. 3.

[4] Cf. *Lettre autobiographique,* published by N. Van Daell in *Extraits choisis des oeuvres de Paul Bourget,* p. 5.

[5] *Ibid.,* p. 5.

[6] G. Renard, *Les Princes de la jeune critique,* p. 232.

[7] *Lettre autobiographique,* p. 13.

[8] *Andre Cornélis,* Introduction, p. VIII.

[9] *Le Disciple,* p. 308.

[10] Jules Sagaret in *Les Grands convertis,* is inclined to belittle the conversion of Bourget, Brunetière, Coppée, and Huysmans.

[11] F. Brunetière, *Nouvelles questions de critique,* p. 331.

[12] R. Lalou, *Histoire de la littérature contemporaine,* p. 107.

[13] G. Deschamps, *La Vie et les livres,* I, p. 69.

[14] *L'Emigré* et *Un Divorce* had been dramatized in 1908.

[15] R. Lalou, *op. cit.,* p. 300.

[16] *Le Démon de midi,* II, p. 375.

[17] E. Bowman, *Early Novels of Paul Bourget,* p. 48.

[18] *La Geôle,* p. 297.

[19] *Nos actes nous suivent,* II, p. 255.

[20] *La Vengeance de la vie,* p. 116.

[21] E. Dimnet, *op. cit.,* p. 116.

[22] R. Doumic, *Ecrivains d'aujourd'hui,* p. 36.

[23] *Nouveaux Essais de psychologie contemporaine,* pp. 28, 29.

[24] *Lettre autobiographique,* p. 13.

[25] R. Doumic says that Bourget's *Physiologie de l'amour moderne,* is "one of the most wicked books that I know." *Op. cit.,* p. 15.

[26] E. Dimnet, *op. cit.,* pp. 113, 114.

[27] *Idem.*

[28] *Lettre autobiographique,* p. 14.

[29] B. Fäy, *Panaroma de la littérature contemporaine,* p. 120.

[30] V. Giraud, *Les Maîtres de l'heure,* I, pp. 254, 255.

[31] C. Le Goffic, *La Littérature française aux XIXe et XXe siècles,* II, p. 242.

[32] Turquet-Milnes, *Some Modern French Writers,* p. 129.

[33] *Le Sens de la mort,* p. 57.

CHAPTER V

[1] *Contes de Bonne Perrette,* Preface.

[2] *Ibid.,* pp. 3, 4.

[3] One of his daughters, Mme Sainte-Marie Perrin, translated the works of Henry Van Dyke into French.

[4] C. Des Granges, *Histoire de la littérature française des origines à 1930,* p. 900.

[5] *Contemporary Review,* LXXIX (1901), pp. 270, 267.

[6] *Correspondant,* CXCV (1890), p. 581.

[7] Cunliffe and De Bacourt, *French Literature during the Last Half Century,* p. 354.

[8] R. Doumic, *Études sur la littérature française,* III, p. 186.

[9] *Le Blé qui lève,* p. 184.

[10] *Les Nouveaux Oberlé,* p. 113.

[11] *L'Isolée,* p. 133.

[12] R. Doumic, *op. cit.,* p. 186.

[13] Quoted in *Les Oberlé,* edited by C. Cabeen, Introduction, p. XVIII.

[14] D. Mornet, *Histoire de la littérature et de la pensée françaises contemporaines, 1870–1927,* p. 130.

[15] *Les Nouveaux Oberlé,* p. 278.

[16] *Contemporary Review,* LXXIX (1901), p. 272.

[17] In speaking of "La Vendée," we mean, not the present department created in 1789, but the ancient Vendée, the military Vendée, which included some 2,000 square miles of western France south of the Loire.

[18] *Correspondant,* CXCV (1899), pp. 37–54.

[19] Quoted by Noëlia Dubrule in her introduction to *Une Tache d'encre,* p. VIII.

[20] R. Doumic, *op. cit.,* p. 188.

[21] J. Calvet, *Le Renouveau catholique,* p. 124.

[22] *Questions littéraires et sociales,* p. 86.

[23] J. Calvet, *op. cit.*, p. 107.

[24] B. Fäy, *Panorama de la littérature contemporaine*, p. 121.

[25] *Month*, CLX (1932), p. 258.

[26] *Contemporary Review*, LXXIX (1901), p. 267.

[27] *Bookman*, LXXV (1932), p. 645.

[28] R. Doumic, *op. cit.*, p. 170.

CHAPTER VI

[1] *Les Caractères*, adapted and edited by E. Pellisier, p. 3.

[2] A. Britsch, *Henry Bordeaux, Biographie critique*, p. 6.

[3] He has also written a few dramas, most of which are his novels dramatized, as *L'Écran brisé, Un Médecin de campagne*, etc.

[4] The first edition did not contain the articles on A. France and P. Bourget, which were written and added later.

[5] Published in his *Vie au théâtre, 3e série*, p. IV ff.

[6] Cf. *Revue bleue*, XVII (1902), pp. 307–310.

[7] Cf. "Sur *Le Pays Natal*," *Journal des debats*, March 12, 1901.

[8] *Les Roquevillard*, p. 106.

[9] L. Cardon, in the introduction of his edition of *La Maison*, p. V.

[10] J. Ferchat, *Le Roman de la famille française*, p. 225.

[11] M. Ligot, *Le Sens de la vie et l'idée de l'ordre dans l'oeuvre d'Henry Bordeaux*, p. 92.

[12] Cf. *La Peur de vivre*, Introduction, p. V.

[13] *La Peur de vivre*, p. 341.

[14] *Les Roquevillard*, p. 363.

[15] *Revue des deux mondes*, XIII (1933), p. 512.

[16] M. Ligot, *op. cit.*, p. 103.

[17] This story was later published as the third part of *Les Trois Confesseurs*, 1935.

[18] *Revue Latine*, June 25, 1904, p. 368.

[19] A. Britsch, *op. cit.*, p. 47.

[20] Address given by H. Bordeaux at the *Semaine des écrivains catholiques*, 1922. Quoted by Ligot, *op. cit.*, p. 258.

[21] *Blackfriars* XII (1931), p. 124.

[22] This letter is dated Jan. 27, 1918, and is published at the beginning of Bordeaux's *George Guynemer*, translated by Louise Sill, 1918.

CHAPTER VII

[1] L. Bertrand, *Idées et portraits*, p. 154.

[2] *Mon Frère le Dominicain*, p. 16.

[3] *L'Immolé*, p. 193.
[4] *Ibid.*, p. 96.
[5] *Le Baptême de Pauline Ardel*, p. 229.
[6] *Ibid.*, p. 230.
[7] L. Levaux, *Romanciers*, p. 24.
[8] *Le Fer sur l'enclume*, p. 43.
[9] *Le Signe sur les mains*, p. 26.
[10] *Ibid.*, p. 240.
[11] Cf. *Études religieuses*, CXXCVIII (1926), p. 337.
[12] *Mon Frère le Dominicain*, p. 25.
[13] F. Vandérem, *Le Miroir des lettres*, VI, p. 45.
[14] *Minerve Française*, Aug. 15, 1919, p. 832.
[15] J. Calvet, *Le Renouveau catholique*, p. 253.
[16] A. Thérive, *Opinions littéraires*, p. 61.
[17] *L'Immolé*, p. 193.
[18] L. Levaux, *op. cit.*, p. 22.
[19] L. Bertrand, *op. cit.*, p. 166.
[20] A. Thérive, *op. cit.*, p. 59.
[21] L. Levaux, *op. cit.*, p. 34.
[22] *Revue hebdomadaire*, Sept., 1925, p. 103.

Chapter VIII

[1] *Bordeaux*, p. 3.
[2] *Commencements d'une vie*, p. 1.
[3] *Ibid.*, p. 19.
[4] *Ibid.*, p. 22.
[5] *Nouvelles littéraires*, June 26, 1926.
[6] One other small volume of poems, *Orages*, was published in 1925.
[7] *Nouvelles littéraires*, March 14, 1925.
[8] *Le Baiser au lépreux*, p. 62.
[9] *Ibid.*, pp. 52, 53.
[10] *Ibid.*, p. 134.
[11] *Ibid.*, p. 173.
[12] *Genitrix*, p. 155.
[13] Cf. *Journal des débats*, July 10, 1925, p. 64.
[14] *La Fin de la nuit*, p. 119.
[15] *Ibid.*, End of preface.
[16] *Destins*, p. 265.
[17] Cf. Gide's letter to Mauriac, quoted at the end of *Dieu et Mammon*, p. 199.

[18] *Annales politiques et littéraires*, XCVIII (1932), p. 283.

Le Mystère Frontenac, p. 125.

[20] *Ibid.*, p. 291.

[21] *Les Anges noirs*, pp. 291, 292.

[22] *Revue hebdomadaire*, Feb. 1, 1936, p. 111.

[23] *Nouvelles littéraires*, May 26, 1923.

[24] *Dieu et Mammon*, p. 151.

[25] R. Gillouin, *Esquisses littéraires et morales*, p. 6.

[26] *Le Renouveau catholique*, p. 322.

[27] *Nouvelles littéraires*, May 26, 1923.

[28] *Dieu et Mammon*, p. 102.

[29] *Ibid.*, p. 157.

[30] *François Mauriac et le problème du romancier catholique.*

[31] *Ibid.*, pp. 47, 49.

[32] *Ibid.*, p. 67.

[33] *Revue des deux mondes*, Dec. 1, 1933, p. 708.

[34] *Journal des débats*, Nov. 24, 1933, p. 868.

[35] *Le Roman*, p. 41.

[36] G. de Catalogne, *Une Génération*, p. 37.

[37] *Études religieuses*, CCXXII (1935), p. 468.

[38] *Journal des débats*, April 15, 1932, p. 591.

[39] *Le Romancier et ses personnages*, p. 96.

[40] *Études religieuses*, CXCIX (1929), p. 682.

[41] *Étude de Ramon Fernandez*, preceding *Dieu et Mammon*, p. 23.

[42] *Revue générale*, CXXIX (1933), p. 322.

[43] *Revue hebdomadaire*, March 17, 1928, p. 362.

[44] *Vie de Jésus*, p. 48.

[45] *Nouvelles littéraires*, Feb. 23, 1935.

[46] *Annales politiques et littéraires*, C (1933), p. 634.

CHAPTER IX

[1] *De l'âge divin à l'âge ingrat, L'Amour, les Muses, et la chasse,* and *Les Caprices du poète.*

[2] The preface to *La divine douleur.*

[3] Cf. *De l'âge divin à l'âge ingrat*, p. 53.

[4] *Ibid.*, p. 10.

[5] *Ibid.*, p. 16.

[6] *Ibid.*, p. 22.

[7] *Ibid.*, p. 28.

[8] He especially resented the fact that one professor made him the subject of a psychological experiment. *Ibid.*, p. 100.

[9] *Ibid.*, p. 117.

[10] *Ibid.*, p. 159.

[11] *Ibid.*, p. 222.

[12] *L'Amour, les Muses, et la chasse*, p. 4.

[13] *Ibid.*, p. 182.

[14] Published in the volume *Le Roman du lièvre*.

[15] Quoted in *Les Caprices du poète*, p. 6.

[16] *Ibid.*, p. 13.

[17] *Le Deuil des primavères*, p. 147.

[18] Quoted in *Les Caprices du poète*, p. 87.

[19] *Ibid.*, p. 119.

[20] Cf. *Mercure de France*, XLVI (1903), p. 327.

[21] *Ma Fille Bernadette*, p. 269.

[22] *Le Testament de l'auteur.*

[23] *De l'Angelus de l'aube à l'Angelus du soir*, p. 127.

[24] *Le Deuil des primavères*, p. 179.

[25] *De l'Angelus de l'aube*, p. 60.

[26] A. Lowell, *Six French Poets*, p. 259.

[27] E. Pilon, *Francis Jammes et le sentiment de la nature*, p. 52.

[28] Cf. L. Rush, *Catholic World*, CXXIII (1926), p. 168, and H. Clouard, *La Poésie française moderne*, p. 251.

[29] H. Clouard, *op. cit.*, p. 252.

[30] J. Calvet, *Le Renouveau catholique*, p. 205.

[31] *L'Arc en ciel des amours*, p. 128.

[32] A. Lowell, *op. cit.*, p. 220.

[33] R. Lalou, *Histoire de la littérature française contemporaine*, p. 242.

[34] Cf. *Premier livre des quatrains*, Preface.

[35] *De Tout temps à jamais*, Preface.

CHAPTER X

[1] R. A. Eric Shepherd, *Religious Poems of Richard Crashaw*, p. 16.

[2] *Pierres sacrées*, p. 215.

[3] Quoted by F. Gohin, *Le Poète Louis Mercier*, p. 7.

[4] *Pierres sacrées*, p. 149.

[5] F. Gohin, *op. cit.*, p. 2.

[6] *Petites géorgiques*, p. 15.

[7] R. Lalou, *Histoire de la littérature française contemporaine*, p. 401.

[8] *Pierres sacrées*, p. 116.

[9] F. Thompson, *Hound of Heaven* (edited by Rev. F. P. Lebuffe), p. 22.

[10] Cf. *Monde illustré*, CXXVII (1920), p. 66.

[11] *Pierres sacrées*, p. 9.

[12] C. T. Winchester, *Some Principles of Literary Criticism*, p. 136.

[13] *Voix de la terre et du temps*, p. 68.

[14] *Ibid.*, pp. 187, 188.

[15] P. Gesell, *Art by Auguste Rodin*, p. 47.

[16] A. de Musset, *Namouna*, Chant II, Stanza IX.

[17] *Pierres sacrées*, p. 24.

[18] *Poème de la maison*, p. 108.

[19] F. Gohin, *op. cit.*, p. 100.

[20] *Minerve française*, V (1920), p. 58.

[21] *Correspondant*, CCXXXIII (1908), p. 914.

[22] *Monde illustré*, CXXVII (1920), p. 66.

[23] *Lazare le ressuscité*, p. 59.

[24] *Pierres sacrées*, p. 208.

[25] *Voix de la terre*, p. 121.

[26] *Études religieuses*, CLI (1917), p. 356.

[27] *Ibid.*, p. 357.

[28] *Minerve française*, V (1920), p. 59.

[29] *Pierres sacrées*, p. 269.

[30] *Commonweal*, May 27, 1925, p. 72.

[31] *Mois littéraire et pittoresque*, June, 1903, p. 741.

[32] *Ibid.*, p. 750.

CHAPTER XI

[1] T. Quoniam, *De la Sainteté de Péguy*, p. 1.

[2] H. Daniel-Rops, *Péguy*, p. 26.

[3] E. Mounier, *La Pensée de Charles Péguy*, p. 5.

[4] V. Boudon, *Avec Charles Péguy de la Lorraine à la Marne, Août-Septembre, 1914*.

[5] E. Mounier, *op. cit.*, p. 286.

[6] *Oeuvres complètes*, V, p. 329.

[7] Cf. *Ibid.*, I, pp. 35, 36.

[8] P. Pacary, *Un Compagnon de Péguy, Joseph Lotte*, p. XVII.

[9] Cf. J. Calvet, *Le Renouveau catholique*, p. 143.

[10] H. Daniel-Rops, *op. cit.*, pp. 232, 233.

[11] Quoted by D. Halévy, *Charles Péguy et les Cahiers de la Quinzaine*, p. 178.

[12] J. Tharaud, *Notre cher Péguy*, II, p. 153.

[13] A. Suarès, *Charles Péguy*, p. 39.

[14] H. Daniel-Rops, *op. cit.*, p. 190.

[15] C. Sénéchal, *Les Grands courants de la littérature française contemporaine*, p. 133.

[16] A. Gide, *Nouveaux prétextes*, pp. 208, 209.

[17] *Oeuvres complètes*, VI, pp. 360, 376, 377.

[18] Cf. V. Boudon, *op. cit.*, p. 170.

[19] P. Pacary, *op. cit.*, p. 302. Lotte wrote this, say the critics, under the direction of Péguy.

[20] *Oeuvres complètes*, VII, p. 162.

[21] *Ibid.*, XIII, p. 198.

[22] J. Tharaud, *op. cit.*, I, p. 35.

[23] A. Suarès, *op. cit.*, p. 27.

[24] *Oeuvres complètes*, III, p. 185.

[25] Cf. V. Boudon, *op. cit.*, Preface.

[26] Quoted by R. Lalou, *Histoire de la littérature française contemporaine*, p. 370.

[27] Quoted by Pacary, *op. cit.*, p. 346.

[28] Quoted by E. Mounier, *op. cit.*, p. 137.

[29] Turquet-Milnes, *Some Modern French Writers*, p. 236.

[30] *Oeuvres complètes*, IX, p. 24.

[31] H. Daniel-Rops, *op. cit.*, p. 12.

[32] A. Gide, *op. cit.*, p. 213.

[33] E. Mounier, *op. cit.*, p. 16.

[34] F. Porché, *Poètes français depuis Verlaine*, p. 149.

Chapter XII

[1] Cf. H. Massis, *La Vie d'Ernest Psichari*, pp. 38 ff., and L. Aguettant, *Ernest Psichari*, p. 67.

[2] H. Psichari, *Ernest Psichari, mon frère*, p. 210.

[3] *Ibid.*, p. 23.

[4] E. Renan, *Feuilles détachées*, p. 419.

[5] H. Psichari, *op. cit.*, pp. 100 ff.

[6] *Terres de soleil et de sommeil*, pp. 93, 94.

[7] A. Goichon, *Ernest Psichari, d'après des documents inédits*, p. 113.

[8] *Terres de soleil et de sommeil*, p. 249.

[9] *Idem.*

[10] *Revue de Paris*, VI (1924), p. 99.

[11] C. Péguy, *Oeuvres complètes*, IV, p. 505.

[12] Introduction to *L'Appel des armes*.

¹³ *L'Appel des armes*, p. 200.

¹⁴ *Les Voix qui crient dans le désert*, pp. 310, 311.

¹⁵ *Ibid.*, p. 4.

¹⁶ *Ibid.*, p. 172.

¹⁷ *Ibid.*, p. 195.

¹⁸ *Le Voyage du centurion*, p. 242.

¹⁹ *Ibid.*, Preface, p. XXVI.

²⁰ *Revue de Paris*, VI (1924), p. 109.

²¹ A. Goichon, *op. cit.*, pp. 286, 287.

²² *Revue des deux mondes*, Dec., 1932, p. 883.

²³ A. Loisy, *Mors et vita*, p. 60.

²⁴ *Les Voix qui crient dans le désert*, p. 243.

²⁵ H. Psichari, *op. cit.*, p. 84.

Chapter XIII

¹ L. Delpit, *Representative French Lyrics, 1885–1925*, p. 228.

² *Carmina sacra*, pp. 80, 81.

³ *Ibid.*, p. 77.

⁴ *Ibid.*, p. 81.

⁵ H. Clouard, *La Poésie française moderne*, p. 222.

⁶ J. Calvet, *Le Renouveau catholique*, p. 258.

⁷ Cf. *Revue des deux mondes*, June 1, 1936, p. 650.

⁸ *Oeuvres*, I, p. 22.

⁹ *Ibid.*, p. 12.

¹⁰ *Ibid.*, p. 13.

¹¹ *Ibid.*, p. 91.

¹² *Ibid.*, p. 22.

¹³ *Carmina sacra*, p. 59.

¹⁴ *Ibid.*, p. 45.

¹⁵ *Ibid.*, p. 12.

¹⁶ *Ibid.*, p. 10.

¹⁷ *Ibid.*, p. 64.

¹⁸ *Ibid.*, p. 89.

¹⁹ *Ibid.*, p. 164.

²⁰ *Ibid.*, p. 164.

²¹ E. Schuré, *Femmes inspiratrices et poètes annonciateurs*, p. 330.

²² G. Duhamel, *Poètes et la poésie*, p. 191.

²³ *Carmina sacra*, p. 140.

²⁴ In a letter to Calvert, he says: "J'avais achevé auprès de Stéphane Mallarmé, de développer le goût inné en moi d'un certain tour poétique, un peu sibyllin, un peu augural, mais en lui conservant

la clarté nécessaire, et sans exagérer la tension." Cf. *Mercure de France,* CCLXIX (1936), p. 290.

[25] *Oeuvres,* I, p. 100.

[26] Quoted by Mary Ryan, *Dublin Review,* CLXX (1922), p. 259.

[27] A. Praviel, *Du Romantisme à la priere,* p. 251.

[28] Cf. *Revue des deux mondes,* June 1, 1936, p. 664.

CHAPTER XIV

[1] Sheed and Ward, *This Publishing Business,* II (No. 1), p. 22.

[2] Cf. Turquet-Milnes, *Some Modern French Writers,* p. 155; G. Duhamel, *Paul Claudel,* p. 6; E. Dimnet, *Outlook,* CXLV (1927), p. 337; G. Cattaui, *Dublin Review,* CXC (1932), p. 268; J. Madaule, *Le Génie de Paul Claudel,* p. 20.

[3] F. Strowski, *La Vie catholique dans la France contemporaine,* p. 465.

[4] *Cinq grandes odes,* p. 108.

[5] Cf. *Revue de la jeunesse,* Oct. 10, 1913, pp. 158 ff.

[6] Louis Chaigne gives many interesting biographical details in *Le Chemin de Paul Claudel.*

[7] Cf. J. Benoist-Méchin, *Bibliographie des oeuvres de Paul Claudel.*

[8] He wrote *L'Endormie,* a short satirical drama, at the age of fifteen, but it was not published until 1925.

[9] *Théâtre,* IV, p. 90.

[10] Written in 1913–14.

[11] Written in 1916. *La Nuit de Noël,* a short mystical drama in no way connected with this trilogy, was published in 1915.

[12] English translation by Rev. John O'Connor, p. XI.

[13] *Ibid.,* p. 23.

[14] It is in reality the text of the opera composed by Darius Milhaud and produced in 1929 at the Opera House in Berlin. Claudel himself made the English translation.

[15] *Études,* p. 74.

[16] J. de Tonquédec, *L'Oeuvre de Paul Claudel,* p. 22.

[17] Prologue, p. 9.

[18] English translation, p. XXVI.

[19] K. Brégy, *Poets and Pilgrims,* p. 203.

[20] *Théâtre,* II, p. 203 ff.

[21] *Théâtre,* IV, pp. 58, 59.

[22] *L'Annonce,* pp. 39 ff.

[23] *Ibid.,* pp. 52–57.

[24] *Théâtre,* II, p. 116 ff.

[25] *L'Annonce*, pp. 114 ff.

[26] *Le Soulier de Satin*, First day, scene 11.

[27] Cunliffe and De Bacourt, *French Literature during the Last Half Century*, p. 298.

[28] Besides the plays already mentioned, Claudel published two lyric farces, *Protée* and *L'Ours et la lune*.

[29] *L'Annonce*, pp. 126 ff.

[30] *L'Otage*, pp. 116 ff.

[31] *Le Père humilié*, p. 79.

[32] *Théâtre*, III, pp. 259 ff.

[33] *Le Soulier de Satin*, Second day, scene 11.

[34] *Ibid.*, First day, scene 12.

[35] *Ibid.*, Third day, scene 13.

[36] Quoted by E. Goldbeck, *Bookman*, LXVII (1928), p. 501.

[37] *L'Agamemnon* (1896), *Les Choéptores* (1920), and *Les Eumènides* (1920).

[38] Cf. *Correspondance avec J. Rivière*, p. 142.

[39] *Études*, p. 123.

[40] *Cinq grandes odes*, p. 17.

[41] *Ibid.*, p. 156.

[42] *La Messe là-bas*, p. 46.

[43] J. de Tonquédec, *op. cit.*, p. 92.

[44] The best known of these poems is probably the one to the Infant Jesus of Prague, translated into English by Henry Van Dyke.

[45] *Corona benignitatis*, p. 30.

[46] *Ibid.*, p. 149.

[47] *Théâtre*, II, p. 305.

[48] It is defended by the author in *Les Réflexions et propositions sur le vers français*, published in *Positions et propositions*.

[49] Cf. *The Living Age*, CCCXLIII (1932), p. 227.

[50] *La Connaissance de l'Est*, p. 11.

[51] *Ibid.*, p. 123.

[52] Rev. John O'Connor translated it from the author's manuscript. Several of the essays had appeared in French periodicals.

[53] *La Connaissance de l'Est*, p. 31.

[54] *Corona benignitatis*, p. 26.

[55] *Feuilles de saints*, p. 158.

[56] *Études*, p. 71.

[57] Cf. *Revue des deux mondes*, Feb. 15, 1914, p. 877.

[58] Cf. L. Chaigne, *Le Chemin de Paul Claudel*, p. 51.

Chapter XV

[1] He began writing poetry in 1897 when he was only twenty-two, and has produced four volumes: *Chansons d'aube, Algérie, Foi en la France,* and *Le Miroir de Jésus.*

[2] He has published two novels: *La Vieille Dame des rues,* the fictional biography of an old lady living in Paris, and *Jeux de l'enfer et du ciel,* which tells in three volumes the story of fifteen persons who visit Ars during the lifetime of its saintly curé.

[3] His two principal works of criticism are: *Nos directions,* a collection of lectures and essays on poetry and the drama, and *Partis pris,* reflections on the art of writing.

[4] He judges his own poems when he says: "They are worth what they are worth. But, I insist, never has a cry more sincere, more spontaneous, more impossible to restrain, gone forth from me. It is for this reason they are dear to me." *L'Homme né de la guerre,* p. 120. Their sincerity is, in fact, their greatest merit.

[5] *L'Homme né de la guerre,* p. 10.

[6] *Ibid.,* pp. 10, 11.

[7] *Ibid.,* p. 11.

[8] *Ibid.,* p. 28.

[9] He had studied medicine in Paris, 1901–1909, and practiced it in Bray-sur-Seine, where he was born in 1875.

[10] *Foi en la France,* pp. 113, 114.

[11] *L'Homme né de la guerre,* p. 212.

[12] He has also written an excellent study of the life and genius of Mozart, *Promenades avec Mozart.* It has been translated into English by Alexander Dru.

[13] *Saint Jean Bosco,* Preface.

[14] Three other plays which belong to the profane theater are: *Les Propos interrompus, La Joyeuse farce des Encore,* and *Les Contes de Perrault en action.*

[15] *Jeux et miracles pour le peuple fidèle,* I, Preface.

[16] He has written over forty dramas since 1920.

[17] May Bateman calls it the finest of all his plays. Cf. *Dublin Review,* CLXXX (1927), p. 83.

[18] *Catholic World,* CXXX (1929), p. 8.

[19] *Jeux et miracles pour le peuple fidèle,* II, pp. 39, 40.

[20] We have called all these plays *miracles,* though Ghéon makes a distinction. In the preface to *Saint Maurice ou l'obéissance,* he

explains that a *miracle* is a play in which the supernatural intervenes visibly. A *jeu* is one which is based on legend rather than on authentic historical documents.

[21] *Jeux et miracles pour le peuple fidèle*, I, Preface.
[22] *Trois miracles de Sainte Cécile*, p. 120.
[23] *Triomphe de Notre Dame de Chartres*, pp. 14, 15.
[24] *L'Impromptu du charcutier*, p. 44.
[25] *Marriage of St. Francis*, p. 62 (Translation by Rev. C. C. Martindale).
[26] *Jeux et miracles pour le peuple fidèle*, II, pp. 233, 234.
[27] *Ibid.*, II, pp. 17–36.
[28] Cf. *Chronique des lettres françaises*, II (1924), pp. 675–677.
[29] *Marriage of St. Francis*, Preface.
[30] A. Praviel, *Du Romantisme à la prière*, p. 196.

CHAPTER XVI

[1] M. Braunschvig, *La Littérature française contemporaine*, p. 271 ff.
[2] Talvart et Place, *Bibliographie des auteurs modernes*, II, p. 368.
[3] *Faut-il supprimer le gynécée*, p. 4.
[4] *Ibid.*, p. 41.
[5] *Ibid.*, p. 94.
[6] *La Mère*, p. 32.
[7] J. Ernest-Charles, *Grande Revue*, C (1919), p. 684.
[8] *Attente*, p. 13.
[9] *Les Heures du foyer*, p. 65.
[10] *Ibid.*, p. 174.
[11] *Nouvelles Littéraires*, April 24, 1926.
[12] *Mercure de France*, CCIV (1928), p. 418.
[13] *Ibid.*, CCV (1928), p. 650.
[14] *Mon Seigneur et mon Dieu*, p. 121.
[15] *Ibid.*, p. 25.
[16] *Nouvelles Littéraires*, April 28, 1928.
[17] *Revue hebdomadaire*, Aug. 7, 1920, p. 94.
[18] *Correspondant*, CCCIV (1926), p. 790.
[19] *La Littérature française contemporaine*, p. 69.
[20] See *Nouvelles Littéraires*, Sept. 29, 1928.
[21] *Les Chansons et les heures*, p. 44.
[22] *Ibid.*, p. 38.
[23] *Revue des jeunes*, Feb. 25, 1921, p. 43.
[24] *La Vie littéraire*, Feb., 1931, pp. 117, 120.

[25] *Les Chants de la merci*, p. 16.

[26] *Le Rosaire des joies*, p. 9.

[27] *Correspondant*, CCCXXI (1930), p. 134.

[28] *Les Chansons et les heures*, p. 82.

[29] *Nouvelles Littéraires*, Sept. 29, 1928.

[30] *Les Chansons et les heures*, pp. 12, 13.

[31] In 1930 she published *Un d'Artagnan de plume, Jean-François Bladé*.

[32] Quoted by Louis Bethleem in *Revue des Lectures*, XXII (1934), p. 1187.

[33] *Nouvelles Littéraires*, June 2, 1928.

[34] *Revue hebdomadaire*, April, 1926, p. 502.

[35] *Nouvelles Littéraires*, June 30, 1923.

[36] *Princesses de science*, p. 19.

[37] *Ibid.*, p. 13.

[38] *Femmes d'aujourd'hui*, p. 207.

[39] *Mercure de France*, CCLV (1934), p. 136.

[40] *Études religieuses*, CXXXV (1913), p. 822.

[41] *Ibid.*, CCIX (1931), p. 251.

General Bibliography

Alexander, Calvert, *The Catholic Literary Revival*, Milwaukee, 1935.

Archambault, Paul, *Jeunes Maîtres*, Paris, 1926.

Barbey d'Aurevilly, Jules, *Le Roman contemporain*, Paris, 1902.

Bertrand, Louis, *Idées et portraits*, Paris, 1927.

Billy, André, *La Littérature française contemporaine*, Paris, 1928.

Braunschvig, Marcel, *La Littérature française contemporaine étudiée dans les textes*, Paris, 1928.

Brégy, Katherine, *Poets and Pilgrims*, New York, 1925.

Bremond, Henri, *Manuel illustré de la littérature catholique en France de 1870 à nos jours*, Paris, n.d.

Brunetière, Ferdinand, *Nouvelles questions de critique*, Paris, 1898.

Calvet, Jean, *Le Renouveau catholique*, Paris, 1931.

Catalogne, Gérard de, *Une Génération*, Paris, 1930.

Clouard, Henri, *La Poésie française moderne des romantiques à nos jours*, Paris, 1924.

Crawford, Virginia, *Studies in Foreign Literature*, Boston, 1899.

Cunliffe, J. W. and De Bacourt, P., *French Literature During the Last Half Century*, New York, 1927.

Delpit, Louise, *Representative Contemporary French Lyrics, 1885-1925*, Boston, 1927.

Deschamps, Gaston, *La Vie et les livres*, Paris, 1894.

Des Granges, Charles, *Histoire illustrée de la littérature française des origines à 1930*, Paris, 1933.

Doumic, René, *Écrivains d'aujourd'hui*, Paris, 1903.

——— *Études sur la littérature française*, 6 series, Paris, 1896–1909.

Dubech, Lucien, *Les Chefs de file de la jeune génération*, Paris, 1925.

Duhamel, Georges, *Les Poètes et la poésie*, Paris, 1922.

Ellis, Havelock, *Affirmations*, London, 1898.

Fäy, Bernard, *Panorama de la littérature contemporaine*, Paris, 1925.

Germain, André, *De Proust à Dada*, Paris, 1924.

Gide, André, *Nouveaux prétextes*, Paris, 1925.

Gillouin, René, *Esquisses littéraires et morales*, Paris, 1926.

Giraud, Victor, *Les Maîtres de l'heure, essais d'histoire morale contemporaine*, 2 vols., Paris, 1911–14.

Guérard, Albert, *Five Masters of French Romance*, New York, 1916.

Huneker, James, *Egoists*, New York, 1909.

Lalou, René, *Histoire de la littérature française contemporaine (1870 à nos jours)*, Paris, 1922.

Lasserre, Pierre, *Les Chapelles littéraires, Claudel, Jammes, Péguy*, Paris, 1920.

Le Goffic, Charles, *La Littérature française aux XIXe et XXe siècles*, 2 vols., Paris, 1920.

Lemaître, Jules, *Les Contemporains; Études et portraits littéraires*. 8 vols., Paris, 1897–1918.

Levaux, Léopold, *Romanciers*, Paris, 1929.

Loisy, Alfred, *Mors et vita*, Paris, 1916.

Lowell, Amy, *Six French Poets; Studies in Contemporary Literature*, New York, 1915.

Mornet, Daniel, *Histoire de la littérature et de la pensée françaises contemporaines, 1870–1927*, Paris, 1927.

Peck, Harry T., *The Personal Equation*, New York, 1898.

Porché, François, *Les Poètes français depuis Verlaine*, Paris, 1929.

Praviel, Armand, *Du Romantisme à la prière*, Paris, 1927.

Renard, Georges, *Les Princes de la jeune critique*, Paris, 1890.

Rigné, Raymoɳd de, *Dans le style de Huysmans, Conan Doyle, Paul Bourget*, Paris, 1922.

Sagaret, Jules, *Les Grands convertis*, Paris, 1906.

Schuré, Edouard, *Femmes inspiratrices et poètes annonciateurs*, Paris, 1908.

Sénéchal, Christian, *Les Grands courants de la littérature française contemporaine*, Paris, 1933.

Stansbury, Milton, *French Novelists of Today*, Philadelphia, 1935.

Strowski, Fortunat, *La Vie catholique dans la France contemporaine*, Paris, 1918.

Symons, Arthur, *Figures of Several Centuries*, London, 1915.

—— *The Symbolist Movement in Literature*, New York, 1919.

Talvart, H. and Place, J., *Bibliographie des auteurs modernes (1801–1927)*, Paris, 1928.

Thérive, André, *Opinions littéraires*, Paris, 1925.

Thibaudet, Albert, *Histoire de la littérature française de 1789 à nos jours*, Paris, 1936.

Thieme, Hugo, *Bibliographie de la littérature française de 1800 à 1930*, Paris, 1933.

Turquet-Milnes, *Some Modern French Writers*, New York, 1921.

Vandérem, Fernand, *Le Miroir des lettres*, 8 series, Paris, 1918–1929.

Vincent, François, *Âmes d'aujourd'hui*, Paris, 1911.

Index